THE GOSPEL
MESSAGE
of

THE BIBLE

New Testament, Psalms & Proverbs

arranged for straight-through, front-to-back reading
paraphrased · condensed · cross-referenced
complete outline headings

"A QUIET TIME COMPANION"

Presented to:

_____

_____

_____

By:

_____

_____

Date: _____

Comment: _____

_____

_____

_____

_____

THE COVER
Cover art by Gregg Mann

The cover shows **light** radiating from the Gospel Message because scripture says the entrance of God's Word brings light and life, and illuminates our path. (Ps. 119: 130, 105) The Gospel is needed light in the darkness all around us.

The cover shows **power** because the Gospel is the power of God unto salvation to all who believe. (Rom. 1: 16) The shield represents the shield of Faith, and Faith comes by hearing the Word of God.

A hand is **offering** The Gospel Message. In like manner, let's share the light. (2: Tim 2: 2 *page 103*) The Gospel is to be shared, and the best way of sharing is word-of-mouth, person-to-person, one individual telling another.

This book is not The Bible, but it contains *the Gospel Message of The Bible*, especially from the New Testament, in an easy to read format.

◆ ◆ ◆

Worry causes one to look all around
Fear causes one to look behind
Guilt causes one to look within
Faith causes one to look up

COMMITTED

Have you ever wondered how best to serve the Lord?
How best to live the Christian life, a doer of the word?
How best to share with others your substance and your faith?
How best to do God's business, until you see His face?

He said, "Just be committed. That's all I require today.
Ready to follow the Word, to witness and pray.
Just be committed. Willing to trust and obey.
Just be committed each step, each decision, each day."

You want to share God's message, but neither sing or preach?
To make a mark on others' lives, but neither write nor teach?
Do you want to make a difference, but haven't much to give?
Do you want to be a blessing, to please God as you live?

He said, "Just be committed. That's all I require today.
Ready to follow the Word, to witness and pray.
Just be committed. Willing to trust and obey.
Just be committed each step, each decision, each day."

Now, I'm not saying it's easy, I'm saying it's right -- worthwhile.
By faith it will be easier during the second mile, so smile....

Each of us can put our own life story in this verse.
Some have been a little better -- some a little worse.
When we come to God with questions, no matter why we came,
Specifics will be different; the basic answer is the same.

He'll say, "Just be committed. That's all I require today.
Ready to follow the Word, to witness, to pray.
Just be committed. Willing to trust and obey.
Just be committed each step, each decision, each day."

Printed by:
GILLILAND PRINTING, INC.
Arkansas City, Kansas

THE GOSPEL
MESSAGE

from

The New Testament

of

THE BIBLE

paraphrased · reorganized · condensed
with selected Psalms and Proverbs

"an owner's manual for human beings"

THE TRUTH CONTAINED HEREIN

CAN CHANGE YOUR LIFE

Editor: J. E. Foy
PUBLISHED BY
Send-A-Message Company
5126 East 21st Street
Tulsa, Oklahoma 74114-2210
© copyright 1995
James Elwood Foy Trust
ALL RIGHTS RESERVED

ISBN # 1-888300-47-7

Library of Congress Catalog Card Number: 95-92756

DEDICATED

TO THE LORD

AND

TO GOSPEL TRUTH

WHY THIS BOOK

PURPOSES:

To put an easy to read digest of the Bible Message in convenient form. Read it straight through, cover to cover, over and over to become saturated with The Gospel Message. Keep a copy in the car, another at work, one beside your bed or breakfast table. It's small in size to fit pocket, purse or glove box.

To be a gift which will enable the receiver, including new converts, unbelievers, seekers, young people and longtime believers, to quickly comprehend the basic concepts of Scripture.

To be a convenient appetizer for study of The Bible. This work is not an interpretation nor a version of the Bible, nor a technical study guide. It is an *hors d'oeuvre*, an enticement and an invitation to in-depth investigations.

To read and reread. The hour is late, the message vital.

Front-to-back reading. The books of The Bible are arranged herein by subject matter as follows:

1 - Who Christ really is
2 - The basic precepts of the gospel
3 - The primary doctrinal issues
4 - Broader aspects of faith, worship and living the Christian life
5 - Looking back - looking forward: the Historical and Future
6 - Inspirational selections from the Old Testament
7 - Helps and References

When I've given a Bible to a new believer or started young people on a Bible reading plan, I've suggested they begin by reading *1 John* because it's short and gives an overview of just who Jesus is. Follow with *The Gospel of John* to gain fuller understanding of the Gospel plan. Next, *Colossians* provides a brief doctrinal overview, and *Romans* gives insight into the sin problem and solution. Never have I said to anyone, "Here is a Bible. Start at the front and read through to the end." But I have wanted a book with which I could do just that. That is a primary purpose of this book. It can be read straight through to give one quick insight to the scriptural message. I trust you will benefit from reading it, that you'll read it again and allow its message to grip you, and that you will pass along a copy to others.

Since this book places the biblical books in an order different from the Bible, it may be helpful to recall that the original manuscripts were not a book. The New Testament Books were letters and texts written to a specific person or church, and circulated among the believers because they were recognized as divinely inspired Scripture. They were brought together in sequence in the form of The Holy Bible hundreds of years later.

The Bible was originally written in mostly Hebrew and Greek, with a smattering of Aramaic. No original manuscripts still exist, but we have some 5,000 ancient manuscripts which are painstakingly accurate copies of the originals. Because of the numerous manuscripts, language experts are able to know beyond a reasonable doubt that less than one word in 100 is subject to question. None of the 1% of potentially questionable words are important to any major doctrine of Christianity.

By way of illustration, in the eighteen hundreds, no copy machines existed, and families were large. Suppose a mother wrote a family history and sent it to the oldest of her fifteen children, who copied it and sent the copy to the next oldest child, who copied that and sent it to the next oldest, and so on until each child had a handwritten copy of the family history. After the mother's death, the original history document could not be found, but at a family reunion, each of the children brought their copy of the family's past. It was discovered that in the copying, errors were made in spelling, omitted words, and one child had left out an entire sentence. But, comparing the fifteen copies, it was easy to determine exactly what the mother had originally written, for none of the fifteen texts contained exactly the same errors and most agreed exactly on most words. By using the preponderance of evidence on each word, there was no doubt of the precise wording of the original writing. In similar manner, by comparing the many carefully-handwritten, ancient copies, an accurate, correct reproduction of the original text is possible.

The King James Version translated in the common language of the day. But we don't speak now with *"thee, thou, hast, wert"*. We say *"you, have, were"*. *Thee* and *thou* are not more holy or more religious, but are more confusing today. Therefore, this paraphrase from the King James uses modern day wording. It's easier to grasp the message in today's English.

FOOTNOTES AND HELPS

Throughout **THE GOSPEL MESSAGE**, phrases correlating to the following subjects are underlined and footnoted.

1) God loves you. **2)** God wants the best for you. **3)** The sin problem. **4)** Jesus is the answer. **5)** Faith is the key. **6)** Good works won't save anyone. **7)** God's Word is needed. **8)** Prayer is vital. **9)** Obedience is expected. **10)** The remedy of confession. **11)** Salvation can be sure. **12)** Share your faith. **13)** Warnings. **14)** Jesus is God. **15)** Live a new life as a re-born Christian. **16)** Overcoming Temptations. **17)** Living in Heaven.

To assist in the finding of comments related to these subjects in **THE GOSPEL MESSAGE**, a _Footnotes and Helps Index_ is provided starting two pages ahead. In that index, page numbers are given to guide you to pages on which comments are made regarding each topic. The applicable comment on the indicated page will be underlined and marked with a topic number as numbered above and in the index. In some cases, disconnected underlinings of one or more verses in the same paragraph will be footnoted with only one reference. In other cases, one underlining will be numbered to refer to more than one of the above subjects.

· · ·

Regarding Paragraphing: **The standard form of paragraphing has not been followed in this book.** For example, when the text quotes individuals speaking, a new paragraph is not created for each change in speaker. One continuous story or thought is often contained in one paragraph under one topic heading although there is more than one speaker and there would normally be several paragraphs.

Reading Plan Suggestions

A WEEKEND FEAST

It's possible to read completely through THE GOSPEL MESSAGE in one weekend. *Friday evening*, read from the beginning to page 72. This is the gospel and letters written by the apostles. *Saturday* read from page 73 to 120 and from 217 to 247. This gives the reader both New Testament and Old Testament, the past and the future, on Saturday. *Sunday* read from page 121 to 216 which is primarily historical examples of Jesus and the Apostles. The pages are small -- it's not easy but you can do it once.

AN ENJOYABLE WEEK

Day 1: Read from front to page 38. **Day 2:** Read pages 39 - 72. **Day 3:** Read pages 73 - 112. **Day 4:** Read pages 113- 151. **Day 5:** Read 152 - 216. **Day 6:** Read pages 217 - 224. **Day 7:** Read 225 - 247.

A MONTH OF BLESSINGS

Day 1: From the beginning to page 6 -- Intro & 1st John. **Day 2:** pages 7 - 29 -- John's Gospel. **Day 3:** pages 30 - 38 -- Isaiah & Colossians. **Day 4:** pages 39 - 50 -- Romans. **Day 5:** pages 51 - 62 -- James & 1 Peter. **Day 6:** pages 63 - 72 -- 1 Thessalonians & Ephesians. **Day 7:** pages 73 - 86 -- Corinthians. **Day 8:** pages 87 - 94 -- 2 Peter & Galations. **Day 9:** pages 95 - 106 -- 2 Corinthians, Timothy & Titus. **Day 10:** pages 107 - 112 -- Philippians. **Day 11:** pages 113 - 120 -- Hebrews. **Day 12:** pages 121 - 130 Acts (early days of the Church). **Day 13:** pages 131 - 134 Acts (primarily Peter). **Day 14:** pages 135 - 151 -- Acts (primarily Paul). **Days 15 - 22:** pages 152 - 214 -- The Combined Gospels as The Biography of Jesus (Read about eight pages each of these days). **Day 23:** pages 215 - 224 -- Jude, Revelation, Ecclesiastes. **Day 24:** pages 225 - 236 -- Psalms. **Day 25:** pages 237 - 247 -- Proverbs and a Personal Commitment. Then review or repeat.

A STUDY PLAN

Use the HELPS AND REFERENCES Section which follows as a study guide. Each day for seventeen days take one Topic looking up each verse in The BIBLE and in THE GOSPEL MESSAGE. Read the entire context. Make notes as you go (it's okay to write in the book). Outline what you read to add clarity and understanding. You may wish to discuss these topics with others.

HELPS AND REFERENCES

Each of the following scriptures, grouped by the Topics stated, are underlined in the text and appear in THE GOSPEL MESSAGE on the *page* indicated by *italic numbers in parenthesis* before each reference. Book, Chapter and Verse are given so the scripture can be found in the Bible. With most references is a concise statement of their content. Verses should be read in context.

1)   **GOD LOVES YOU:**

(4)   I John 3:1   He wants you as His child.
(5)   I John 4:7   God IS love.
(11)   John 3:16   everyone in the world.
(23)   John 15:3   enough to die for you.
(43)   Romans 5:8   even though you sin.
(24)   John 16: 27   assurance of God's love
(3)   I John 1: 4   wants joy for you

2)   **GOD WANTS GOOD, THE BEST, FOR YOU:**

(45)   Romans 8:28   He works for your good.
(47)   Romans 12:2   His will is good, perfect.
(18;23;3) John 10:10; 15:11; I John 1:4   a full life.
(5)   I John 4:18   eliminating fear.
(23)   John 14:27   with peace of heart & mind.
(24)   John 16:33   even in difficult times.
(111)   Philippians 4:19 He'll supply your needs
(41| Romans 2:4   His goodness leads to Him
(52)   James 1: 17   all good is from God

3)   **SIN IS THE PROBLEM:**

(42;30)   Romans 3:23; Isa. 53: 6   All have sinned
(93)   Galatians 3:22   All are condemned.
(43;220)   Romans 6:23; Rev. 21:8,27 Sin pays off in
                                      \ eternal death.
(3)   I John 1:5, 8   God can not tolerate sin.
(78)   I Corinthians 6:9   No sin in heaven.
(97; 116) II Cor. 5:l0, 11; Heb. 9:27   Judgment
(53)   James 2:10   Breaking one law is total guilt.
(49)   Romans 14:23 Anything not of faith is sin.
(70)   Ephesians 5: 3 - 14   Symptoms of sin
(58;97)   I Pet. 1: 17; II Cor. 5: 21   Christ is sinless

4)   **JESUS IS THE ANSWER:**

(22; 18;126 ;100) John 14:6; 10:9; Acts 4: 12;
I Tim. 2: 4   The only way.

(10; 29) John 3:16,18, 36; 20:31   He gives
\ everlasting life.

(13;14;36) John 5:40, 47; Col. 1: 20 Without Him,
\ no eternal life.

(9) John 1:12, 29   He makes you God's child

(24;15) John 17:3; 6: 57   To know Him is
\ eternal life.

(219) Rev. 3:20   Invite Him into your life.

(59;97) I Peter 2:24; II Cor. 5:21   He took our sin.

(60;22) I Peter 3:18; John 14:2,3   He'll take us to
\ heaven.

(20) John 11:25 He is the resurrection and life.

Others: *(43)* Rom. 6:23; *(29)* John 20:31; *(93)* Gal. 2:
20, 21; *(37)* Col. 2:14; *(76)* I Cor. 1:30; *(65)* I Thes. 5:
9; *(68)* Eph. 1:3-7; *(114-116)* Hebrews 2:16-18; 5:9;
9:28; 10:19-25; *(30)* Isaiah 53: 6

5)   **FAITH IS THE KEY:**

(69) Ephesians 2:8,9   by faith because of grace.

(43) Romans 5:12-21   made right by faith.

(46) Rom 10:9, 19,17   believing God necessary

(93;116) Gal. 3:11; Heb. 10:38;11:1-6   Only faith

(139) Acts 16: 32 Believe   \ gives life.

(46) Romans 9:32   Believers not rejected

(6; 114) 1 John 5: 4; Heb. 4: 2 overcoming by faith

(93) Galations 2: 16   faith, not deeds

6)   **GOOD WORKS ARE WORTHLESS TO EARN SALVATION:**

(41;42) Romans 3:20, 27; 4:5,6 No salvation in
\ good deeds.

(106) Titus 3:5, 6   By mercy, not good works.

(5;15) I John 3:23; John 6:29 The saving "work" is
\ belief.

(93) Galatians 3:10 One bad deed condemns

(110) Phil. 3:7-9 Paul didn't rely on good works

(93) Galations 2: 16 Good deeds inadequate.

(93) Galations 3: 11   The just live by faith.

7) **GOD'S WORD NEEDED:**

(29;31)   John 20:31; Isa. 55:1-11 Written to give life
(46)   Romans 10:17   for faith
(58)   I Pet. 1:23   for spiritual birth
(59)   I Pet. 2:2   for spiritual nourishment
(15)   John 6:63, 68   for spiritual living
(104-5)   II Tim. 2:15; 3:16,17   study & teaching
(102;38) I Tim. 4:15, 16; Col. 3:16   for safety
(53)   James 1:22   for obedience
(139)   Acts 17:11   for intelligent faith
(72)   Eph. 6:17   for warfare
(114)   Heb. 4:12   for spiritual insight
(38)   Col. 3: 16   let it fill you

8) **PRAYER IS NEEDED:**

(24)   John 16:24   for joy
(110)   Phil. 4:6   to replace worry
(72;65)   Eph. 6:18; I Thes. 5:17   continually
(55)   James 5:13-16   in good times and bad
(100)   I Tim. 2:8   with a good conscience
(60)   I Pet. 3:7   specifically for spouses

9) **OBEY:**

(23)   John 14:12, 21, 23 Out of love, fellowship
(5;44)   I John 3:14, 18, 19; Rom. 8:14, 16
                                    \ for assurance
(58)   I Peter 1:14   Be Holy

10) **CONFESSION IS THE REMEDY FOR FAILURE AND SINNING:**

(3)   I John 1:9   admission brings cleansing
(46)   Rom. 10:9,10 admission brings salvation
(234)   Ps. 51:17   confession restores inner
                    \ contentment and peace with God.

11) **THE BELIEVER'S SALVATION IS SURE:**

(6)   I John 5:13 can know you have eternal life
(5)   I John 3:20 even when you don't feel like it
(15)   John 6:37   you will not be rejected
(19)   John 10:27-30   God will not let you go
(45)   Romans 8:33-39   inseparable from Christ
(115)   Heb. 6: 18-20 anchored in God

	(120)	Hebrews 13:5 He will never leave you
	(103-4)	II Tim 1:12; 2:13 He is able and faithful
	(58)	1 Peter 1: 5 it's God's power that keeps us

12) **SHARE YOUR FAITH:**

	(60)	I Peter 3:15 be ready
	(123)	Acts 1:8 the Holy Spirit will assist you
	(213)	Mat. 28:19, 20 it's our job
	(103 -5)	II Tim. 2:2; 4:2 train others
	(36;38)	Col. 1:28,29; 4:17 work at it

13) **WARNINGS:**

(114;119) Heb. 2:3; 12: 25-29 no escape outside Jesus
(97) II Cor. 6:2   no promise of other time to be saved
About false religions: *(218)* all Jude; *(221-2)* Rev. 2
& 3; *37)* Col. 2:18-23; *(114;120)* Heb. 3:12: 13:8-9;
(106) Titus 3:10,11; *(77)* I Cor 3: 18-20; *(97-8)* II Cor
5:10,11; 11:13,14;   *(92)* Gal. 1:8,9

14) **JESUS IS GOD:**

	(3)	I John 1:1 was before the beginning
	(6)	I John 5: 20 is True God and eternal life
	(9)	John 1:1-4,10,14 is Creator, is Life, \ is glory of God
	(13)	John 5: 18 religious leaders say Jesus \ claimed to be God
	(19;109)	John 10: 30-33; Phil 2: 6 Jesus same as, \ equal to God
	(22)	John 14: 9 to see Jesus is to see God
	(24)	John 17: 5 Jesus is Deity before creation
	(129)	Acts 9: 5 God tells Saul God is Jesus
	(37)	Col. 2:9 all of God is bodily in Jesus
	(36)	Col 1: 15 Jesus is the image of the \ invisible God
	(219)	Rev. 19: 11; 20:11 Jesus is God, The Judge
	(218;221)	Rev. 1: 17; 22: 9 accepts worship as God
	(30)	Isaiah 45: 21 no other God beside \ the Savior - Creator

(100 -103) I Tim. 1:17; 3:16; 6: 15, 16   *(79)* I Cor.
8: 6; *(216)* Jude vs 25; *(105)* Titus 2:13, 14;
(110) Phil 2:6 Jesus the one & only God of salvation

15)   LIVE A NEW LIFE AS A CHRISTIAN:

(97)	II Cor. 5:17	Be different
(79)	I Cor. 6:19,20	Glorify God
(77)	I Cor. 3: 11-15	Work which will endure
(36)	Col. 1:10	Live pleasing to God
(37)	Col. 3:1-5	Live for eternal values
(37-38)	Col. 3: 15,17	Do all worthy of Jesus
(59; 60)	I Pet. 2:21; 4:1	Follow the example of Jesus
(119)	Heb. 12: 1, 2, 28, 29	Persevere
		\ (ex. Heb. 11: 24-26 *pg 118*)
(94)	Gal. 6:7-8	Don't fool yourself
(70;71)	Eph. 5 & 6	Specific instructions for all
(109)	Phil. 2:3-8; 1: 21-27	with Humility
(110)	Phil. 3:14-4:1	work at it
(65)	I Thes. 5:14-23	do this and don't do that
(37)	Col. 2:6	all by faith
(43)	Rom. 6: 1-7	freed from serving sin
(47)	Rom. 12: 1	by different thinking
(49)	Rom. 15: 1-7	don't just please yourself
(53; 55)	James 1:27; 2:16,20; 4:4	do practical,
		\ realistic charity
(106)	Titus 3: 8	do good for others
(94)	Galations 5: 22-25	value fruitfulness
(105)	Titus 2: 11-13	moderation
(97)	II Cor. 7: 1	Different in body, soul, spirit

16)   OVERCOMING TEMPTATIONS:

(81)	I Cor. 10:13	there is always a way to win
(115)	Heb. 4:14-16	through prayer
(103-4)	I Tim. 6:11, 12; II Tim. 2: 22	flee evil,
		\ fight for good

17)   LIVING IN HEAVEN:

(84)	1 Cor. 15: 51-57	Our bodies will be changed
(65)	1 Thes. 4: 13-18	Both the dead & living changed
(29,213)	John 20: 19-27; Luke 24:36-43	
		\ Jesus' resurrected body - we'll be like Him.
(213)	Lk. 24: 36-43; Jn. 20: 19-29	Able to eat & touch
(97)	2 Cor. 5: 1-8	Immediately at physical death
(220)	Rev. 21: 22 - 22: 5	Life in God's City

Topic 14 is about the fact that Jesus claimed to be God in the flesh. He claimed to be the Creator and an infinite Savior. He said God is His Father; that He, Jesus, is God the Son; and that there is also God the Holy Spirit. In doctrine, this fact is referred to as The Trinity. In order for Jesus to be the Savior spoken of in the Gospel Message, He of necessity must be God.

The concept of the Trinity is not an idea our minds can fully comprehend, but it is something we can basically grasp. One way of thinking of it is to consider the illustration of thoughts and words themselves. Lets use the concept of God.

The concept or idea of God is a thought we can register in our minds. The neurons of our brain can handle the concept of the reality and the essence of God. This basic concept of God as reality can be likened to God the Father.

We put the concept of God in a different form when we verbalize the word God and say out loud, "God". When our vocal cords, lips and tongue speak the word "God", a unique set of vibrations is set up in the atmosphere which carry the idea of God to the ears of those around us. This verbal sound pattern of the word "God" could be likened to the Holy Spirit.

We can write the word "God" on paper and see it in tangible form. "*GOD*" in solid print. This physical expression of the word "God" can be likened to Jesus, God the Son.

So, we can comprehend the concept of God in three ways: As a basic thought of reality held in our brain; as a voiced set of vibrations sent into the atmosphere by our mouth and caught by our ears; and as a visible and tangible printed form on paper such as this page. "GOD" expressed in three forms.

This is merely a paltry illustration of three-in-one, and another illustration of a more physical nature follows. The reality of God The Trinity is far above and beyond these illustrations, but they do serve to help us understand that even in our limited, finite world, a "trinity" is possible. We accept the Trinity by faith, but it's not an ignorant or foolish faith. It's reasonable faith.

"CIRSQUATRI" ™

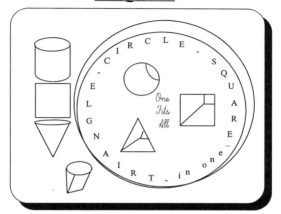

To help conceptualization of the three-in-one idea, imagine one solid object which is at the same time a triangle, a circle and a square. It's the round peg that fits a square hole, and a triangular.

You can make a three-in-one object. The end of a dowel is a one-inch circle. Cut the dowel one inch from the end. The ends together with the sides at their widest point become a one-inch square.

Clamp the one-inch piece on its side. Cut it from the outside edge of one end to the center of the circle's radius on the other end. Do the same to the other side. You are now looking down on a triangle.

From this position as a triangle, turn the dowel piece in the clamp one quarter turn and you are looking at a square. Stand the dowel piece on its circular end, and looking down you see a circle.

Even to us, three-in-one is possible. For God to make something three-in-one is easy. For God, Himself, to be a three-in-one Entity is no problem.

THE GOSPEL MESSAGE

a paraphrased, reorganized digest of

THE HOLY BIBLE

CONTENTS & ORDER OF BOOKS

<u>CONTENTS</u> <u>OF</u> <u>PICTURES</u>

As a young lad walks in the footprints of his dad,
similarly, we can follow the footsteps of Jesus.

The artists herein are
Greg Mann and **George Porter**,
both of Tulsa, Oklahoma.

THE MESSAGE IN BRIEF

FROM

1st John

JESUS IS ETERNAL AND WE CAN KNOW HIM PERSONALLY

Jesus Christ existed with God the Father in the beginning. [14) I John 1:1] He is called The Word, The Life, The Way, The Creator, The Son, The Savior. We heard Him with our own ears, scrutinized Him with our own eyes, and touched Him with our own hands. We are sharing His message with you so that you may, together with us, have fellowship with Him and with God His Father. This fellowship will bring you complete joy. [1) I John 1:4]

JESUS IS LIGHT AND CAN REMEDY DARKNESS

This is THE MESSAGE we heard from Jesus and share with you: God is absolute light and in Him is no darkness at all. [3) I John 1:5] If we say that we are fellowshipping with Him, yet continue living in sin's darkness, then we are lying. If we live in light as He lives in light, then we truly have fellowship with Him and with each other, and the sacrifice of Jesus Christ continues to cleanse us from every sin. If we claim to have no sin, [3) I John 1:8] we are deceiving ourselves, for God's light makes sin apparent. If we insist that we have never sinned, we are calling Him a liar and His word does not possess us. If we admit our sins, then He never fails, and is within God's law to forgive us the judgment of all our sins, cleansing us from every shortcoming. [10) I John 1:9]

I write this in order that you not sin. Yet, if we sin, we have a go-between with God the Father, Jesus Christ the perfect One. He is the payment for our sins, and for the sins of the entire world.

LIVING LIKE JESUS

The way we can have assurance that we know Jesus as Savior and Lord is by obeying Him. One who says I know Him personally, yet does not obey Him, is a liar. Those who unconditionally obey Him, will literally feel God's love, which gives them added assurance that they really do know Him. One who says that Jesus lives in him ought to live as Jesus lived.

LIVING IN LOVE

I write an ageless commandment: Love your brother. One who says he lives in God's light while hating his brother is self-deceived. One who lives in God's light loves his brother, and will not trip, nor cause others to stumble.

LIVING FOREVER

Do not love the world nor the treasures of the world. If you love the world, the love of the Father is crowded out. All that the world offers, the lust of the flesh, the lust of the eyes, and the pride of life, is not of the Father, but relates only to the world. This world is terminal and everything it offers, but one who does the will of God lives forever.

A STANDARD FOR BELIEVERS

It is the last age. Many who had professed to be part of us have left demonstrating that they never were truly one of us. We have insight from the Holy Spirit and a standard to discern who is genuine. One who denies that Jesus is the risen Christ is denying both the Father and the Son, and is not one of us.

You continue in the faith and you will receive the promised eternal life. Live in Him. Let Him live in you. Then, when He appears again, you will have confidence and not be ashamed before Him.

BEING LIKE THE GLORIFIED JESUS

What amazing love the Father shows to make us His children. [1] I John 3:1 We are the children of God. It isn't yet clear what we will be like in eternity, but we know that when He appears in eternal glory, we will be changed to be like Him. If you have this assurance, you'll strive to be like Him here and now.

RESULTS OF LIVING IN JESUS

The eternal God-the-Son became a sinless man, Jesus, to remove our sins. Therefore, whoever lives in Jesus will not continually sin. Living in Jesus results in righteousness. By contrast, the devil has sinned from the beginning and entices us to sin. One who sins continually is living for the devil. Jesus came to destroy the work of the devil. One who is born of God will not go on continually living for the devil, because Jesus is within him and Jesus cannot sin. True children of God can not enjoy habitually sinning.

Love each other. It is natural for the world to hate you, but for you to hate your Christian brother is equivalent to murder. We saw the love of God in His willingness to die for us. Similarly, our love is to be unselfish. If you have enough of this world's goods and are unwilling to give to your brother who is

4

hungry or naked or homeless, how could you love your brother? Show your love, not by words or theory, but by helpful actions and practical deeds.

When you practice love-in-action, you will know that Truth is living in you and you will have a peaceful heart before God. [9) I John 3: 14-23] If your heart condemns you, God is wiser and bigger than your heart, forgiving you your shortcomings. But when your heart does not condemn you, then you will experience peace and confidence, and not be afraid even though knowing you will one day face The Holy God. [11)] Meanwhile, our requests of Him are granted because we obey Him and are living to please Him. Of course, His primary commandment is that we believe in His Son, Jesus Christ. [6) I John 3: 23]

A STANDARD FOR TRUTH

Do not believe every religious teaching, but examine them to know whether or not they are what they claim. There are many false prophets. Only those who teach that Jesus is the Christ, the Messiah come in the flesh, are of God! Whoever does not teach this is not of God. You believers are of God and have overcome false spirits because greater is the true Spirit in you than the false spirit in the world.

GOD IS LOVE

You are loved. [1) I John 4:7] Love each other, for love is of God, and those who are born of God are branded by love. God is love. Love sent His only begotten Son into the world that we might live eternally through Him. We did not initiate that love; He did when He came and paid for our sins.

Since God loved us that much, we ought to be able to love each other. Although no one has ever seen God, we can see His essence reflected in us as we love because of His Spirit within us.

The Father sent His son to be the Savior of the world. Whoever admits that Jesus is the risen Son of God is indwelt by God and by God's love. [1&2) I John 4: 18,19] This love removes fear, so that we need not tremble in the presence of God. If you still tremble at the thought of facing God, then you don't have within you the love of God. You can love Him because He first loved you.

5

FAITH ENABLES A RELATIONSHIP WITH GOD

Whoever is born of God overcomes the world by faith. [5) I John 5:4] We believe by faith the witness of a man in court. Is not the witness of God more reliable? The witness of God is confirmed to these who believe in Jesus by an awareness of the Spirit within them. Those who do not believe God, by that disbelief, call God a liar.

GOD SAYS JESUS IS ETERNAL LIFE

This is the witness of God: God says He gives us eternal life through His Son. He who has the Son has eternal life. He who does not have the Son does not have eternal life. You who believe on the Son of God may know for sure that you do have eternal life. [11) I John 5: 9-13] I write this so you'll have confidence in your salvation, and so you will continue to believe.

JESUS IS IN FACT GOD THE SON

We testify personally that the Son of God has come and enlightened us to know Him who is true, even Jesus Christ. He is the true God and eternal life. [14) I John 5:20] Amen.

THE PERSON
AND SOURCE
OF THE MESSAGE

FROM

The Gospel of John

In the beginning, Jesus, sometimes called The Word, did not just exist with God, but was God. He was Creator, and made everything that was ever made. He was Life itself, and the Light of all humanity, penetrating the darkness. He became the physical expression of the invisible God. [14) John 1:1-4]

A man named John was sent by God to identify Jesus and to explain that Jesus is Light -- the true light for everyone. The eternal Jesus became flesh and lived among us. We witnessed His glory and deity, [14) John 1:14] and saw that He was the personification of grace and truth. Yes, God, as Jesus, came to live in the world He created, among the people He had made and through whom He was born, but He was neither recognized nor accepted. They did not know who He was. But, those who by faith do accept Him will be made children of God because they recognize Him and believe that He is the eternal One. These believers who know Him are spiritually born again, [4) John 1:12] not by physical conception or natural processes, nor because of human desire, but by God, supernaturally.

THE MESSAGE OF JOHN THE BAPTIZER

John said, "Jesus of Nazareth was born after I, though as Creator He was always here. As Messiah, He will benefit us all because His omnipotence, grace and truth will complete the law of Moses. Jesus came to us from the heart of God, and, being God's only conceived Son, is God in a human body."

One day, seeing Jesus, John exclaimed, "Look, the Lamb of God who atones all sin. [4) John 1:29-34] He is the Messiah, the unique Son of God."

JESUS RECRUITS DISCIPLES

Two of John's followers began following Jesus. Jesus turned to them and asked, "What do you wish?" They responded, "Master, where do you live?" Jesus replied, "Come and see."

One of these, Andrew, found his brother, Simon, and took him to Jesus, saying, "We have found Messiah, the Christ."

Seeing Simon, Jesus said, "You have been going by Simon, but now you will be called Peter, meaning stone."

Thereafter, Jesus saw Philip and said, "Follow me." Philip got Nathaniel and said, "We have found the Messiah. He is

Jesus of Nazareth, Joseph's son." Nathaniel questioned, "Can any good come from Nazareth?" Philip replied, "Come and see."

Jesus saw Nathaniel and said, "There is a true Israelite without guile." "How do you know me?" asked Nathaniel. Jesus said, "I saw you before you and Philip talked under the fig tree." Nathaniel said, "You are the Son of God, King of Israel." Jesus said, "You will see much greater things than this."

FIRST MIRACLE OF JESUS

Jesus was invited to a wedding in Cana of Galilee. When the wine was gone, the mother of Jesus said to Him, "They are out of wine." Then to the servants she said, "Do whatever Jesus tells you." The servants turned to Jesus who said, "Fill the water pots to the brim with water." They filled them. Jesus then said, "Serve it to the host." When the host, unaware of its origin, tasted the water, it was wine. The host said, "This is excellent wine. It should have been served first." This miracle confirmed His disciples' belief in Jesus.

JESUS DEMONSTRATES HIS AUTHORITY

Jesus went to the Jewish Passover feast in Jerusalem. There He found in the temple merchants selling to be sacrificed oxen, sheep and doves; and money changers exchanging foreign currency. With a whip Jesus drove them all out saying, "Do not make my Father's house a marketplace."

The Jews said, "Prove to us that You have the authority to do this." Jesus replied, "Destroy this Temple and in three days I will raise it up." Said the Jews, "It took 45 years to build this temple; could You rebuild it in three days?" But Jesus spoke allegorically of His own body, which after His death and resurrection His disciples remembered, reconfirming their belief in Jesus.

At this Passover, many believed in Jesus because of His authoritative teaching and miracles.

A RELIGIOUS LEADER INVESTIGATES JESUS AND BELIEVES

Nicodemus, a Pharisee, a ruler of the Jews, came to Jesus one night. "Teacher, we know You are from God because of Your miracles." Jesus said, "Truly, unless one is born again he cannot see the kingdom of God." Asked Nicodemus, "How could a man be born a second time? It is impossible."

Jesus said, "Unless one is born both physically and spiritually he cannot enter the kingdom of God. That which is flesh relates to the physical and that which is spirit relates to the spiritual. Don't be put off because I said you must be born again. I have come from heaven so that humanity can ascend to heaven. As Moses impaled before the people a snake in the desert, so I will be impaled before the world so that whoever believes Me will not be destroyed but will have eternal life. <u>God loves mankind so much that He sent His Son, conceived of a virgin, that whoever believes in Me should not be destroyed but have everlasting life.</u> [1] & 4) John 3: 16-18 <u>God did not send Me to condemn the world but to save it. One who believes Me is not condemned, but one who does not believe Me is already condemned</u> because he doesn't believe and because Light is come into the world, and he loves darkness and his evil deeds more than Truth and Light. <u>One who believes on the Son of God has everlasting life. One who does not believe on the Son shall not see life, but will instead see the wrath of God.</u>" 4) John 3: 36

<u>JESUS IS LIKE LIVING WATER</u>

Jesus prepared to leave Judea for Galilee, saying it was mandatory He go through Samaria. When He entered the city of Samaria called Sycar, He saw a well dug by Jacob. Jesus sat on the well to rest while His disciples went into the city for supplies.

Presently there came a woman to get water. Jesus asked, "Would you give me a drink." The woman answered, "Since the Jews will not associate with Samaritans, why would You ask me for a drink?"

Jesus responded, "If you knew who it is asking for a drink, you would have asked a drink of Me and I would have given to you living water." "Sir," she said, "The well is deep and You have nothing with which to draw water." Jesus said, "If you drink of the well's water, you need to drink often. If you drink of the water I give, you will not thirst any more, for My water is an artesian well springing up to everlasting life." The woman said, "Sir, give me that water so I will not have to come back here."

<u>WORSHIP IS AN ATTITUDE</u>

Said Jesus, "Go get your husband and return." She said, "I have no husband." Jesus answered, "I know that you have had five husbands and are living with a man who is not your husband." "You are a prophet," remarked the woman. "Answer this: Should we Samaritans worship in Jerusalem or in our own holy places." Jesus said, "What matters is attitude. God is Spirit. To genuinely worship Him, one must do so in spirit and in truth."

JESUS IS MESSIAH

The woman said, "I know that Messiah is coming, the Christ, to teach us all things." Jesus said, "I am He." The woman forgot her waterpot and ran back to her city. She said to the men, "Follow me to a Man who has told me everything I ever did. He must be Messiah." They followed her.

HARVESTING LIVES FOR ETERNITY

Meanwhile Jesus' disciples returned. Amazed that He'd speak with a woman, they asked Him to eat. He said, "No, thanks. I'm nourished in doing My Father's will and completing His work. One can reap only at harvest time. Look at the opportunity coming now. The field is ripe and ready for harvest. The planter and the reaper celebrate together when the crop is in. I sowed the seed earlier. Now, help Me reap."

As He spoke, a crowd of curious, interested men were approaching, being led by the woman. Many in that city believed in Jesus because of the testimony of this woman.

After Jesus stayed two days with them, many more believed because of His teachings, and these reported, "Now we know that This is indeed Christ, the Savior of the world."

MIRACLES OF HEALING AND BELIEVING

As Jesus journeyed on, a political leader found Him. "I have a sick son back at Capernaum," he told Jesus. "Please heal him, for he is near death." Jesus said, "Go on home. Your son is well." The man took Jesus at His word and went home. When he arrived, he was told the time of his son's recovery, and he noted that it was at the precise time Jesus had assured him. This man and his entire family believed on Jesus.

Jesus went to Jerusalem for a Jewish feast. A pool was there where lay all kinds of handicapped and sick folk, waiting for the water to move. They believed that if someone would put them first in the water after it stirred, that they would be healed of whatever their malady.

A man crippled for thirty-eight years lay at the pool, but had no one to help him quickly into the water when it bubbled. Jesus saw him and spoke, "Would you like to be well?" "Oh, yes," the man replied, "but I have no one to put me into the water in time." Jesus responded to him, "Roll up your bed and walk away." The man believed Jesus, took up his bedroll, and walked away, just as he was told. It was a Sabbath day.

JESUS AND GOD THE FATHER ARE ONE

The religious leaders, seeing him carry his bedroll, reprimanded him for working on the Sabbath, thus technically breaking the law of Moses. He explained to them that when Jesus cured him He told him to take his bedroll and leave the sick area.

When the religious authorities confronted Jesus, He said, "This healing is God My Father's working through Me. I must do My Father's work."

The religious leaders, therefore, wanted to execute Jesus not only for working on the Sabbath and instructing others to do so, but mostly for <u>calling God His Father, making Himself equal with God.</u> [14) John 5:18]

Jesus went on explaining, "My Father will do greater things than this through Me. Even the dead will be raised to life. My Father wants all to honor His Son in the same way they honor the Father. For this reason He has given all judgments to Me. If you do not honor Me, you do not honor My Father. I say to you truly, if you believe what I tell you, then you have everlasting life and will never be judged for your sin but have already been awarded eternal life. There is a time coming when all the dead will hear My voice and come forth to stand before Me to be judged for eternal life or eternal death. John was witness to this fact, and the work My Father is doing through Me is a stronger witness. It is evident that you do not believe either witness for you have not received Me. <u>Study the Scriptures</u> which you believe guide you to eternal life -- <u>they testify of Me.</u> Yet, you still do not <u>come to Me for eternal life.</u> [4) John 5:39-40] I have come in My Father's name and you do not believe Me. Others will come in their own name and you will believe them. Obviously you do not have God's love in you for you have rejected both the testimony of the Scripture and the testimony of the Father's work through Me. If you do not believe the Scripture or the Father,

how will you <u>believe Me that you might have eternal life?</u> [4) John 5:47]
I say all this to give you opportunity to be saved."

MIRACULOUSLY FEEDING A CROWD

A great multitude began following Jesus everywhere, having seen the miraculous healings of the sick and handicapped. Jesus said to one of His followers, "Philip, I'd like to give lunch to this crowd. How would you suggest we do it."

Philip said, "We haven't enough money to provide each one just a bite." Andrew interjected, "There's a lad's lunch of five buns and two dried fish...."

"Have the crowd sit down orderly", said Jesus, "and bring Me the lad with the little lunch."

Having given thanks for the food, Jesus began to break the bread and fish into baskets for the disciples to distribute to the multitude. Everyone ate until they were filled.

"Gather up the leftovers", said Jesus. "Waste nothing."

Twelve baskets full were gathered after more than 5,000 had eaten all they wanted from the boy's lunch. Said the crowd who had participated in the miracle, "Truly This is the promised Messiah."

MIRACULOUSLY CONTROLLING NATURAL FORCES

That evening, Jesus, staying behind to pray alone, sent the disciples across the Sea of Galilee. After dark, an ugly storm came up, and the disciples, rowing into the wind, were getting nowhere. Suddenly, they saw a Figure walking on the sea, getting near the ship. They were scared out of their wits. Jesus spoke, "It is I. Don't be afraid." They welcomed Him aboard, and instantly the water was calm and the ship was at the port of destination.

The next day, some of the crowd from Tiberius near where the boy's lunch had fed so many, took boats across to follow the disciples. They were startled to see Jesus there also. They asked the disciples, "How did Jesus get here? We saw you take the only extra boat last night without Him, and we know He did not come over with anyone else." Then they turned to Jesus and asked Him direct, "Teacher, how did you get here?"

THE GREATEST MIRACLE IS TO BELIEVE JESUS

Jesus responded, "Really, you are following Me because you got a free meal. Don't just look to Me for the

14

physical things I can give you, look to Me for the everlasting life I can give you."

The people asked, "How can we do the works of God as You do." Jesus said, "<u>The work of God for you to do is to believe on His Son.</u>" 6) John 6:29

The people asked, "Can You show us a sign by which we can know for sure You are who You say You are? Could You give us manna from heaven to eat as Moses did?"

Jesus said, "Free food again. Moses gave your fathers bread from heaven and they died. I am the true, living bread from heaven -- the Bread of Life. If you come to Me, you will never have spiritual hunger; if you believe on Me you will never have spiritual thirst. You have seen Me and do not yet believe. <u>Those who believe on Me I will never reject for any reason. Whoever believes on Me has everlasting life.</u> 11) John 6:37-40 I am the Bread of Life which you may take to yourself and live forever. As I live by the Father who sent Me, so <u>you may live by Me.</u> 4) John 6:57

Among the disciples, some questioned, "This philosophy is unusual. Is it believable?" Jesus intuitively knew their doubting and said, "Does the Bread of Life illustration offend or confuse you? <u>Remember, it is the Spirit who gives life. The illustration is spiritual not physical, and if you accept it, it will bring you life.</u> 7) John 6:63 But some of you do not believe. (Jesus knew who did and did not believe and who would betray Him.) Some of Jesus' disciples ceased following Him after this lesson. To the twelve remaining Jesus said, "Why do you not also leave?" Peter responded, "Lord, to whom would we go? <u>Only You have the words of eternal life. We believe and are certain</u> 7) John 6:68 that You are THE Christ (Messiah), THE Son of God." Jesus said, "I choose you twelve to be My close companions; yet one of you is a betrayer."

JESUS FORCES EACH ONE TO MAKE A CHOICE

At the Jew's Feast of Tabernacles, Jesus taught many things. "My teaching isn't Mine, it's My Father's who sent Me. If you truly want to do His will, you will recognize that My teaching is of God. You Jews circumcise a man on the Sabbath Day and say it is keeping the law of Moses. I have healed on the Sabbath Day and you say it is breaking the law of Moses. Be careful in your judgments. Do not judge by traditions or appearances, but according to truth and right.

"I am the true water of life. If anyone thirst, let him come to Me and drink, for whoever believes on Me shall have within himself a spring of living water." Many who heard Him teach believed in Jesus, saying He is the Christ. Others would not believe, causing a division.

JESUS FORGIVES THE GUILTY

While He taught in the temple one day, Jesus was accosted by the Scribes and Pharisees who dragged with them a woman caught in the act of adultery. "Moses' law says to stone an adulteress," they reminded Jesus. "What do You say?" Jesus ignored them and wrote on the ground with His finger. After further cajoling from the leaders, Jesus stood and said, "Let the sinless one among you cast the first stone." Then he stooped and again wrote on the ground. The accusers, convicted by their own conscience, left one by one, leaving Jesus with the adulteress. Jesus stood and said, "Where are your accusers? Does no one condemn you?" "No one," replied the woman. "Neither do I condemn you," said Jesus, "Go your way and stop committing adultery."

TRUTH SETS FREE AND GIVES ETERNAL LIFE

Then Jesus resumed teaching the listeners. "I am the Light of the world. He that follows Me will not live in darkness but will have the Light of life. It is written in your law that the witness of two men is to be believed. I give witness of Myself and My Father gives witness of Me. But you know neither Me nor My Father, for, if you know Me, you know My Father also. Soon I go My way, and you will look for Me, but you will die in your sins and where I go you cannot come. You are from earth; I am from above. You are of this world; I am not of this world. Therefore, if you do not believe in Me, you will die in your sins. However, if you live by My word, then you become truly My people, will recognize the Truth, and the Truth will make you free. Whoever commits sin is the servant of sin, but when I set you free, you will be truly free."

The religious leaders mocked, taunting Jesus with insincere questions. Jesus responded, "You are of your father, the devil, and you perform the lusts of your father. Because I tell you the truth, you do not believe Me. Who among you can convict Me of Sin, yet, if I speak truth, why don't you believe Me? One who is of God listens to Me; the fact that you will not listen to Me is evidence that you are not of God. I tell you truly, one who listens to Me, and believes, will never see eternal death."

JESUS HEALS A BLIND MAN AND GRANTS HIM ETERNAL LIFE

One Sabbath day, as Jesus walked by a man who had been blind since birth, His disciples asked, "Who did sin, this man or his parents, that he was born blind?" Jesus said, "Neither. But in order that the glory of God may be demonstrated, I will today do the work of God through him. I am the Light of the world."

Jesus made mud from dust, put it on the man's eyes, and instructed him to wash off the mud in a pool called Siloam. The man did as instructed and returned with full vision.

When his friends saw him, they said, "Aren't you the blind beggar?" "Yes I am," he replied. "How do you now see?" they asked. "A Man called Jesus healed me," he explained. "Where is Jesus?" they asked. "I don't know," he said. The people took the healed man to the Pharisees who questioned him about his new sight. "Jesus healed me, and now I can see," he said. Some of the Pharisees said, "Jesus is not of God for He doesn't observe the Sabbath."

But they were split over the issue because others said, "How could a sinner do such miracles?" They asked the former blind beggar, "What do you think of the Man who healed you?" "He is a Prophet," he responded.

Some leaders refused to believe the alleged healed man had been blind or cured by Jesus, and pledged that anyone saying Jesus was the Christ, the Messiah, would be excommunicated from the Synagogue.

They called in the parents and interrogated them, "Do you say your son was born blind? Then how does he now see?" The parents, fearful of these religious officials, replied, "This is our son and he was born totally blind. But how it is that he can now see we do not know. He is of age, ask him."

The leaders recalled the man who had been blind. "Give God praise," they said, "not this breaker of religious law, Jesus." Answered the healed man, "Whether or not He is a lawbreaker I don't know. One thing I do know, I was blind, but now I see. Since the world began, no one has been able to make a man born blind to see. If this Man were not of God, He couldn't have done it."

The leaders were furious. "You are a complete sinner. Do you think you can teach us?" And they excommunicated him.

Jesus found the man and asked, "Do you believe in the Son of God." And the man answered, "Who is He, that I might believe on Him?" Jesus said, "I am He." The man responded, "Lord, I believe," and worshipped Him.

Jesus said, "I came into the world that the blind might see, and that those who erroneously think they see might realize they are actually blind."

JESUS IS OUR SHEPHERD

Jesus said, "One who enters the sheep enclosure by some means other than the door is a thief. He who enters by the door is the shepherd. To him the guard opens the door so he can call his sheep by name and lead them out. The sheep follow him because they know his voice. They will not follow a stranger, but will scatter, for they do not know his voice.

"I am the Door. Thieves and robbers come before Me, but the sheep do not recognize them. One who enters by Me will be safe, and can come in and out and find nourishing pasture. Thieves steal, kill and destroy. I am come to give life -- life full, satisfying and eternal. [2 & 4) John 10:9,10]

"I am the good Shepherd and give My life for the sheep. One watching the flock who is not the good Shepherd will run when danger approaches, and the sheep are killed or scattered. I am the good Shepherd and know My sheep and am known by My sheep. There are sheep of Mine not yet in My flock. Those I must find and bring into My flock so there may be one true flock and one true Shepherd. When I give My life for the sheep, I will reclaim it. No one can take My life from Me and no one is needed to give it back. I have received power from My Father to give up My life and to live again."

These teachings caused further division among the people. So they asked Him, "Tell us clearly, straight out, are You the Christ?" Jesus replied, "I have told you clearly, but you won't believe. The works that I do in My Father's name tell you clearly, but you do not believe because you are not part of My flock. <u>My sheep listen to My voice and follow Me. I know them and give them eternal life and they shall never perish. No one can wrench them from Me. My Father who gives them to Me is greater than all, and no one can wrench them from My Father's hand.</u> 11) John 10:27-29 <u>I and My Father are one.</u>" 14) John 10:30

JESUS AND GOD THE FATHER ARE ONE

The Jews began to stone Him. "For which of My works do you stone Me?" asked Jesus. "Not for any of Your works," they replied, "but <u>because You make Yourself God</u>." 14) John 10:33 Jesus said, "If I am not doing the work of God, do not believe Me. But if I am doing God's work, then <u>believe that the Father is in Me and I am in the Father.</u>" For this they again tried to stone Him, but Jesus would not allow it and, walking through the crowd, retreated to the place where John had baptized. Multitudes sought Him out and said, "Everything that John said about Jesus is true." And many believed on Him there.

JESUS RAISES LAZARUS FROM DEATH

Lazarus, brother of Mary and Martha, was seriously ill. His sisters sent word to Jesus that His good friend was sick. Upon receiving the message, Jesus said to His disciples, "The purpose of this illness isn't the death of Lazarus, but the glory of God." Jesus loved Mary, Martha and Lazarus, but He waited two days before starting His journey to their Bethany home.

Let us now go to Bethany to awaken our friend, Lazarus, from sleep," Jesus said. The disciples replied, "Since Lazarus is sick, he needs sleep." Jesus said, "I was using an metaphor to mean Lazarus is dead. It is good for you that I was not there to heal him because now your faith will be increased."

By the time Jesus arrived, Lazarus had been buried four days. Many friends of the family were there from Jerusalem to comfort Mary and Martha. When Martha went out to greet Jesus she said, "Lord, if You had been here my brother would not have died. Still, I know that even now God will give whatever You ask." Jesus said, "Your brother will rise again." "Yes," said Martha, "I know he will rise again at the resurrection." Jesus said, "<u>I am the resurrection and the life. One who believes in Me, though he be dead, will live; and one who is alive and believes in</u>

Me will never really die. Do you believe this?" [4] John 11:25 She said, "Yes, Lord, I believe You are Christ, the Son of God."

When Mary met Jesus, she knelt at His feet and said, "Lord, if only You had been here, Lazarus would still be alive." Seeing her weeping, Jesus ached in His heart and wept. Friends commented, "How He loved Lazarus. Could not this miracle worker have caused him to get well?"

"Where is he buried?" Jesus asked. "Come and see," was the reply. They took Him to a cave closed with a boulder. Jesus ordered, "Remove the boulder." "But Lord," Martha gasped, "he's been buried four days. There will be the stench of decay." Jesus consoled, "Remember how I said if you'd believe, you would see the work of God?" So they removed the boulder.

Jesus prayed, "Father, I thank You that You always hear Me." Then, He commanded, "Lazarus, come forth!" At once, the dead man was standing in front of them, still wrapped in burial cloth head to foot. Jesus said, "Unwrap him, he is freed."

Many family friends, seeing this and other things Jesus had done, believed on Jesus. Others were still skeptical and reported these events to the Pharisees. The Pharisees and Chief Priests called a council to determine what to do in the face of all these miracles, fearing that everyone would believe on Jesus to the extent that the Roman authorities would strip them of their religious titles and even their political power. The high priest said, "It is better for one man to die than for the whole nation to be eliminated." From that meeting forward, they plotted to kill Him and issued an order that, if anyone knew Jesus' whereabouts when not in public, they should inform the council.

PROPER WORSHIP IS A PRIORITY

The Jewish Passover Feast was near, and Jerusalem was full of travelers. Six days before the feast, Jesus went again to Lazarus' home. Martha served supper, Lazarus joined Jesus at the table, but Mary chose an expensive ointment and anointed the feet of Jesus, filling the house with the fragrance. Disciple Judas Iscariot reprimanded her, "You should have sold this ointment for a good price and given the money for the poor." In truth, Judas, who would be the one to betray Jesus, didn't care for the poor, but as treasurer for the group, wanted to get his hands on the money. Jesus rebutted Judas, "Leave her alone. She has been saving this ointment for My burial. The poor will always be here for you to help, but I will not always be here physically."

THE JEALOUSY OF FALSE RELIGIOUS LEADERS

The rumor having spread that Jesus was there, many curiosity seekers came not only to see Jesus but also to glimpse Lazarus whom He had raised from the dead. For this reason, the chief priest consulted how to kill not only Jesus, but also Lazarus, since many people believed on Jesus due to Lazarus.

So many knew of this miracle that as Jesus came to Passover, a crowd formed, took palm branches to shade Him and to pave the path He rode on a donkey, and shouted, "Hosanna. Blessed is He who comes in the name of the Lord." All of this fulfilled Messianic prophecies. The Pharisees worried among themselves, "We failed! The whole world has gone after Him."

BELIEVE WHILE THE OPPORTUNITY IS PRESENT

Jesus taught His disciples, "The time has come for Me to be glorified. Unless a kernel of wheat be planted in the ground, it will remain just one kernel of wheat. But if the seed germinates, it yields bushels of wheat.

"He who cherishes his life so that he will not let it go, will lose it. He who lets go of his life in this world will keep it eternally. If anyone wants to serve Me, let him obey Me and stay with Me, and he will receive honor from My Father.

"My soul is grieved, yet it is for this specific time and cause that I came into the world. Father, glorify Your name. Now, this world is judged; now, satan, the prince of this world, is cast out. When I am crucified, I will draw everyone to Me.

"Only a little longer is the Light with you. Believe in the Light that you may be children of Light. When you believe on Me, you believe on Him who sent Me; and when you see Me, you see Him who sent Me. I am Light to the world so that those who believe in Me should not exist in darkness. I came to save the world, but those who don't believe will be judged by the words that I have spoken. What I speak is from the Father and gives everlasting life."

AN EXAMPLE OF HUMILITY AND HONOR IN SERVICE

After supper with His disciples, Jesus began to wash their feet. Peter said, "Lord, You're not to wash my feet." Said

Jesus, "You don't understand the significance of what I'm doing, but if I don't wash you, then you don't belong to Me." Said Peter, "Than wash my hands, my head and my feet." Jesus replied, "Since you have bathed, you need only your feet washed (from the dusty road)." The washings finished, Jesus asked His disciples, "Do you comprehend what I did? If your Lord has washed your feet, you ought to wash each other's feet. The servant is not above his Master. You'll be happy if you follow My example. I don't mean all of you, for there's a betrayer among you." Then said Jesus to Judas, "What you are going to do, do now." The others at the table did not realize what Jesus meant, but surmised Jesus had sent Judas on an errand.

LOVE IDENTIFIES THE DISCIPLES OF JESUS

With Judas gone, Jesus continued teaching. "Now I will be glorified, and the Father in Me. My children, I will be with you only a little longer, for you cannot come where I am going. I want you to love each other as I have loved you. Let the world see that you are My disciples by your love for one another."

Peter said, "Lord, where is it You go that I can't follow? I am willing to die for You." "Are you, Peter?" Jesus said. "Actually, before the rooster crows at sunrise you will three times deny even knowing Me."

TRUST IDENTIFIES THE DISCIPLES OF JESUS

"Don't worry. Trust Me as you trust God," said Jesus. "In My Father's heavenly estate are many homes. That is why I have told you I would go and prepare a mansion for you, then return to take you to live with Me. [4) John 14:2,3] You know where I mean and how to get there."

Thomas asked, "Lord, how can we be sure of the way there?" Jesus replied, "I am the Way, the Truth and the Life. The only way to the Father is through Me. [4) John 14:6] When one knows Me, he knows My Father also." Philip asked, "Would You give us a glimpse of the Father?" Jesus said to him, "Look at Me. Don't you know Me? When you see Me, you see the Father. I am in the Father and the Father in Me. [14) John 14:9] He is speaking and working through Me. You can believe both His words and works in Me. In truth, one who believes in Me will do even greater works than I have done because I am going to the Father to grant the petitions you will make to the Father in My name."

OBEDIENCE IDENTIFIES THE DISCIPLES OF JESUS

"<u>Demonstrate your love for Me by keeping My commandments.</u> [9) John 14:12] When I am gone, the Father will send the Holy Spirit to comfort you. Unbelievers cannot receive Him, nor understand Him, because they do not recognize truth. But you I will not leave companionless. I, by the Spirit, will come to you and be alive within you. <u>You who obey My commandments are the ones who love Me, and whom are loved by Me and My Father.</u> [9) John 14:21,23] <u>You are the ones to whom We will make Ourselves known, and the ones to whom the Holy Spirit will teach spiritual truths,</u> and the ones who will be enabled to remember what I have taught you. <u>I give you My peace.</u> I do not give as the world gives, <u>so do not be worried or afraid.</u>" [2) John 14:27]

PRODUCTIVENESS IDENTIFIES THE DISCIPLES OF JESUS

"I am like a grapevine, you are like branches and My Father is like a caretaker. Unfruitful branches are taken away, and fruitful branches are pruned so they will be more fruitful. The word that I speak is the nourishment that keeps you healthy. Stay in Me and allow Me to produce through you, for only then can there be fruit. Without Me you can do nothing. In Me you produce glory to the Father. <u>The Father and I love you</u> -- stay within Our love. You will stay within Our love when you obey My commandments. I command you to believe on Me and to love one another. <u>Greater love has no one than to give his life for his friend.</u>" [1) John 15:3]

JOY IDENTIFIES THE DISCIPLES OF JESUS

"<u>I say all this so My joy may stay within you and so your joy may be complete.</u> [2) John 15:11] I have chosen you to bring forth fruit, to be those whose prayers are answered, and to love each other. Those in the world will detest you as they detested Me, because you are not one of them. Just as they hated and persecuted Me, so they will you because of Me and because they do not know the Father. Those who hate Me, hate My Father. Those who would have believed Me will believe you also. You are My witnesses because you have personally been with Me.

"So you will not be caught off guard or confused, I tell you in advance that religious leaders will excommunicate you, and even kill you, saying they are working for God; but they are not acquainted with God the Father nor Me."

THE HOLY SPIRIT IDENTIFIES THE DISCIPLES OF JESUS

"While I have been with you, you didn't need the Holy Spirit. It's good that I am leaving, for I will send the Holy Spirit to comfort you, and to convict the world of sin, of My righteousness, and of coming judgment. Those in the world who don't believe in Me will be convicted of sin because of their unbelief. They will be convicted by My righteousness because I have been raised to live again with My Father. And they will be convicted at the judgment because satan is judged and defeated by My death and resurrection. The Spirit will guide you into truth and show you things to come. He will glorify Me."

PRAYER AND PEACE IDENTIFY THE DISCIPLES OF JESUS

"You will be sorrowful when I leave you, but that sorrow will be turned to joy when I see you again, and that joy cannot be taken from you. Meanwhile, <u>whatever you ask the Father in keeping with My name He will give. Ask, and you will receive that which will make your joy full.</u> [8) John 16:24] <u>Be assured that the Father loves you</u> [1) John 16:27] because you have believed that I am of the Father, that I came from the Father and that I am returning to the Father. <u>I tell you this so that you may have peace. In the world you will have testings and troubles, but be optimistic and happy, I have conquered the world.</u>" [2) John 16:33]

A PRAYER OF JESUS WITH HIS DISCIPLES

Jesus looked toward heaven and said, "Father, this is the time. Glorify Me so I can bring glory to You and can <u>give eternal life to My own. My own are those who know You, the only true God, and who know Me,</u> [4) John 17:3] Your only Son whom You sent for this purpose. I have glorified You and finished the work You assigned Me here. <u>Demonstrate the glory that I had with You before I created the world.</u> [14) John 17:5]

"I pray for these who know I am uniquely of You. I am not staying in the world with them, but am returning to You. Keep these secure in My name, as I, while I was with them, kept them secure in Your name. Let My joy be realized in them. The

24

world will reject them, because they are not of the world. Set them apart to truth -- Your Word is truth. I am sending them out into the world as You sent Me, dedicated to truth.

"I also pray for those who will believe on Me through their work and testimony. Let us all be one, that, by this evidence of Your love, the world can believe in Me and can know that You love the believers just as You love Me. I want these to be with Me eternally, to see My glory and to understand My eternal nature. O, Father, the world has never known You, but these believers know that You have sent Me and that I am in You and You are in Me. I have given them Your name, that the love We share may be in them and that I by My Spirit may dwell in them."

BETRAYED BY JUDAS

Jesus and His disciples went to a familiar garden where they often found quiet. It was there Judas brought the mercenaries from the chief priests and Pharisees. When they approached, Jesus, knowing their intent, said, "Whom do you seek?" They said, "Jesus." Jesus responded, "I am He." At this, the men fell down backward. Jesus asked again, "Whom do you want?" "Jesus of Nazareth," they said. Jesus answered, "I am He. Let these others go their way." But Peter slashed out with a dagger and cut off the right ear of Malchus, the high priest's servant. Said Jesus to Peter, "Put away your weapon. Should I resist My Father's plan." And He healed the severed ear.

The soldiers bound Jesus and led Him away.

DENIED BY PETER

Peter and John followed surreptitiously. Knowing the high priest, John was allowed into the palace where Jesus was taken, and permitted to bring Peter into the courtyard. A girl said to Peter, "You're one of His followers." "I am not," assured Peter.

Peter moved to an open fire in the courtyard. "Aren't you one of His disciples?" asked someone there. Peter denied it.

Meanwhile, the high priest interrogated Jesus. Jesus replied, "I taught openly in the temple and synagogues, and did nothing secretly. Ask about Me of those who heard." At this, an officer of the priesthood slapped Jesus.

About this time, Peter was asked by a relative of the man whose ear he had cut off, "Didn't I see you in the garden with

Him?" Peter vehemently denied again -- and immediately heard the cock crow.

A MOCKERY OF A TRIAL

Jesus was led to Pilate's judgment hall. Pilate asked, "What's charged against this man? Why not judge Him by your own law?"

Said the Jews, "If He were not a lawbreaker we would not have brought Him to you. But Roman law forbids us to crucify a man."

Pilate asked Jesus, "Are You The King of the Jews?" Jesus answered, "Is that your own question or did others suggest it?" Pilate replied, "I am not a Jew. Your own nation and chief priests have brought You here. What have You done?"

Jesus said, "My Kingdom is not of this world, but I am a King. For that purpose I was born. I came into the world to declare truth. One who cherishes truth will listen and recognize My message." Pilate said pointedly, "What is truth?!" Then, not waiting for an answer, he reported to the Jews, "I find no fault in this man. But you have a custom that I should release to you a convict during the Passover season. Would you like me to release The King of the Jews?" The wrought up crowd yelled, "Not Jesus, but Barabbas." Barabbas was a robber and murderer.

A FALSE SENTENCE OF DEATH

Pilate had Jesus beaten. The soldiers shaped a crown of thorns and forced it onto His head. Then, putting a purple robe on Him, they mocked Him, "Hail, King of the Jews," while they slapped Him. Then, as Jesus with the thorn crown and purple robe stood there, Pilate said to the Jews, "I find no fault with Him. Look at this man." But the chief priests and officers cried out, "Crucify Him, crucify Him!" Pilate capitulated, "You take Him then and judge Him in your courts, for I find no fault in Him."

The Jews replied, "By our law, He ought to die because He says He is the conceived Son of God. But we are not authorized to crucify anyone."

Pilate asked Jesus, "Do You know I have power to crucify You or to release You? Tell me, what is Your origin?"

Jesus replied, "You have no power at all over Me except as is allowed from above."

Pilate thereafter tried to release Him, but the Jews cried out the more, "Crucify Him. If you let Him go, you are no friend of Caesar, for whoever calls Himself a King is treasonous to Caesar." Said Pilate, "Look at your King! Should I crucify your King?" The crowd yelled, "Away with Him. Crucify Him. We have no king but Caesar." Pilate then delivered Him into their hands and they led Him away, compelling Him to drag His cross.

THE CRUCIFIXION

On a hill called The Skull, or Calvary, they crucified Him between two others. On Jesus' cross, Pilate had posted in three languages, "KING OF THE JEWS, JESUS OF NAZARETH." The Jews asked Pilate to change the charge to read: *He claimed to be King of the Jews*, but Pilate refused them on this issue, saying, "What I have written, I have written."

INADVERTENTLY FULFILLING PROPHECY

The soldiers at the execution took Jesus' garments and tore them into four sections, one for each soldier. Noticing His coat was seamless, they said, "Let's not tear this. Let's gamble for it." Unwittingly they fulfilled a prophecy, "They part My raiment among them and for My vesture they cast lots."

AT THE CROSS

Jesus' mother was near the cross and John beside her. In the throes of death, Jesus said to His mother, "There is your son." And to John He said, "Look after your new mother." From that moment, John counted her as family.

Jesus said, "I thirst." A sponge was soaked in vinegar and lifted to His lips. Jesus called out with a will, "It is finished," and He bowed His head and dismissed His spirit.

ACTS OF RELIGIOUS MURDERERS AND GODLESS SOLDIERS

The Jews who wanted Jesus crucified did not want the bodies of those executed to be hanging on the cross the next day, their High, Holy Sabbath Festival. Therefore they petitioned Pilate to break the legs of those crucified, to hasten their death so they could be removed. The soldiers did break the legs of the two others, but when coming to Jesus, they observed that He was dead already. Instead of smashing His legs, one of the soldiers ran a spear into His side, and out poured blood mixed with water. The writer is an eyewitness. This incident fulfilled the prophecies of scripture, "Not a bone of Him shall be broken", and "They shall look on Him whom they pierced."

THE BURIAL

Soon after this, Joseph of Arimethaea, a Pharisee and secret believer, asked of Pilate permission to bury the body of Jesus. Pilate consented. Then Joseph, with Nicodemus (the Pharisee who visited Jesus surreptitiously one night), prepared the body for burial according to Jewish practice. They placed the body in a new sepulcher located in a nearby garden, and closed the tomb before the beginning of the Sabbath.

THE RESURRECTION

Before sunrise Sunday morning, Mary Magdalene came to the sepulcher and saw that the stone was rolled away from its door. Immediately she ran to Peter and John, and said to them, "The Lord's body has been taken out of the tomb!"

Peter and John ran to the tomb. John stooped down, looked in and saw the linen wrappings lying in place. Peter went into the tomb and saw the slumped linen wrappings still wound as if around a body, but the face napkin folded in a place by itself. Then John went in also and saw the evidence close up. *(A natural body could not have vacated the empty, undisturbed wrappings; and had thieves stolen the body, even if friends of Jesus, they would have taken it wrapped not leaving the linen behind, and not taking time to fold the face napkin. The disciples died as martyrs to verify their belief in the literal resurrection of Jesus.)* Both disciples went home, convinced Jesus was alive from death.

Mary, however, stayed, and through her tears kept watch outside the sepulcher. Then, stooping and looking again into the tomb, she saw two angels by the linen wrappings, one at the head and one at the foot where Jesus' body had been.

The angels said, "Woman, why do you weep?" Mary answered, "Because Jesus is gone and I do not know where His body has been taken."

Then she stood and turned, and saw a man quite near her who said, "Woman, why do you weep? Whom do you seek?"

Mary, thinking this the gardener, pleaded, "Sir, if you know where the body is, tell me so I can take care of Him." The man spoke her name, "Mary." At once she knew it was Jesus, and exclaimed, "Master!"

Jesus said quickly, "Do not embrace Me now for I have not yet ascended to My Father. Go to My followers and tell them that I ascend to My Father and your Father, to My God and your God." Mary Magdalene hurried to the disciples, telling them what she had seen and what Jesus had said.

RESURRECTION PROOFS

That same Sunday, in the evening, the disciples assembled and secured the doors, fearing the Jews. <u>Jesus materialized among them and said, "Be at peace." He showed them His hands, feet and side.</u> [17) John 20: 19,20] The disciples were thrilled to know that this was the Lord. Jesus spoke again, "Yes, be at peace. Just as My Father sent Me, so I send you."

But Thomas was not there that evening. When the other disciples reported that they had seen the Lord, Thomas said, "Unless I see for myself the nail prints in His hands, and put my finger into the nail scar on His feet and examine with my own hand the wound in His side, I will not believe He lives."

Eight days later, the disciples again were together behind secured doors and Thomas was with them. <u>Jesus again materialized among them and said, "Be at peace. Thomas, reach out and examine for yourself My scarred hands and feet and side. Do not be without faith -- believe! Thomas examined the healed wounds and exclaimed, "My Lord and my God!"</u> [17) John 20: 19- 27]

"Because you have seen Me in person," Jesus said, "you believe. Blessed are those who are not privileged to see Me physically, yet believe."

BELIEVE AND LIVE

The one recording these events is John. I am the one at the cross to whom Jesus gave the responsibility of His mother; the one next to Him at the last supper, and the first disciple at the open tomb. This is a true, eyewitness account.

Jesus did many other signs in the presence of His disciples which are not written here. <u>But these are recorded so that you may believe that Jesus is the Christ, the Son of God, and through believing, you will have eternal life in Him.</u> [7 & 4) John 20:31]

THOUGHTS FROM

Isaiah

Come. Let us reason together before it is too late. Though your sins be as glaring as day-glow scarlet, you can be as white as snow; though they be as permanent as indelible red, you can be as pure as bleached wool.

In the year that king Uzziah died, I saw the Lord sitting upon a throne, high and lifted up, and his essence filled the temple. Above the throne stood the seraphim, each having six wings. With two he covered his face, with two he covered his feet, and with two he did fly. One cried to the other and said, "Holy holy holy is the Lord of hosts, the whole earth is full of His glory." The door frames vibrated from the voices, and the house was filled with smoke. Oh, the majesty, power, purity and terror of it all!

Then flew one of the seraphim to me, having a live coal in his hand which he had taken with tongs off the altar. He laid it upon my mouth, and said, "Lo, this has touched your lips. Your iniquity is taken away, and your sin is purged." Also, I heard the voice of the Lord, saying, "Whom shall I send? Who will go for Us to warn the people?" Then said I, "I am here, send me."

This is THE GOSPEL MESSAGE He sent me to tell. God is absolute purity. We are all like sheep which have gone astray. We have turned everyone to his own way. But the Lord God has put on our Shepherd, the Savior, the sin and iniquities of us all. [3 & 4) Isaiah 53: 6]

God the Creator has said, "I am God. There is no other God, nor shall there ever be. I am the first and the last, the beginning and the ending -- the infinite One. There is no God and no Savior other than Me." [14) Isaiah 45: 21]

The Lord says, "Come to Me. No money is required. Why do you spend your earnings on that which does not nourish or satisfy? Why do you work for that which does not endure? Come to Me that you may live -- forever.

"Seek Me while there is opportunity, call on Me while you have the inclination. Turn away from evil ways and wicked thoughts. Turn to Me, for I will have mercy, yes, come to Me, for I will freely pardon without limitation.

"My thoughts are not as your thoughts nor are My ways as your ways. As distant as the stars are from earth, so are My ways and My thoughts higher than yours. When My word is given, it is not an empty promise nor a powerless expression. My word will accomplish its purpose and succeed in My intent. I have given My word that whoever comes to Me shall be saved."
Isaiah 55: 1-11

How do you conceive of God? What is your idea of your Creator? Does your image of God measure up to reality.

God, the only true God, poured out all the oceans of earth from the cup of His hand. He measured the vast stretches of space with the span of His thumb and little finger. From His teaspoon He sprinkle all the dust of the globe. All the hills and mountains were proportioned on His kitchen scales. All the nations of the world combined are as insignificant to Him as the smallest droplet of water in a reservoir. All the continents are less than a speck of dust on His mantel. All the forests on earth together are insufficient to fuel His fireplace. To God, the endless canopy of sky is less than a pup tent to a man, the sphere of earth like a small camp stool. The rulers among men are comparatively less in stature than a locust. All the instincts, intelligence and laws of the universe are simple, even incidental and trivial to Him. God calls each one of the endless trillions of stars by an individual name. There is no way to comprehend His mind. There is no limit to His power. Effortlessly He holds the entire universe together and causes it to function. He is never tired or strained.

By contrast, even youths quickly tire and athletes are easily exhausted. But God gives inexplicable endurance to the weak, and power to the weary. Those who worship the Lord will have supernatural resources, and those who rely on Him will find new strength. They will know genuine highs, flying like eagles. They shall run the contests of living without exhaustion. They shall keep walking through life able to endure without despair. They shall have eternal life.

THE TEN COMMANDMENTS

Have no other god than the one true God.

Do not put anything above God in value, honor, priority, fear, respect, worship, love, obedience or any other way.

Do not use the name of God in any empty way or for an oath.

Set a day of worship apart unto God.

Give honor and respect to your father and mother.

Do not murder.

Do not commit adultery.

Do not steal.

Do not lie.

Do not covet, and have no jealousy.

JESUS' SUMMARY OF THE COMMANDMENTS

Love the Lord God with all your energy and with every part of your being.

Love your neighbor as you love yourself. As you would have others do to you, do the same toward them.

CHRIST IS
OUR ULTIMATE NEED

FROM

Colossians

From Paul, an apostle of Jesus Christ by the will of God, and from Timothy, to the saints and faithful believers at Colosse. Grace and peace to you from God our Father and from the Lord Jesus Christ.

We pray constantly for you, giving thanks for your faith and the love you have for all believers. We are thankful that your belief of the Gospel has given you the assurance of going to heaven and has made you fruitful believers. We pray that you will have insight into God's will and grow in your understanding of God. We pray <u>that you will live pleasing to God</u>, [15) Col 1:10] spiritually productive because of genuine Christian lives. We pray that you will have strength proportionate to God's glorious power, making you patient, able to joyfully endure inconveniences and hardships, grateful to God that you share in His inheritance.

FOCUSING ON THE PREEMINENT CHRIST

You have been delivered from the power of darkness and are part of the kingdom of Christ who has redeemed us and has forgiven our sins. <u>Christ is the image of the invisible God,</u> [14) Col 1:15] <u>the Creator</u> of every material thing and of every power, energy and authority. Christ created all, and holds it all together. He is the head of the church, He is the beginning, the first alive from the dead to never die again. He is in every way preeminent. God the Father focused all purposes in Christ, and <u>through Christ alone can anyone be reconciled to God</u>. [4) Col 1:20]

You who were at odds with God are now reconciled to Him by the death and resurrection of Christ, and have been made blameless in His sight. Continue in the faith, stable, not able to be led away from the truth of the gospel.

Christ in you is the hope of glory. <u>That is why we preach Christ, warning everyone, teaching everyone, so that everyone has an opportunity to be made perfect in Christ. In fact, I work hard at it, responding to the urgency of His conviction and power within me.</u> [12) Col. 1: 28,29]

I want you to know how earnestly I desire to teach you the truths of God which are difficult to understand. In Christ is all the treasure of wisdom and knowledge. I am happy for your steadfastness in the faith. Just <u>as you received Jesus by faith, continue to live your life in Him by faith</u>. 15) Col 2:6   Your foundation is Christ. Build your life on Him with thankfulness.

Beware! There are philosophies of egotistical, self-deluded leaders which can deceive you. Some follow traditions and socially accepted institutions, but are not of Christ. <u>In Christ is all of the only true God. You are absolutely complete in Christ</u>. 14) Col 2:9   Furthermore, He is over all powers or governments or entities, so what more could you need. He has made you alive with Himself by the power that raised Him from death, and <u>has forgiven you every wrong, having paid on the cross for all sin</u>. 4) Col 2:14

Beware not to let men judge you about what you eat or drink or wear, or what day you worship, or what days you celebrate as special. <u>Don't be fooled</u> by someone with false humility to follow angels. You won't be gullible if you keep Christ alone as your head, not the doctrines and covenants of angels or men. <u>They may seem wise and appear to be religious</u> 13) Col 2:18-23   because of a forced humility and a code of discipline, <u>but these false gospels appeal</u> to your old nature, teaching that you have some inherent ability to earn God's favor. <u>They are not of God</u> nor honoring to God.

PREPARE FOR HEAVEN BY LIVING LIKE CHRIST

Since you are risen with Christ, <u>seek heavenly things</u> where Christ rules at the Father's right hand. <u>Set your affection on heavenly objectives, not earthly</u>. 15) Col 3:1-5   For we are dead, and our life can only be found in Christ who is above. Christ is our life. When He returns, we shall go with Him to glory.

<u>Be deathly afraid in regard to certain actions</u> -- fornication, evil lusts, uncleanness, unnatural love, covetousness. God judges these. You may have practiced these in the past, but now renounce them. Also renounce anger, hate, malice, mocking God, filthy talk, lying and similar deeds. Emulate the image of Christ. <u>Ask yourself, what would Jesus do; and do it. Be set apart for God</u>. Show mercy. Be kind, humble, meek, patient, enduring of hardships, forgiving just as Christ forgave you.

Primarily, live love. <u>Let your heart be controlled by the peace of God</u>. 15) Col 3:15   If something would disrupt that peace, don't do it. If something brings that peace, do it. Live so that you can be thankful to God in all you do. <u>Let the wealth of God's word possess you</u>. [7) Col 3:16]   Instruct and challenge each other in this principle. Keep a song in your heart to the Lord.

EVERYDAY EXAMPLES OF LIVING EMULATING CHRIST

<u>Whatever you do, in talk or action, only say and do that which can be done in the name of the Lord and for which you can give God thanks</u>. [15) Col 3:17]

Wives, submit to your husband in the Lord.

Husbands, love your wife and do not mistreat her.

Children, obey your parents, for this pleases God.

Fathers, don't drive your children to discouragement or anger.

Employees, follow the rules of your employer; not just when you are being observed or just to get by, but with the single purpose of pleasing God. Work enthusiastically, to honor God. It is the Lord who will give eternal rewards, and it is the Lord who will, without respect of person or position, punish the wrongdoer, so it is the Lord whom we serve.

Employers, be fair and equal with your employees, remembering that your "Employer" is in heaven.

WISE COUNSEL

Pray; be on your guard; and be grateful. Live wisely, perceptively with the unbelievers around you. Use time well and wisely. Make your conversation compassionate, yet containing helpful truths (that might hurt), discerning how to best respond to each one with whom you talk.

<u>Take care that whatever mission God has given you, you complete it</u>. [12) Col 4:17]   Remember that I have set the example, for I have written this with my own hand from prison. Grace be with you. Amen.

THE GOSPEL
DETAILED AND DEFENDED

FROM

Romans

From Paul, a servant dedicated to the gospel of Jesus Christ our Lord. Jesus, a descendant of king David by human lineage, by Divine lineage is The Son of God as proven when He was raised from death. Through Him you have grace and peace.

EXEMPLARY FAITH

You Romans are loved by God who has made you saints. In my unceasing prayers, I thank God for you and that your faith is an example throughout the world. I ask that God will allow me to visit you, for I long to bring a spiritual gift that will anchor you more firmly in the faith.

I am indebted to everyone, sophisticated and unsophisticated, highly intellectual and average thinker, so I stay ready to preach the gospel. I'm never ashamed of the gospel of Christ, for it is God's powerful means of salvation to everyone who believes and it demonstrates God's righteousness so that those with only a little faith will see that faith increase. "The just shall live by faith."

GOD IS AGAINST THE FAITHLESS

God has warned of His anger against all who label truth ignorance. Men intuitively realize God exists, and they see His existence demonstrated. God is invisible, but evidences of His existence, power and deity are clearly seen in His creation. There is no excuse to miss God who is so obvious in nature. Yet some do not acknowledge God and are not grateful to Him, but instead become contradictory and egotistical in their theories. Trying foolishly to replace God, they label truth false. Calling themselves intelligent, they become fools, changing the glory of God The Creator into an imitation of a created thing. Therefore, God writes them off. Some degrade themselves, becoming homosexuals and lesbians, reaping appropriate results of this erroneous lifestyle. Some do not want to have even a thought of God, so God gives them up to a filthy life, filled with evil, sexual promiscuity, jealousy, love of money, one-upmanship, hatred, arguing, murder, deceit, back stabbing, bragging, lacking natural affection, having no mercy or pity. These degenerates realize the judgment of God is coming and that their sins deserve the death sentence, yet they not only continue to live in their vile manner, but find entertainment in watching the godless living of others.

You who are judging others have no excuse, for you condemn yourself by the things which you do. Remember that the judgment of God is based on truth -- on reality. Don't be deluded to think that you will escape judgment.

JUDGMENT IS COMING

Some of you think God is weak, or soft on sin, because His judgment hasn't yet fallen after so long a time, or because He is good to sinners. Take note. <u>God's patience and goodness are intended to lead you to repent.</u> [2) Rom 2:4] <u>Don't go on sinning, taking advantage of His goodness,</u> for you are stock-piling God's wrath when the day of His holy judgment does come. In unbiased judgment He will sentence everyone without respect of their person or position. Not the ones who agree intellectually with God, but the ones who obey and follow Him shall be justified in that judgment day. Jesus will be the Judge and the gospel will be the standard by which all will be tried.

TRUE GODLINESS

Do you profess to be religious, even a teacher? Do you practice what you teach, or are you a hypocrite so that the name of God is mocked? True godliness is both inward and outward (that which is believed AND practiced), not only of the letter, but also of the spirit of the gospel, seeking praise of God, not one's peers.

EVERYONE IS GUILTY AND WILL STAND IN FRONT OF GOD

It is written, "No one is righteous. No one seeks after God as they ought. No one does only good, no not one." Dirty talk, cursing, bitterness, deceit, murders, destruction of reputation and property, wars, making others miserable -- these are what people do. They do not fear God. But the law of God shuts the mouth of everyone. <u>All are guilty before God. By trying to keep the law, no one will ever be justified before God. The law only makes obvious one's sins and the need of a savior.</u> [6) Rom 3:20]

ANYONE CAN BE MADE INNOCENT IN THE EYES OF GOD

But now God demonstrates His righteousness in a new way, without the law. By faith in Jesus Christ, one can have the righteousness of God. It is given without bias or prejudice to everyone who believes. <u>All have sinned and fallen far short of</u>

God's glory; but all can be redeemed from sin freely by God's goodness. [3) Rom 3:23,24] God accepts the perfect life and sacrificial death of Jesus as payment for all sin. Thus, God is just when He forgives and makes righteous those who believe in Jesus.

FORGIVENESS IS FREE

No one can brag because he is forgiven of sin and made acceptable to God. The forgiveness is a free gift from God, not something earned by the one forgiven. [6) Rom 3:27,28] Jesus paid the price. The forgiven one had only to put faith and trust in Jesus, and accept His free gift of salvation.

FORGIVENESS IS BY FAITH

The patriarch Abraham was justified by faith. He relied on God's promise, confident that God would do as He said. Scripture is clear: "Abraham believed God and his belief was credited to him for righteousness." Also, David records: "Happy is one to whom God credits unearned righteousness." No one can earn favor with God. [6) Rom 4:6]

To one who does not work for it but truly believes on Jesus who justified the ungodly, that one's faith is credited to him as righteousness. [6) Rom 4:5] If we believe on God who raised Jesus from the dead, then our believing will be credited to us as righteousness. Justified by faith, we have peace with God through our Lord Jesus Christ. Through faith, Jesus gives us God's grace and glory. Just trust Jesus. [6) Rom 4:23 - 5:1]

REALISTIC PROGRESS IN THE CHRISTIAN LIFE

With these thoughts in mind, we can actually feel honored when we face hardships. Hardships build patience. Patience during hardships develops experience and expertise in overcoming. That experience of seeing God bring us through hardships builds confidence in His promises to be with us in all of life's circumstances. That confidence makes us bold in our Christian walk and allows the love of God to permeate our hearts through the Holy Spirit.

GOD PROVIDES A PLAN OF SALVATION

When we were weak sinners, at the proper time in God's plan, Christ died for us. Few of us would give our life for a good person or even for a charitable person. But in Christ, God demonstrated His love by giving His life for us when we were His enemies. [1] Rom 5:8

By Adam, sin and death entered the world; and all sin. Now, by Jesus, perfection and eternal life are available to the world, a free gift to all who will believe. Sin fills the world, but God's grace engulfs the world and covers sin. Sin has produced guilt and death, but God's grace makes available forgiveness and everlasting life to those who put faith in Jesus Christ our Lord. [5] Rom 5:12-21

ALLOW JESUS TO LIVE IN AND THROUGH YOU

Shall we go on sinning so that God's grace may flourish? Of course not! We are dead to sin. We, who are by faith identified with Jesus, are vicariously identified with His death, so that, like Christ was raised from death, we also would have new life. [15] Rom 6:1-7

Our old nature was crucified with Him to destroy sin and to free us from serving sin. One who is dead does not sin. [15] Since we died with Christ, we shall also live with Him who is resurrected never to die again. Through Jesus Christ we are actually dead to sin and alive to God. Don't let sin rule you. Don't let yourself be a tool of error. Be a tool of right, as one alive from the dead. Sin has no power to subdue you. You are not under law but under grace.

Shall we take advantage of God's grace and go on sinning because we are not under law? Of course not! You surrender your freedom to whomever you serve. Serving sin results in death. Serving righteousness results in life. Thank God that though we did serve sin, we have obeyed from our hearts the true doctrine and have been made free from sin and have given our loyalty to righteousness. Yes, sin earns death, but God freely gives eternal life through Jesus Christ our Lord. [3 & 4] Rom 6:23

Reason with me. Law has authority over one as long as one is alive. A wife is bound to her husband while he lives, but if he dies, she is free from her husband and can lawfully remarry.

Similarly, true Christians have become dead to the Old Testament Law through the death of Christ. Now we are bound to Him and able to produce fruit for Him. Before, under law, we could only produce the fruits of sin, resulting in death. Now, under grace, we serve Christ, resulting in eternal life.

WE ARE ALL LAWBREAKERS

Is the law evil? Of course not. The law exposes sin and awakens us to our need of a redeemer. So the law is holy, and serves its purpose.

By the standard of the spiritual law, I am a slave of sin. I do things I hate and would not condone in others. I omit things I want to do. Obviously then, I am not in control, but am controlled by sin. In my body is nothing good enough, for I do not have the power to follow my own good intentions. Instead, I do acts about which I feel guilty. My mind delights in the law of God, but my body delights in glandular pleasures and social wrongs which I do not approve. It is a constant battle that the flesh often wins. I am miserable, heading for spiritual death because of physical lusts! Who shall deliver me? I thank God that He has provided deliverance through Jesus Christ our Lord.

JESUS IS THE SOLUTION TO THE PROBLEM OF GUILT

There is no condemnation to those in Christ Jesus who live controlled by the Spirit instead of controlled by their physical desires. Life in Christ sets us free from the death in sin.

The law could only condemn me because I continued to break the law's standard. But God's Son became a person like me and broke the power of sin by fulfilling the law's standard and by paying for me sin's sentence of death. Now, vicariously, I have the righteousness of Christ, just as if I myself had been able to keep the law; and His Spirit lives in me. The sentence of guilt and death has been replaced by the Spirit of peace and life.

SUBMIT TO THE SPIRIT OF GOD WITHIN

Thinking like the World cannot please God, for it makes one unresponsive to God, and kills the soul. Godly thinking is the result of the Spirit of God living within (which is true of all believers), and produces life in the soul. Since God's Spirit lives in you, He will raise you from the dead just as He did Jesus. We are obligated to live in obedience to the Spirit, silencing sinful lusts. <u>When God's children are obedient to the Spirit of God, they feel an assurance within that they truly are children of God who will share Christ's inheritance and glory</u>. [9)]
Rom 8:14,16 This glory and inheritance which awaits in heaven makes any suffering we must endure on earth pale by comparison.

44

GOD IS ON YOUR SIDE

We are saved by Faith, trusting in that which is not visible. If it were visible, then faith would not be required. But since it is by faith, we patiently wait for the fulfillment. During our faith-life, the Spirit aids us when we do not know how to pray. The Spirit makes intercession for us as no man could, for He knows the heart and mind of both men and God, and His intercession is according to God's will. With this assurance, we know that everything works together for good for those who love God, who are His chosen believers. [2) Rom 8:28] He always knew these would believe and He prearranged for them to become like a reflection of His Son in order that Jesus would have many adopted sisters and brothers. These whom He knew would believe, He made sure heard the gospel, and cleansed them and made them saints fit for heaven. There is nothing else to say; since God is for us, no one and no power can prevail against us. [1)] [Rom 8:31] Since God was willing to give His only Son for us, it is certain He will give us anything else we truly need.

YOU CAN BE SECURE IN GOD THE SON

Who could convict of sin one of God's chosen believers? It is God, the lawgiver Himself, who has justified us. Who could condemn us? It is Christ, the judge Himself, who died, rose again, and is in heaven interceding for us. What could separate us from the love of Christ? Could tribulation, or distress, or persecution, or famine, or poverty, or peril, or death? NO! In all these we are more than conquerors through Christ who loves us. Not death, nor life, nor angels, nor devils, nor powers, nor things present, nor things future, nor height, nor depth, nor any other creature or thing shall be able to separate us from the love of God which is in Christ Jesus our Lord! [11) Rom 8:33-39]

GOD IS SOVEREIGN

I would give up my own salvation if it helped my Jewish kin recognize Jesus as their Messiah. They have had many advantages, even being the people through whom Christ was born. But not all born Israelites physically have been chosen by God to be Israelites spiritually -- a part of His true family.

A potter selects some clay to make a waste container which will become contaminated and destroyed, and other clay to make an exquisite vase to decorate kings tables which will be valued indefinitely. Similarly, God has chosen some within His creation to be His children to share eternal glory with Him, and others He has not so chosen. He shows mercy on whomever He in His sovereignty elected.

This is difficult to comprehend, but neither a bed pan nor a crystal vase can say to its creator, "Why did you make me into this form and use." We, similarly, can't question God. Nevertheless, in humans, salvation is a function of faith. Those rejected by God are rejected because they did not seek Him by faith but by trying to earn His favor with good works. It is written, "Some will misunderstand or be offended over Christ, but whoever believes on Him will not be disappointed or rejected." Faith is the victory. 5) Rom 9:32,33

Yes, my heart's desire and prayer is that all Israel be saved. But their zeal for God is based on error. Misunderstanding the requirements of God, they tried to create their own righteousness, and in so doing have failed to accept the righteousness which God wants to freely give them. Christ is the fulfillment of the law, giving His perfection to everyone who believes on Him.

THE GOSPEL

This is gospel faith: If you make a verbal admission 10) Rom 10:9 that Jesus is your Lord, believing in your heart that God raised Him from the dead, you are saved. For it is the heart which must believe 5) Rom 10:10 to appropriate Christ's righteousness, and it is the mouth that makes the statement of faith which produces salvation. As the scripture says, "Whoever believes on Him will not be disappointed or rejected." There is no discrimination or bias; whoever calls on the name of the Lord is saved. Faith comes by hearing the gospel message, the Word of God. 7) Rom 10:17

IT IS BEYOND EXPLANATION

How deep and rich are the wisdom and knowledge of God! How unimpeachable are His conclusions, and His methods past discovering! No one comprehends the full reasoning of the Lord, let alone has ever been His counselor. The Lord never obtained anything from anyone -- He is the infinite Source. It is because of Him and through Him and for His purpose that everything exists. To Him be glory forever.

I implore you because of God's mercy, <u>offer your body as a living sacrifice to God, dedicated to Him, for it is the reasonable thing to do. Do not be poured into the mold of society, but let God mold you into an original creation by changing the way you think and the things on which you meditate.</u> [15) Rom 12:1] Then <u>you can demonstrate the results of God's plan for you, that it is good, desirable, and perfect.</u> [2) Rom 12:2]

FULFILL YOUR ASSIGNMENT IN THE PLAN OF GOD

Be neither egotistical nor self-debasing, but think realistically about yourself, remembering that God has provided saving faith to all. All believers form a body in which not every member has the same function. We are one in Christ and belong to one another, but we have different responsibilities. One is gifted to preach, one to help others, another to teach, or to give constructive criticism, or to contribute funds to the work, or to befriend. Let everyone fulfill their gift with humility, diligence, cheerfulness, and with sincere love.

Despise evil, cling to good. Show kind affection to each other as brothers and sisters with mutual humility and respect. Be prudent in business, enthusiastic in spirit, serving the Lord. Be joyful in your salvation, patient in testings, and continue in a prayerful attitude. Take care of needy believers, be hospitable, bless those who persecute you, rejoice with those who rejoice, weep with those who weep, and get along with each other.

Don't be impressed with wealth, fame or power. Don't snub the poor and powerless. Don't be conceited. Don't trade evil for evil. Be honest to all. Live peaceably with everyone with whom it is possible. Don't try to get even. The Lord has said, "I will repay; vengeance is Mine." Therefore, if your enemy is hungry, feed him; if he is thirsty, give him water; for in doing this you activate his conscience. Don't allow evil to wear you down, but wear down evil with good.

BE A GOOD CITIZEN

Be subject to authority, for order and authority are ordained of God, and you don't want to resist God's structure. Proper authorities protect the good and prosecute the evil.

Give to all their due: taxes to the entities owed taxes, customs to the customs officials, respect to whom it is due, honor to whom it is due, and such like. Do not be in debt to a man for anything, except the debt of brotherly love which fulfills the entirety of God's law.

BE LIKE JESUS

Our salvation is nearer every day. Conduct yourself as in daylight, in transparent honesty, not in dark deeds. Drench yourself in Jesus Christ and do not give sinful lusts any chance to drown you.

ALLOW FOR DIFFERENCES IN NONESSENTIAL CONVICTIONS

Accept one who is weak in the faith, but don't argue with him all the time. If you believe that all things God has made are beneficial in proper perspective, but a weak brother believes that some things are taboo in every instance, do not judge him for staying away from the thing that offends him. It is to God, not you, that he must answer, and God is able to strengthen him.

BE SINCERE BEFORE THE LORD

Be sure you are fully convinced in your own mind about what you believe, not two-faced or double-minded. Some reserve one special day for the Lord, some another. Some drink wine worshipping the Lord, others abstain from wine to honor the Lord. Be sure that whatever you do or don't do, it is for the Lord. Do not get into arguments, judging your brother. It is Christ who is the judge. We will all stand before His judgment. There, every knee shall bow and every tongue shall confess to God, and shall give an account of himself.

DO NOT BE SPIRITUALLY EGOTISTICAL OR STUBBORN OR SELFISH

While we should not judge our brother, neither should we offend or confuse him. Nothing is unclean by itself, but if one considers a thing unclean, then to him it is unclean. We then, to whom the thing is neutral, should not disappoint the faith of our weaker brother who sincerely considers that thing unclean. Give it up for your weaker brother's sake. Don't let something you think of as neutral, or even as good, make you appear evil to a person for whom Christ died. Don't hold out for your rights, but hold out for righteousness, peace and joy in the Holy Spirit for the entire family. A believer who lives this way will be praised by God and by fellow believers.

EMPHASIZE FAITH AND FOLLOWING THE EXAMPLE OF CHRIST

In summary, if your faith is strong enough to allow you to do things that others consider offensive, then do not flaunt your faith. You will be happy when you don't feel guilty because you offended a brother by some act which he believes is sinful. If you have doubt about any activity, do not participate in it, for you couldn't do so in faith, and <u>whatever is not done in faith is sin.</u> [3)] [Rom 14:23] You strong in faith, help carry the weaker ones, and teach them sound doctrine that will make them stronger. <u>Do not live just to please yourself, but follow Christ's example</u>. [15) Rom 15:1-7] As you are patient with each other, you will begin to agree on these unclear issues, resulting in glory to God.

WORDS OF WISDOM

May God fill you with all joy and peace in believing, that you may have prolific hope through the Holy Spirit, full of goodness and knowledge, able to teach, to correct and to encourage one another. Note those who cause divisions, teaching false doctrines. Avoid them. They serve only themselves, but with sweet talk and cunning speeches they deceive many simple-hearted.

WORDS OF WORSHIP

Now to Him who is able to secure you according to the gospel and the scriptures, to the everlasting God, infinitely wise, be glory through Jesus Christ forever. Amen.

A MESSAGE OF VALIDATION

FROM

James

TESTING HAS A PURPOSE

Believers, accept difficulties with contentment, understanding that the testing of your faith develops patience. Allow patience to finish its work in you so that you can become mature and complete, lacking nothing.

PRACTICE CONSISTENT FAITH

When you lack wisdom, ask of God. He gives generously and does not criticize. But ask in faith without wavering. A wavering person is like a wave which is driven and tossed by the wind. Such a one will not receive anything from the Lord. A double minded person is unstable in all of life.

A believer of meager position should be delighted when honored, and a rich person should be delighted when humbled. The experience will remind him that, like the flowers on grass, he will soon wilt and be gone.

ENDURE THE PROCESS OF TEMPTATION

Happy is the one who endures temptation, for after overcoming the enticement, he will be awarded the crown of life which the Lord promises to those who love Him. However, do not say when you are enticed that you are being tempted by God. God can not be tempted by evil and He does not tempt anyone. We are tempted when we are drawn away from God by our lusts and longings. The lusts germinate and produce sin. Sin ripens into death.

GOD IS GOOD AND ONLY GOOD CAN COME FROM GOD

God gives only good and perfect gifts, and every good thing comes from God who is light. [2) James 1:17] His light never changes, and its encompassing, permeating radiance overcomes shadows of doubt and deceit.

OBEY GOD

God made us His children through the word of truth. Therefore, be quick to listen to His word, but slow to speak and slow to anger. The wrath of men can not carry out the righteousness of God. Give up evil and humbly receive the word of God which is able to save your soul.

Do what the word teaches, don't just acknowledge its truth. Don't fool yourself. If you hear the word but don't put it in action, you are like someone who sees his dirty face in a mirror but leaves without washing, forgetting how he looked. One who looks in the mirror of God's word and <u>takes the corrective action called for, shall be happy because of his obedience</u>. 7) James 1:22-25

TRUE GODLINESS PRODUCES GODLY RESULTS

One who thinks he is religious but can't control his tongue is deceived and has false religion. Pure, <u>true religion results in caring for orphans and widows in need, and in being different from the rest of the world</u>. 15) James 1:27

TRUE GODLINESS IS NOT HAUGHTY

Don't give preferential treatment to persons of wealth or position. If you give the best seats and other favors to rich people, yet pay little attention to, or give "standing room only" to poor people, you are showing favoritism! Listen. God selected primarily those who are poor in this world to be the ones rich in faith and to be the inheritors of His kingdom. But you shame the poor. If you genuinely fulfill God's command to love your neighbor as yourself, you are living right. But if you show partiality, you are sinning. <u>If you keep the entire law, except one point, you are a lawbreaker</u>. 3) James 2:10

GENUINE FAITH LOOKS ALIVE AND ACTS ALIVE BECAUSE IT IS ALIVE

If someone claims to have faith, but has no good works, will his "faith" alone save him?

If a brother and sister are starving and naked, and one of you says to them, "God bless you; I will pray that God will feed and clothe you;" but you do not give them what they so desperately need; what good is it? That kind of faith, in theory only, which does not produce any godly action, is dead faith. <u>Living, genuine faith takes care of those in need, believing that God will supply for the faithful one who makes godly sacrifices to help the poor</u>. 15) James 2:16

ACTIONS MIRROR FAITH AND DEEDS DESCRIBE FAITH

Someone may say, "I have faith, but you are relying on good works."

I respond, "How can you show me your faith without demonstrating it by your actions? I show my faith by my godly deeds. What I really believe is proven by what I do. Actual belief is revealed by believable actions."

You may say, "I believe in the one true God." I reply, "That's good. But the devil also sincerely believes, and trembles for fear of God."

<u>Faith which does not produce godly results is not godly, living faith</u>. [15] [James 2:20] On the other hand, works without faith are also dead. Abraham was an example of how faith and works go together -- are mutually inclusive. His deeds were the outworking of his faith, and his faith was completed by his actions.

As the body without the spirit is dead, so faith without corroborating activity is dead.

THE RESPONSIBILITY OF GREATER INSIGHT

Teachers, having had more knowledge, will be held more strictly accountable than students.

OUR CONVERSATIONS REVEAL THE NATURE OF OUR REAL FAITH

There are many ways we stumble, but the mouth is the most common. If anyone can control his mouth, he is able to control his total person. Just as a small fire can start a great conflagration, so the little tongue can open a world of trouble. Our tongues are unruly and full of poison. They bless God and curse a man who is made in the image of God. Blessing and cursing out of the same mouth. That should not be. Let wholesome conversation demonstrate your faith in action.

IDENTIFY THE SOURCE OF YOUR INWARD CONDITION

If there is bitterness, envy and quarreling in your heart, realize that it is from satan and will lead to evil deeds. God's wisdom is pure, peaceable, gentle, ready to help, merciful, good, impartial, and not hypocritical. Those who make peace will have peaceful times in which to do good.

GET CLOSE TO GOD

Why do you have wars? It is from lust and greed. You fight to get what you want. Don't fight, just ask.

When you have asked, you didn't receive some requests because you asked for the purpose of satisfying your evil lusts. Don't you know that <u>friendship with the world is enmity</u>

with God. [15) James 4:4]   If you ask to be close with the world, you seek to be distant from God. God's spirit in us is jealous of our friendship. God doesn't grant requests that would endear us to the world system.

God resists the proud, but gives more grace to the humble. Submit to God. Resist the devil and he will flee. Draw near to God and He will embrace you. Cleanse your hands, purify your minds, be serious and sincere, be humble before God, and He will honor you.

A PROPER ATTITUDE

You who boast, "I will do this and that, and make a lot of money", consider this. You have no idea what shall happen tomorrow, or if you will even be here. Your life is but a vapor, here today and gone tomorrow. Bragging like that is wrong. Say, "If the Lord allows, I will do this and that." Since you know to have this attitude, if you do not have it, to you it is sin.

A PROPER PERSPECTIVE

You who are trusting in your riches are going to be miserable. If you cheated those who worked with you or for you, the Lord is aware of it. You live the lifestyle of the rich and famous on earth, while you have damaged honest folks within your business, and you have gotten away with it. But the coming of the Lord is ahead.

You who have been hurt, be patient. Do not judge or begrudge, but rather forgive. The Lord is full of pity and tender mercy. He is the judge.

EXAMPLES OF AN EFFECTIVE BELIEVER

Believers, don't take oaths. When you hurt, pray. When you are bubbling over, sing to the Lord. When you are sick, call the elders of the church to pray for your healing. Confess your faults to one another and pray for one another, that you may be reconciled to each other. The genuine, fervent prayer of a righteous man is very effective. [8) James 5:13-16]

If one of you is living in sin, and another of you converts him, know this: the one who converts a sinner is instrumental in the forgiveness of many sins and in saving a soul from eternal death.

CHRISTIANS SHOULD MODEL THE MESSAGE

FROM

I Peter

GOD CHOSE US

From Peter to those selected by God, whom He knew from eternity past would be set apart to Him because of their belief in the atoning blood of Jesus and their obedience to the gospel. May God's grace and peace be your experience time and time again.

GOD GIVES US ETERNAL LIFE BY FAITH

Praise God, who, in overflowing mercy, has given us a new birth with the anticipation of everlasting life, based upon the resurrection of Jesus Christ from the dead. As His children, we have awaiting in heaven an inheritance that will not decay nor lose its perfect glory. His power keeps us, sustains our saving faith, and prepares us for heaven. 11) 1 Peter 1:5

Knowing this truth produces inner joy though we may be enduring hardships. Such trials are for a comparatively short time and serve a purpose. Though they can be discouraging, these tests prove the quality of our faith and demonstrate it to be more precious than pure gold.

By faith we love Him whom we have not seen and rejoice in Him with contentment beyond expression. Such faith will result in praise, honor and glory when Jesus comes for us.

BE SELECT

Live as obedient children. 9) 1 Peter 1:14 Do not conform your lifestyle to spiritually ignorant lusts. Be pure, set apart unto God in everything. Scripture says, "Be Holy, for I am Holy."

BORN FROM ABOVE

The Father, to whom we look for salvation, is One to respect and fear. He judges without partiality and cannot be bribed. Only the sacrifice of the infinite and sinless Christ can save us from His judgment. 3) 1 Peter 1:17

Before He created the universe, God planned salvation for us through His Son alone in order that our trust and hope would be solely in Christ and nothing else.

We are born again (born spiritually), not of mortal generation, but by immortal, by the seed of the word of God which is eternal living truth. 7) 1 Peter 1:23 All flesh is temporary and mortal but God's Word is eternal and immortal.

NOURISHED BY THE WORD OF GOD

Put away all malice, cunning, hypocrisy, jealousy and vile talking. Be like a newborn baby looking for milk and <u>desire the nourishment of the word which will make you grow in the Lord</u>. [7] 1 Peter 2:2

UNIQUE PEOPLE

You believers are spiritual stones built into a spiritual temple. You are a unique priesthood set apart by Jesus Christ to offer within that temple spiritual sacrifices which are made acceptable to God by Jesus. Christ is the Cornerstone of that temple, cast away by men but chosen by God. Whoever believes on this Cornerstone will not be disappointed. Whoever builds on this Cornerstone will have a fireproof temple. You are a chosen generation, a royal priesthood, a unique people, intended to dramatize the praises of Jesus who has made you the people of God and has given you light in place of darkness, and mercy instead of judgment.

INSTRUCTIONS FOR LIVING

Refrain from evil lusts which war against the soul. Live so that people glorify God because of your good works. For the Lord's sake, be subject to the law of the land, for it is the Lord's will to silence the ignorance of foolish people by your righteous living. In Christ you are free, but don't use this freedom as a cover for maliciousness or immoderation. Give honor to all. Love other believers. Fear God. Respect the government.

Employees, respect your employer and fulfill your commitments to them -- the fair ones and the unfair. If you do a good job even when your boss is unfair, you will bring praise to God. If you do well and still suffer for it, this is especially noticed by God.

Remember how <u>Christ suffered, leaving us an example to follow in His steps.</u> [15] 1 Peter 2:21 He was neither sinful nor deceitful. He didn't return evil for evil. <u>He carried our sins in His own body on the cross, in order that we could live in righteousness.</u> [4] 1 Peter 2:24 By His stripes we are healed. We are as sheep that went astray, but now have returned to the Shepherd of our souls.

Wives be subject to your husband. If he is an unbeliever, let him see God's word lived in your life so he may be converted. Do not rely so much on outward beauty as on inner beauty -- a sweet and quiet spirit -- which to God is very precious.

Husbands, honor your wife and be understanding, for in some ways she is not as strong. Together you share the blessing of procreation, so <u>don't forget to pray</u>. [8) 1 Peter 3:7]

As believers, be harmonious, have compassion for each other, love as family, be kind, be courteous. Don't give evil for evil, but rather give blessing, and you will be blessed.

If you would like to live prosperously and long, don't consider evil and cunning. Flee evil; do good; desire peace and pursue it. The Lord watches over the righteous and hears their prayers, but He is against evil doers.

<u>Let the Lord control your heart and be prepared at all times to give a reason to anyone who asks why you are certain of eternal life. Answer with humility and respect, having a clear conscience that even though they may have been mocking you,</u> [12) 1 Peter 3:15] you gave a true answer backed up by godly living. Your false accusers will ultimately be ashamed of themselves, and you are better off to suffer for doing good than for doing evil.

<u>Christ also suffered once for sin, the pure One suffering for the impure, that by His death and resurrection He might bring us to God</u>. [4) 1 Peter 3:18] (Baptism is a picture of this death and resurrection.) Now Christ is at the right hand of God ruling over angels, governments and all powers.

Since Christ suffered for us, <u>let us live for God</u>. [15) 1 Peter 4:1] Be done with unrestrained living, evil lusts, too much wine, wild partying, gluttony, putting material things above God, and riotous living. God will judge the living and the dead, and the end is near. Be self-controlled, prayerful, and loving among yourselves, for love overlooks many faults. Be hospitable without complaining, as good stewards of God's blessings.

Whatever gift God has given you, use it for the benefit of others and to enhance their concept of God.

<u>EXPECT TESTING</u>

Don't be surprised when you are tested as if by fire, thinking such hardships strange. Instead, be glad to participate in Christ's suffering. When His glory is revealed to all, you will be delighted beyond imagination for He will share with you His glory.

Be happy if you suffer for the name of Christ, but be sure you're not suffering because of some evil act (not just "big" sins such as murder or robbery, but "little" sins such as gossiping or envy).

Don't be ashamed to suffer as Christians; but we believers should examine ourselves to be certain our own house is clean. And since judgment starts at the house of God, where does that leave those who do not believe the gospel? Having no savior, they have no hope. But you who truly suffer for Christ, commit the security of your souls to Him, a faithful Creator and Savior.

HUMILITY IS FOR EVERYONE

Elders, feed the flock of God and be a leader. Not because you have to, but because you want to. Not for money, but with a servant's attitude. Not as a cocky egotist, but as a humble example. Then when the chief Shepherd returns, you shall receive a reward that never loses value.

Young people, submit to the elders.

All of you be humble with one another. God resists the proud but gives grace to the humble. Humble yourself before God and let Him exalt you at the proper time.

Place all your concerns on Him, for He is concerned over you.

BE PREPARED

Be alert. Be poised. Your enemy, the devil, walks around like a roaring lion looking for someone to devour. Resist him with intense faith.

May the God of all grace, who has called you to share His eternal glory after you have suffered on earth for a short time, make you mature, season your faith, strengthen and calm you. To Him be glory and praise and dominion for ever and ever. Amen.

A MESSAGE OF HOPE

FROM

1 Thessalonians

From Paul, Timothy and Silvanus to the Thessalonian church: Grace and peace to you from God and the Lord Jesus Christ.

EXEMPLARY LIVES

We give thanks for you in prayer, remembering constantly your work of faith, labor of love and patience in looking for the return of the Lord Jesus Christ. You have been chosen by God, and when the gospel was preached with conviction among you in the power of the Holy Spirit, you became followers of the Lord and of us. Others have heard how you turned from idols to serving God, waiting for the resurrected Jesus to return. With your example, it is easy to find new believers of the gospel.

You recall that we came to you after being imprisoned at Philippi. We preached, not trying to please men, but God who controls our conscience. We did not flatter, nor did we covet your money. God knows. We imparted not only the gospel but also part of our own souls. We lived honorably among you, and as a father instructs his children, we exhorted, comforted and challenged you to live worthily of God.

EXEMPLARY FAITH

We are further thankful that when we preached, you accepted the message as from God, which it is. It is this faith of yours which makes the message so effective. You are our joy and crown of rejoicing! Yes, you, when we all stand before Jesus at His coming.

Now, like so many before, you have the opportunity to suffer for Christ. You are secure in Christ and have found comfort in the faith so that you are not confused by the suffering you are experiencing. Your confident faith and love are a comfort to us.

REMAIN FAITHFUL

Continue to live pleasing to the Lord. Abstain from fornication, be honorable and set apart unto God, not controlled by lusts.

Do not cheat your brother in any matter, but love him. You are known for your brotherly love, but let it grow even more.

Make it your practice to be quiet, minding your business, being industrious with honesty. Then you will never be in poverty.

YOUR FAITH BRINGS ETERNAL HAPPINESS AND TOGETHERNESS

Regarding the dead, I want you to understand God's plan so that you will not be hopeless in your sorrow over their absence. Just as Jesus died and rose again, so also believers who have died will rise again. When He returns, Jesus will bring them with Him. 17) 1 Thes. 4: 13

Those believers alive on earth when Jesus returns will not have an advantage over those who have already died. For the Lord Himself (not a *stand in* but Jesus, Himself) shall descend from Heaven announced by a shout from the highest angel and a blast from the trumpet of God. Then the dead bodies of believers will be resurrected, renewed and rejoined to their owners who as spiritual beings are accompanying Jesus, and we still physically living ones shall be changed and shall join them all in the air, clouds of believers to be forever with the Lord and with one another. 17) 1 Thes. 4: 13 -18 Comfort each other with this truth.

As to when this will occur, it will come as a thief in the night. Watch and be ready. Hold on to faith, love, and the hope of salvation, remembering that God has not scheduled us for destruction but for eternal life. Jesus Christ died for us that whether we live or die, we will always be with Him. 4) 1 Thes 5:9,10 Comfort and instruct each other on this.

SPECIFIC INSTRUCTIONS

Respect your leaders in the Lord, and warn the unruly. Comfort the handicapped, support the powerless, and be patient with everyone. Don't return evil for evil. Constantly pray and rejoice. 8) 1 Thes 5:17 It is God's will to be thankful in everything. Do not stifle the Holy Spirit, nor despise prophecy. Test all teachings and hang on to truth. Avoid even the appearance of evil. 15) 1 Thes 5:14-23 To have inner peace, be set apart totally for God, body, soul and spirit, ready for the coming of Jesus. Jesus is faithful and can develop this spiritual maturity in you.

Pray for us. Greet each other with an innocent embrace. Read this letter to all the believers. The grace of our Lord Jesus Christ be with you. Amen.

EVERYTHING IN CHRIST

FROM

Ephesians

THE PLAN OF GOD

From Paul, an apostle of Jesus Christ by the will of God, to the believers at Ephesus and all the faithful in Jesus Christ. May you experience God's peace and joy in Jesus Christ.

Let us honor God who has already secured for us every heavenly benefit in Christ. Designing that we should be set apart to Him, He chose us before He created the world. <u>In Christ we are saved from the penalty of sin and forgiven for our acts of sin, made ready to be with Him in heaven.</u> This inheritance [4) Eph 1:3-7] was predetermined by the plan of God for those who trust in Christ, that as His children we should bring praise to God.

A GUARANTEED INHERITANCE

You trusted in Christ, having listened to the word of truth, the gospel of salvation. You have received the official seal of salvation, the Holy Spirit, which guarantees your inheritance.

BY THE POWER OF CHRIST

I've heard of your faith in the Lord Jesus and of your love for all believers. I pray constantly for you, that you'll have wisdom and insight in understanding Christ, confident in your salvation since He has chosen you, and that you'll comprehend just how rich and glorious is your eternal inheritance.

I pray that you'll grasp the excessive greatness of His power that is at work in believers. It is the same surpassing power which raised Christ from the dead and placed Him in heaven, far above powers or beings or governments, and above anything in this present world and in the world to come. That mighty power has put everything under His feet and made Christ the head of the body of believers. Christ is everything to everyone.

BY GRACE THROUGH FAITH

You believers are alive out of death in sin. You once lived by the customs of this world and by the disobedient spirit of satan who now rules the world. You lived for the lusts of the body, fulfilling the urges of your glands and of sinful thinking, deserving judgment as do all unbelievers. But though you were dead in sin, God, in mercy, love and grace, has made you alive in Christ and given you a place with Him in heaven where eternally He will demonstrate in you His surpassing love and kindness.

It is by grace you are saved through faith. This faith is not self-generated but is a gift from God, eliminating any boasting. [5) Eph 2:8-9] Now you are the craftsmanship of God, created through Christ, intended to do good as God has ordered. In the past you were without Christ, having no hope. But now you have Christ, have been reconciled with God, and have peace.

WE ARE IN THE HOUSEHOLD OF GOD

You are no longer strangers, but are saints, members of God's family. You believers form a temple built upon the foundation of Jesus Christ. This temple forms a house of God inhabited by the Holy Spirit.

STRENGTHENED BY HIS POWER WITHIN US

I, Paul, am the apostle for you Gentiles. By special revelation, God made known to me that Gentiles, as well as Jews, can become fellow-heirs of Christ. I, the least of saints, was chosen to share with you the unfathomable riches of Christ.

Through the change He makes in believers, God demonstrates incomprehensible wisdom and gives us confidence, even boldness, in our faith.

Because of all this, I kneel before God the Father of our Lord Jesus Christ, asking that He give you strength by His Spirit in your inner man; that you will continue to have faith that Christ dwells within you; that you remain secure in His love, grasping the greatness of that love (though it surpasses understanding); and that you may be controlled by the awareness that God Himself is in you.

RECOGNIZING INFINITE POWER PRODUCES WORSHIP

To Him who is able to do exceedingly beyond any thing that we could ask or imagine as we allow His power to work in and through us, to Him be glory in the church through Jesus Christ our Lord, now, and throughout an endless eternity. Amen.

WE HAVE RESPONSIBILITIES TO FULFILL

I ask you to live the life believers ought to live, practicing patience and humility, keeping harmony and peace. Believers are one body, with one Spirit, and have one eternal hope, one Lord, one faith, one baptism, one God and Father of all, who is above all, through all and in you all.

To each member of the body He gives different abilities: apostles, or prophets, or evangelists, or pastors, or teachers. These diverse capabilities are individual responsibilities for the maturation of the believers, for the work of the ministry, for the good of the whole body of Christ.

We are to have unity in the faith, forming a complete body that measures up to the standard of Christ.

BECOME MATURE CHRISTIANS

We are not to be unlearned like children -- unstable and confused by every new philosophy of doctrine taught by slippery leaders who deceive many. But telling the truth in love, we are to be mature in Christ, our head, and we are to perform well our own function in the body so that it will grow in numbers, strength and love.

Don't be vain. Don't allow your heart to be blinded so that you are alienated from God. Don't allow lusts to warp your conscience. Don't be greedy or unclean in thought or action. As you have been taught in Jesus, drop these sinful ways and let the Spirit control you with new thoughts, making you a new person set apart to God.

Be truthful; don't go to sleep angry; don't give the devil an opening; don't steal but work hard so you can give to the needy; don't talk filthy but make what you say of value to others; and don't disappoint the Spirit of God who is the guarantee of your salvation. Be done with bitterness, anger, ranting, evil talking and malice. Be kind to each other, tenderly forgiving one another just as God because of Christ has forgiven you. Be followers of God [15) Eph 5:1,8] much as a young child follows a parent.

Live out love, just as Christ did, even sacrificing Himself for us. Sexual sins, unclean actions, covetousness, and harmful or filthy jokes should not be part of your lifestyle. People who practice this kind of life are not inheritors of heaven. Don't be fooled. God will judge. Don't participate in dark acts, but live in the light. Your life should prove what is acceptable to the Lord, reproving sin. In fact, don't even gossip about the sin going on around you, for those kinds of conversations can become a kind of vicarious participation. Be a light that exposes sin. Wake up! Christ will give you light. [3) Eph 5:3-14]

Live prudently, not foolishly. Live wisely, using time well and understanding the will of the Lord,[15) Eph 5:15] for the days are evil. Don't be controlled by chemicals or alcohol, but be controlled by the Holy Spirit. This will result in psalms and hymns and spiritual songs filling your mind, and you will sing in your heart to the Lord. You will give thanks to God for everything. You will submit yourselves to each other due to reverence for God.

Wives, submit to your husband as if to the Lord. The husband is head of the wife as Christ is the head of the church.

Husbands, submit to Christ and love your own wife as Christ loved the church and gave Himself to save it, that He might set it apart for Himself and make it pure and without blemish. Love your wife as you love yourself, caring for her and nourishing her as you do your own body.

A man shall leave his father and mother, and be made one with his wife. This is a picture of Christ and His church, therefore, let every man love his wife as himself, and let every wife honor her husband.

Children, submit to your parents in the Lord, for this is right. Honor your father and mother, and you will have a good and long life.

Fathers, do not encourage your children to do evil, but train them and nurture them with godly teaching.

Employees, submit to your employer with respect and loyalty, as if you worked directly for Christ, not just when others are watching, but consistently, doing the will of God from a sincere heart. Remember, those who do right, whether an employee or an employer, shall be rewarded by the Lord.

Employers, be loyal and honest with your employees, without threats. Remember, you have a Superior in heaven who judges without respect of person or position.

BE STRONG AND TAKE A STAND

In conclusion, be strong in the Lord, relying on the supreme power of His strength. Use the weapons provided by God so you can stand against the devil's deceitful ways. [15) Eph 6:10] Our real battle is not physical but spiritual, against satan and his cohorts. Therefore, it is crucial that you take God's defenses to withstand evil.

Having prepared properly, take a stand protected by righteousness, truth, the gospel of peace, faith, the assurance of salvation, and <u>the word of God</u>. 7) Eph 6:17

<u>Pray constantly in the Spirit</u>, 8) Eph 6:18 not just for yourself but for all believers, watching with patience for the answers. <u>And pray for me</u>, that I will have boldness to preach the gospel.

GODLY CONTENTMENT

May peace be yours together with confident love that springs out of faith from God the Father and the Lord Jesus Christ. Grace is with all who love our Lord Jesus Christ in sincerity. Amen.

A MESSAGE FOR MATURITY

FROM

<u>I Corinthians</u>

From Paul, an apostle of Jesus Christ by God's will, to the church of God at Corinth, and to all those everywhere who have become saints by faith in Jesus. May grace and peace be your experience from the Lord Jesus Christ.

TRUE WEALTH

I thank God that He has enriched you in everything. He has given you all the spiritual gifts as you wait for the coming of our Lord. At that time He will give you the final confirmation of the work of Christ in you, presenting you sinless at the judgment. God is faithful.

BE UNITED IN CHRIST

I ask you to be harmonious, not divisive. Don't form cliques around favorite spiritual leaders. Christ is not divided. Christ is the only one who died for you, and you were baptized only in the name of Christ. I am glad that I baptized just a few, for my mission is to preach the gospel, not to baptize.

CELEBRATING THE GOSPEL

The preaching of the gospel is foolishness to unbelievers, but to believers it is the unchangeable power of God that saves from destruction. Look at the godless philosophies and scientific theories of the past. Men's wisdom of the ages, with time, becomes recognized as foolishness. Men's intelligence has never enabled them to know God, but God in His wisdom has chosen the foolish act of preaching to save those who will believe. We preach that Christ's crucifixion demonstrated the power and wisdom of God.

If God had any, His "foolishness" would be wiser than the intelligence of men, and His "weakness" would be stronger than the strength of all men combined.

Look around. Not many of the intelligencia, or powerful, or wealthy are believers. God has chosen the seemingly foolish to confuse the so-called wise. He has chosen the weak things to frustrate those apparently strong in this world. He has chosen the simple, insignificant things to bring to insignificance those who think they are something. No one will brag in front of God. But you believers have been placed by God into Jesus Christ, and have been credited with all of Christ's wisdom, righteousness, position with God, and inheritance. [4) 1 Cor. 1:30] God says, therefore, "If you want to brag or celebrate, do so about the Lord."

When I preached among you, I didn't use great oratorical technique or skillful argumentation. I relied only on the truth of Jesus crucified and alive again. I was humble, mild and respectful. My message was not composed of pompous words or human wisdom. For effectiveness, I relied on the power of the Holy Spirit so that your faith would not be based on men but on God.

SPIRITUAL REASONING IS FOREIGN TO UNBELIEVING MINDS

On the other hand, when teaching believers, we instruct with logic and reasoning. We don't necessarily use the accepted wisdom of the world, for much of that has been proven through the ages to be incorrect. We teach the wisdom of God which the spiritual rulers of this world do not understand, for had they understood it, they would not have fulfilled God's plan by crucifying the Lord of glory.

Eyes have not seen, ears have not heard and minds have not conceived the things prepared by God for His people. But God reveals them to us by His Spirit. We do not have the spirit of the world, but the Spirit of God in order that we may understand godly truths.

The man born only physically, but not spiritually, cannot accept the truths of God. They seem foolish to him since he cannot grasp them. To comprehend God's truth, one has to understand their spiritual connotation. A truly spiritual man has discernment in all areas of life, but the unbeliever can't figure him out. Christ is the originator of intelligence, the source of wisdom, and we have the mind of Christ.

Realize that, when with you, I was unable to speak to you as spiritually mature, but rather as babies in Christ. You were only ready for milk, not meat. Your immaturity is evidenced by the envy among you, the infighting and your cliques. Childishness! Don't choose sides over spiritual leaders. One plants, one waters, one prunes or weeds, but God produces the fruit. Those who plant, water, prune and weed are united in effort, and everyone will individually receive his own reward based on his own performance.

SPIRITUAL BUILDERS

We are coworkers in joint endeavor with God. Coworkers, yet we are also His building. God chose me to lay the foundation, Jesus Christ, which cannot be replaced. No other foundation is acceptable.

Everyone must use care how they build on this foundation. Whether they build with gold, silver and precious gems, or with wood, hay and stubble will be obvious when the work is tested by fire. Those whose work survives fire shall have reward, but those whose work is consumed will have no reward. However, they themselves will be saved, but just as if escaping a house fire with only the shirt on their back. [15) I Cor 3: 11-15]

Don't you know that you are the building, the temple, of God and that God lives in you by His Spirit? If you debase and corrupt the temple of God, your body will be destroyed, for God who lives in you is holy.

TRUE WISDOM IS IN CHRIST

Don't fool yourself! How dangerous to deceive self! Do you think you are smart in the modern trend of thought? Just as a simpleton should seek instruction, you better seek instruction from God so you can be wise. By comparison, the wisdom of the world is stupidity to God. [13) 1Cor. 3:18-20] God snares the so-called wise in their own arrogance. God understands the vanity in the minds of the worldly wise. Therefore, don't exult in men -- yourself or others. It is in Christ that you have mastery of every thing important -- death, life, the present, the future. It is all yours in Christ, and Christ is God.

PROVEN LEADERSHIP

Think of us as ministers of God and trustees of the truth of God. The obligation of a trustee is to be faithful. Now, it's insignificant to me if you or anyone else judge me. I don't even rate myself. I report to the Lord. Don't set yourself up as a premature judge. When the Lord comes, He'll judge knowing secret things and even hidden motives and thoughts. At that time each one shall seek praise from God.

We apostles are made examples. We are called fools for Christ's sake, but it has resulted in your becoming wise in Christ. We have been made to look weak, but by it you have become strong. We are despised, but you are still respected. We sometimes lack the basic necessities of life -- nutrition, liquids, proper clothing. We are tossed around and have no place to call home. We work for a living. Those who mock us, we bless. When we are persecuted, we accept it. When false rumors are spread about us, we only ask that inquiry be made for the truth. We are treated like criminals and bums. I am not pleading for sympathy, but to warn you. You may have many spiritual teachers in your lifetime, but only one like me who has suffered much to become your spiritual father. In a sense, you are my offspring, so follow my example. The kingdom of God is not just talk, but action empowered of God!

DO NOT BE FRIENDS WITH THOSE WHO FLAUNT SIN

Rumor is that one of you is sexually involved with his stepmother. I hear you are proud of the fact you tolerate this sin rather than being sad for the man and excommunicating him. Your pride is ill-conceived. Don't fool yourselves.

Don't you know that just a little leaven leavens a whole ball of dough? Sin is like that. Get rid of the sin so that sinfulness does not permeate the whole church. Do this with sincerity and honesty, not with malice or a double standard. Do not be friends of fornicators, homosexuals, covetous, idolaters, extortioners, drunkards, habitual criminals, or abusive persons who claim to be believers. In the world you can not escape these completely, but in the church you can and should. No one who lives unrepentant in these sins will inherit heaven. 3) 1 Cor. 6:9 Some of you may have practiced these sins in the past, but now you have been cleansed by Christ. God is the ultimate judge, but do not fellowship with blatant sinners.

WHY BRING LAWSUITS AGAINST EACH OTHER

Why take a Christian brother to court over a dispute instead of settling the matter within the church? Don't you know that the Lord will set you up as judges for the entire world at the end of the age? Are you not then able to arbitrate even the most intricate problems? Why must a brother take a brother to court?

HONOR GOD WITH YOUR CONDUCT

Everything legal is not beneficial, and I do not want to be controlled by anything. Don't be addicted to anything, good or bad. Don't you know that your bodies have been made members of Christ's body? Don't make the body of Christ intimate with a prostitute! Run from fornication. Other sins are outside the body, but fornication is a sin against your body which is the temple of the Holy Spirit. <u>You don't belong to yourself; you're bought and paid for, therefore, glorify God in your body and spirit both of which belong to Him</u>. 15) 1 Cor. 6:19-20

MARITAL INSTRUCTIONS

Let each man and woman who marry be faithful to their own wife and husband, respectively. And faithfully take care of your mate's sexual needs. It helps prevent your mate from being unduly exposed to sexual temptation if you don't deny each other regular sexual intimacy. Conduct yourself toward your mate as if your mate had control of your body.

A husband and wife should not divorce. If a Christian has an unbelieving spouse, let them stay together. Their relationship is special. Perhaps the believing mate will be instrumental in the spouse's salvation. But if the unbeliever leaves the marriage, let it be. The Christian will not be bound by the marriage vow in that case. We are called to peace.

Whether you are married or single, remember that the time may be short. Be more conscious of the next world than of this world. This is not the main event. Make your priority the service of the Lord. The states of being married and of being single are both honorable when one lives in the Lord.

BASIC KNOWLEDGE

Knowledge is good but can make one callous, proud and arrogant. Love is better. Regardless of how much someone thinks he knows, there is much about which he is ignorant. The best knowledge is to know that God loves you, and you love God.

MATURE KNOWLEDGE

We have the knowledge that <u>there is only one true God</u>. 14) 1 Cor. 8:6 All the false "gods" and false religions taken together are nothing. But not every genuine believer is this confident in their faith in God. These weaker brothers are offended if Christians use anything tainted by false religions. For example, meat which has been offered to idols and then sold at a bargain is certainly good food. But if eating inexpensive meat which was previously an idol's offering hurts my brother, then I will not eat that meat even though I have the confident knowledge that the eating of it is not a sin. The nonentity idol has no moral or spiritual effect at all on meat offered to it. But I do not want to hurt my weaker brother by my more seasoned knowledge, nor allow my stronger faith to injure the body of Christ.

Don't just seek your own benefit, but also the benefit of others. Every thing in the whole earth is the Lord's and intended for good. Yet, if my enjoying something offends the conscience of another, I will abstain from it in order to help him. The objective, whether eating or drinking or anything whatsoever, is to give glory to God in all we do, and simultaneously avoid offending people. I try to please God, not just for my own good, but also for the good of others. Be followers of my example as I follow Christ.

SUPPORT YOUR MINISTERS

It's proper to support ministers of the Lord in the work of the gospel. Soldiers are supported at war. A gardener eats the produce of his garden. A shepherd lives off the flock he keeps. The law of Moses instructs not to muzzle the ox which grinds the corn. God does not mean this only to allow the oxen to eat from the corn they are working, but intends it as an allegory for us. We share with you spiritual things, and it is right for you to share with us material things. The priests of the temple under Moses' law lived from the sacrifices and bread used in the temple. Likewise, God has ordained that those who preach the gospel should be materially sustained by those to whom they preach.

I don't say this so you'll support me. I preach because I can't help it. There's a message in me that forces its way out. I'm miserable if I don't share the gospel. I haven't taken your material support. I get satisfaction knowing that I have given you God's truth without charge. I support myself so I am free of everyone and offend no one, thus gaining more converts.

WISE AND FLEXIBLE MINISTERING

My method of preaching is to assume the manners and customs of those I am trying to convert. To the Jews, I become a Jew in order to win the Jews. To those outside the Mosaic law, I become as one not under the Mosaic law (but still living

according to the law of God in Christ) in order to win those who
do not recognize the law of Moses. To weak individuals who are
easily offended I live inoffensively so I might win these weak
ones. For the sake of the gospel, I am all things to all people in
order to win a few everywhere.

All entrants in a race run, but only one gets first place.
Run to win. To win this race, be moderate in everything. I use an
illustration of those who seek an earthly award, but we seek a
heavenly reward that will never fade away. Therefore, I run
confidently, boldly. I fight without wasting punches. I maintain
control of my bodily passions lest, after having coached others, I
myself should be thrown out of the game.

WARNING AND ENCOURAGEMENT

Brothers and sisters, be aware that what happened to
our forefathers when Moses led them from Egypt to Canaan is a
warning to us. They all experienced the miracles of God to
protect and nourish them, but still they displeased God and,
therefore, died in the wilderness, not entering into the promised
land. We are not to do as they did, lusting after evil things,
worshipping idols, committing fornication, tempting God,
complaining. Let their failure teach us to examine ourselves
when we think we are secure and to be alert so we will not fall as
they did. No temptation will test you that has not tested others.
And God is always reliable. He will never allow you to be
tempted beyond your ability to resist, but will with every
temptation make a way to escape it, so that you are able to
overcome. Run from sin. [16] 1 Cor 10:13

COMMEMORATING THE DEATH OF JESUS

The proper way to partake of the Lord's supper is to
follow His example. He took bread and said, "This is My body
which is broken for you; do this in memorial of Me." Similarly,
He took the cup and said, "This cup is the new testament in My
blood; do this in memorial of Me." When you break the bread
and share the cup in this manner, you memorialize the Lord's
death until He returns.

Let an individual examine his own self and motives,
and in a contrite attitude let him participate. When one
participates in this ordinance in an unworthy manner, showing

disrespect for the Lord, he will be disciplined by God. Each of you judge yourself in order that God need not judge you. When God does judge believers, He disciplines you as children, but doesn't condemn you with the world.

INSTRUCTIONS REGARDING SPIRITUAL GIFTS

Don't be ignorant about spiritual gifts. In summary, no one speaking by the Spirit can curse Jesus, and no one can genuinely confess Jesus as Lord unless enabled by the Spirit.

In a more detailed examination, there are various gifts, but just one Spirit who performs the outworking of gifts in every believer. The evidence of the Spirit working in and through a believer is given to benefit that believer. The Spirit gives to one person wisdom, to another special knowledge, to another extra faith, to someone else the gift of healing, to another the ability to work miracles, to another the ability to prophesy, to another the ability to differentiate between spirits, to another the ability to speak in languages he has never learned, to another the gift to interpret these languages, and so on, the same Spirit giving each believer the gift God desires.

DIVERSITY OF FUNCTION YET ONE IN PURPOSE AS IN A PHYSICAL BODY

Believers comprise the body of Christ on earth. In our fleshly body, there are many different organs and appendages, each with an individual and important function. Our physical body could not live if all its members performed the same function. In a way, the less obvious members of our human body are the more important ones, and so it often is in the body of Christ. There should be no divisive or envious attitudes among you, but mutual caring for each other just as we care for every part of our physical body.

LOVE IS HIGHEST

Though I'm gifted to speak with languages of men and angels but don't do it in love, I'm just vocalizing meaningless noises. Though I'm multi-gifted -- to prophesy, to understand God's plans, have special knowledge, and faith to remove mountains -- yet, if I do not have love, I have nothing. If I literally sell everything I own and give all the proceeds to the poor, and even though I were a willing martyr, if I have no love, it profits me absolutely nothing.

Love is very patient and kind. Love has no jealousy. Love does not brag on itself and is not haughty or egotistical. Love is not discourteous, is not selfish, is not easily irritated. Love does not assume the worst of others, and does not gloat over someone else's calamity. Love is not lazy, but wants to serve. The body wears down, but love does not wear out. Love delights in truth, accepts responsibility, has a positive attitude, always has hope, holds up under anything and everything. Love forgives. Love never fails.

In the future, gifts of prophecies, speaking in unknown languages, and special knowledge will no longer be granted or needed. Today, we have limited knowledge. When the perfect state arrives, then partial knowledge and prophecy will be a thing of the past, just as when I became a man, thinking and acting as a child was put behind me. For now, we understand things as if seeing through a fog, but in that day we shall understand clearly, face to face. Now we have limited knowledge, but then we shall have infinite knowledge, like God's. At that time, there shall endure faith, hope and love. The greatest is love.

PROPER USE OF SPEAKING IN UNKNOWN LANGUAGES

Pursue Love. In love, also seek spiritual gifts, preferably the ability to prophesy because it is valuable to teach, correct and comfort others. When you pray aloud or sing in a tongue granted as a spiritual gift, interpret the message so everyone can understand and be blessed. I am grateful that I've been given the gift to speak in various tongues more than all of you, but, in the church, I speak so I can be understood.

Tongues are a sign to those who do not believe, hearing you speak in their own languages, knowing you have never learned their tongue. And still, most will not believe. Prophesying is for the believers, to instruct them.

If a stranger visits your church and hears you speaking in several languages, he will think you crazy. But if he hears an understandable message, delivered in the Spirit and power of the Lord, he'll be convicted and converted, and will worship God.

Do all things for teaching. Don't prohibit speaking in an unlearned language. However, when someone speaks in another tongue, let there be an interpretation. If there's no one to interpret the message, let none at that time speak in an unknown tongue. If someone wants to speak a prophecy, let him do so in order, one at a time, that everyone may learn and be blessed. God wants order, not confusion, in the church.

THE GOSPEL IN BRIEF

This is the gospel in summary: Christ died for our sins, was buried, and rose again the third day. He was seen by the disciples, then of over five hundred people at once, most of whom are alive as I write this and can confirm this report. Last, He was seen by me in a special vision.

I am the least of the apostles, and unworthy to be an apostle since I previously persecuted believers. But God in grace made me an apostle. I work hard as God works within me to make His calling of me beneficial to many.

REGARDING RESURRECTION

Some believers fear there may be no resurrection from the dead; but if there is no resurrection, look at the consequences: *1* - Christ is still dead and the gospel is a bad joke; *2* - your faith is worthless; *3* - we are lying to say Christ is alive; *4* - you are still under the penalty of sin; and *5* - the dead have no hope. If that is the case and this life is all there is, then *6* - Christians are abstaining from sinful pleasures for nothing. If there is no resurrection to eternal life, then we should eat, drink and be merry, for tomorrow it may all be over in endless death.

But, Christ is absolutely alive from the dead, the first to be resurrected never to die again. Believers in Christ will be raised at His second coming. Then is the end of the age when Christ will conquer all powers, all entities, and even death. At the resurrection, flesh and bones will be changed. The body is buried a mortal, but raised immortal. It is buried in decay, but raised in glory. It is buried weak and natural, but raised a powerful, spiritual body. The natural body cannot live in heaven, but in heaven we shall be made similar to Christ. [17]

Not all will die, but all will be changed instantly. The trumpet of God will blast and the dead will be raised no longer subject to decay. Those alive will be made immortal. Death is defeated. [17] 1 Cor. 15: 51-57 Eternal life is the victory through Jesus Christ our Lord.

Praise God!

THE RESULT OF KNOWING THERE IS AN EVERLASTING LIFE WITH GOD

Therefore, believers, be consistent, confident, prolific in your work for the Lord, for you can be certain your labor in the Lord is profitable for all eternity.

Be alert! Stand solid in the faith. Be strong, and function from love. The grace of our Lord Jesus Christ be with you, together with my love. Amen.

CHRISTIAN MATURITY GIVES CONFIDENCE

FROM

II Peter

BELIEVERS HAVE IT ALL

From Peter, to all those who have faith in Jesus Christ. May you be aware over and over again of the grace and peace of God through your knowledge of Him in Jesus Christ. This faith-knowledge calls us to virtue and gives us everything that is necessary for true life and godliness.

In Christ we have exciting promises. Two wonderful examples: We have been given part of the divine nature -- We have escaped eternal death. There are many others.

CHRISTIAN GROWTH IS A PROGRESSION

Therefore, be diligent in your Christian life. To your basic faith add virtuousness, then add knowledge, then moderation and balance, then add patience, then more godliness, then brotherly kindness, then complete love. If these qualities possess and control you, you will be productive and rich in Jesus Christ. If you are not growing in these qualities, you will lose sight of your heavenly future and will forget that you have been cleansed from all sins. When you are progressing in Christian growth, you have confidence that you will not be condemned, and you have assurance of your salvation. The result will be a confident and thrilling welcome into the everlasting kingdom of our Lord Jesus Christ.

THE CERTAINTY OF THE MESSAGE

We have not related cunningly concocted fairy tales when we told you the story of Jesus. We were eyewitnesses of His power and majesty when God displayed His glory and deity on the mountain, and there came from heaven a voice which said, "This is My beloved Son in whom I am well pleased."

We not only heard that voice and saw that glory, but we have an even more unmistakable message, the prophetic scriptures which have been fulfilled. Pay attention to this message just as you would to a light illuminating a dark and dangerous pathway. The prophecy of scripture is not from some human source, nor was it given because some man wanted it written. God wanted it written! He, by the Holy Spirit, inspired several holy men to record over several centuries one complementary, consistent, correct, complete message.

There are false prophets teaching false doctrines, damnable heresies, even denying the essence of the Lord Himself who redeemed us. These bring upon themselves sure destruction. However, many good people will follow their deadly ways and will speak evil of the truth. Being jealous of you, they will make sham prophecies at your expense. These will be judged.

Since God did not spare the angels who sinned, but cast them into hell; and since God judged the world in Noah's time, as well as Sodom and Gomorra in Abraham's time; He has given ample warning that He will judge. Remember how He delivered Lot. The Lord will save the righteous, and judge those whom He has not justified.

These false prophets banquet with you and live the lifestyle of the rich and famous. They are covetous and adulterous, and addicted to these sins. Yet, though they are mostly interested in the money, they continue to deceive unstable believers. With skillful words they entice the gullible, promising them freedom while they themselves are slaves of deceitfulness. You must remember the words of the true prophets in scripture and the commands of the genuine apostles of Jesus.

There will be scoffers who will mock saying, "Why hasn't He returned as He promised? Since recorded history, all things continue the same." Of course, they chose to forget previous judgments of God, such as the flood when God punished by water. God will judge the world next time with fire. But be aware, a day with God is as a thousand years, and a thousand years as a day. God is not remiss in His promise, as some think. He is merely patient, not wanting anyone to be condemned, but wanting all to repent and be saved. And so He has waited. But, as He said, He will come to judge.

THE JUDGE IS COMING

It will happen as a thief in the night, surprising the unaware. Then the galaxy shall disintegrate with a great noise, the elements shall melt with terrific heat, and planet earth will be consumed. Realizing that the universe will be dissolved, should we not throw ourselves upon God's mercy, and live holy lives?

Then we can look forward to that day with anticipation, knowing that He has promised us a new heaven and a new earth in which will be only everlasting joy and righteousness.

SUMMATION

In summary, believers, be diligent in your faith and conduct. Realize that the delay in the Lord's judgment means more will find salvation. Do not allow yourself to be led away by false prophets, but grow in grace and in the knowledge of Jesus Christ our Lord and Savior. To Him be glory now and forever. Amen.

BEWARE FALSE
RELIGIONS

FROM

Galatians

From Paul to the churches at Galatia. May the grace and peace of God be your daily experience.

TRUE RELIGION

Jesus gave Himself for our sins and to deliver us from the power of these evil times. Let us give Him glory and praise for ever.

WHY DO YOU LISTEN TO FALSE RELIGIONS

I am amazed that you are so quickly questioning the validity of the gospel of Christ and are considering a different gospel, which is not really the gospel at all, but a perversion of it. Be warned! If I myself, or even an angel from heaven itself, preaches any gospel which is different from the true gospel which I have already given to you, let that one be damned. [13) Gal 1:8,9] Let me emphasize, if anyone teaches any other gospel, let him be cursed.

Do I say this trying to please some group of men? Or to court favor with religious leaders? Absolutely not! I only seek to please God, whose servant I am. The gospel I gave you is not from men, nor subject to revision. It is from God and is unchangeable.

PAUL WAS RESCUED FROM FALSE RELIGION

You know how I persecuted believers of the gospel when I was myself a zealous Pharisee. I terrorized the church more than you could know, and destroyed Christians with a vengeance. But God chose to save me and to use me as His minister. In grace, He revealed His Son to me and commissioned me to preach His gospel. I didn't seek instruction from those who were apostles before me. I went out to the desert where God Himself taught me three years. After that, I was officially joined to the apostles. The believers then heard that I, who had so terribly punished Christians, was now a convert myself, and they glorified God because of my faith and my new mission.

FAITH IN JESUS ALONE PLUS NOTHING IS TRUE RELIGION

There was a time when some Jewish believers wanted those Gentiles who were converted under my ministry to keep the traditional law of Moses and be circumcised. But that error was corrected. We know that one is not saved from sin by trying to do good deeds or by keeping some holy standard. Only by faith in Jesus Christ can one be saved, for by good works or keeping the law shall no one be saved. [5 & 6) Gal. 2:16]

The question arises, if, while I am correctly trusting in faith for Jesus to save me, I find myself giving in to sin, does that make Jesus a party to my sin or does it cancel my faith? Absolutely not. I thereby prove that I am a hopeless sinner, but I am still dead to sin, having died vicariously in Christ on the cross, and I am still alive unto God, having been vicariously raised from death with Christ. It is just as if I were crucified with Christ, yet I still live. Vicariously, it is not I who really lives, but Christ lives in and through me because of my faith in Him who loves me and gave Himself for me.

My slipping into sin does not nullify the grace of God, because forgiveness of sin does not come by being sinless. If it did, Christ would not have needed to die. Forgiveness comes by faith in Christ's atonement. [4) Gal. 2:20,21] His righteousness is given to me by grace through faith.

THE GOSPEL DOES NOT CHANGE

You foolish Galatians. Who has deceived or bewitched you? Some necromancer? You by faith accepted the gospel of grace. Now does it make any sense to rely on self-righteousness for continued salvation?

The Gospel Truth doesn't change! As far back as Abraham, God made it evident that He saved people by faith. The law condemns one who breaks just one commandment one time. No one is made right with God by trying to do good. God has always said, "The just shall live by faith." [6) Gal. 3: 10,11]

Christ, taking the punishment and judgment meted out under the law, rescued us from the obligation of trying to fulfill God's holy law. No one could keep God's law, so all were condemned, until, through Christ, we could receive God's righteousness by faith. The law makes us see how badly we need a savior [3) Gal. 3:22] to rescue us from sin's death penalty. Christ is that savior and more, for He has accepted us as His brothers and sisters in God's family. We have been adopted as equal heirs with Jesus, to live forever with Him in the presence of God the Father. As a child of God, don't throw away your faith.

SPIRITUAL PRODUCE

In Christ, the law is fulfilled by loving God and loving our neighbor as ourselves. <u>Let the Spirit of God produce in you His "fruit"</u>:[15] Gal. 5:22-25 love, joy, peace, endurance, gentleness, goodness, faith, mild manners, moderation. None of these violate any law. (Not civil, criminal, natural or health laws. You will be happy, stress free, content, optimistic, pleasant to live with, healthy, with proper priorities and values, and at peace with God. What could be better?)

MAINTAIN PROPER FOCUS AND PERSPECTIVE

If a fellow believer is caught participating in sin, seek to bring him back to a right relationship with God and men. But be careful that you are not enticed to join in his sin. Help each other work through problems. Support each other. Yet, in truth, each of us bears our burdens alone, for we are individually responsible for our own actions, and no one else can live in our skin.

Be careful not to develop a cocky, conceited attitude, yet be certain you are convinced that what you are doing is important and proper and is your best effort. Don't be dependent upon the praise of others, but <u>do not fool yourself, for you cannot fool God. Whatever you sow, you will reap. Sowing to the desires of the body and the values of this world will bring a harvest of death. Sowing to the will of God and to spiritual values will bring a harvest of eternal life and reward</u>. [15] Gal. 6:7,8 Don't get frustrated doing good, for it will eventually pay off. Therefore, do good for everyone each time you have opportunity, especially for fellow Christians.

Let any feelings of superiority be only in the superior salvation offered through faith in Jesus Christ by His death and resurrection. May you live constantly aware of the grace of our Lord Jesus Christ. Amen.

MESSAGE OF COMFORT

II Corinthians

God is the source of comfort and mercy. He comforts us in the trials of life in order that we, because of our experiences, will be able to comfort others who find themselves in any kind of adversity. When persecution because of being a Christian increases, then the consoling presence of Christ is more apparent. Whether we ourselves are cursed or comforted, we want to be an example to you and to bring you the message of salvation. We are grateful to God that in Christ we know we are always winning.

OUR TRANSFORMATION IS NOT CONTROLLED BY CIRCUMSTANCES

Where the Spirit of the Lord is in control, there is peace and optimism. As we look in the mirror we should see ourselves being changed to be more like the Lord, progressing in glory until the Spirit transforms us into the image of Christ.

FOCUSING ON ETERNAL VALUES

In our ministry, we use no crafty, dishonest tactics. We use no deceit in teaching God's word. The unbelieving do not understand the gospel because satan has blinded their minds. But God has illuminated our minds, giving us knowledge of the glory of God in Christ. God uses human beacons to project His light, demonstrating in us His regal power. In our ministry, we face difficulties, but we do not get depressed; we are frustrated, but not defeated; we do not always understand, but do not quit; we are persecuted, but are never alone; we are knocked down, but not knocked out. In our physical bodies we join in on the sufferings of Christ's death in order that the new life of Christ might also be obvious in us. We know that God, who raised Jesus from the dead, will also raise us and you. We want God's amazing grace to cause thanksgiving in many, and result in prolific praise to God. With this goal in mind, we keep on going. Our bodies get tired, but our souls are refreshed each day. Our trials are small and short compared to the far greater, eternal glory which awaits us. We focus, not on the visible problems, but on the invisible glory. Visible things are temporary; the invisible are eternal.

When our physical bodies decay, God has spiritual bodies for us. This physical body aches and groans, preferring that perfect one which awaits us. Because God's Spirit is within, we are confident and certain in the knowledge that the instant we are absent from this body we are present with the Lord. [17) 2 Cor. 5: 1-8] Our goal, whether here in faith, or there in His presence, is to be pleasing to Him. We will all stand before the judgment seat of Christ in order that everyone may be rewarded for the life lived on earth -- good or bad. Terrorized by God's absolute holiness, we seek to persuade everyone to be prepared. [3 & 13) 2 Cor 5:10,11]

WE ARE MADE NEW IN CHRIST

This is my reasoning: Christ died for everyone, therefore, it's as if everyone died. He died for everyone, in order that those who choose His eternal life would live not for themselves, but for Christ who died for them and rose again. Now, anyone who is truly in Christ is a new person, alive from death. The former existence is gone and everything is new, God-oriented, because God has made us right with Himself through Christ. [15) 2 Cor. 5:17]

It's this message of "being made right with God" that has been given to us by God. Through Christ, God has made the world right with Himself, no longer holding sinners accountable for their sins. Allow yourself to be reconciled to God! God the Father made His son, Jesus, who was absolutely perfect, to actually become the essence of sin, in order that we could be made the essence of perfection in Christ. [3) 2 Cor. 5:21] Do not disregard this message of the grace of God. Now is the right time. Today is the day of salvation. [13) 2 Cor. 6:2] **Turn to God now**, even as you read this gospel message.

LET DEDICATION TO GOD MAKE YOUR LIFE DIFFERENT

You believers, because of all the promises of God, live clean lives -- body, soul and spirit. [15) 2 Cor. 7:1] Out of reverence for God, mature into people set apart to God. Do not be unequally joined to unbelievers. You are the temple of the living God. The Lord says, "Come out from the world and be separate. I am your Father. Be My sons and daughters, ready to be welcomed home."

TRUE RICHES AND THE USE OF WEALTH

You are aware of the grace of our Lord Jesus Christ, that although He was infinitely rich, yet for us He became poor, that we through His poverty might be eternally rich.

In giving to the Lord and His work, first give yourself. As to tithes and offerings, give as you are able. You are not responsible to give beyond your means. Be honest in the sight of God and man in these matters. One who sows sparingly will reap sparingly, and one who sows abundantly will reap abundantly. Give to the Lord according to the plan He puts in your heart, not grudgingly or out of obligation, for God loves a happy giver. God is able to make abundant grace come your way, so that you will have more than you need -- enough to give away. As you excel in generosity, you will praise God for His blessings, and those you help will also be thankful to God. Pray for those to whom you give monetary assistance. Remember that God gave us a gift precious beyond words.

WATCH OUT FOR FALSE RELIGIONS

<u>Don't be corrupted from the simplicity in Christ. Some preach another Jesus, another spirit, another gospel. These are false missionaries, deceitful workers calling themselves apostles of Christ. Don't be surprised, for Satan himself transforms into an angel of light. Don't be fooled.</u> [13) 2 Cor 11:13,14]

Some tell you they've had visions and new revelations. About fourteen years ago I was caught up into God's presence. I heard and saw things beyond expression. I could have become proud, but God gave me a physical infirmity to keep me humble. I asked God three times to remove this, but He told me, "My grace is adequate for you. My strength is better demonstrated through weakness."

Therefore, I gladly delight in my handicap so that through it Christ's power may be obvious. I now take pleasure in handicaps, in being shamed, in distressful situations for Christ's sake, because out of my weakness, Christ's strength explodes.

JUST BE CHRISTIANS

On my next visit, I do not wish to find arguing, envy, anger, strife, backstabbing, gossip, rumors, rebelliousness and unrepented fornication. Examine yourself to be certain you are genuine in your faith. Prove to your own self that Christ is really in you. Be mature believers. Be content. Be harmonious and live in peace. The God of peace and love is with you.

May the grace of the Lord Jesus Christ and the fellowship of the Holy Spirit be your normal experience. Amen.

THE MESSAGE TO LEADERS

FROM

I and II Timothy

&

Titus

From I Timothy

ONLY ONE GOD AND ONE ACCESS TO GOD

Paul to Timothy, my own son in the Faith. May God's grace, mercy and peace through Jesus Christ as Lord fill your consciousness.

Admonish that no one teach any other doctrine, nor give credence to supposed visions and endless genealogies.

The purpose of God's law is to produce love -- love from a pure motive, a good conscience and a genuine faith. Some have strayed from this truth and get high hearing themselves talk. They call themselves authorities and listen to false angles, but they don't understand what they say or to whom they swear allegiance. The law is good when properly used. It identifies sin and sinners and all things contrary to sound doctrine and to the true gospel.

God wants everyone to learn the truth and to be saved. There is only one God, and only one mediator between God and man! It is Jesus, who gave Himself as our ransom. [4) 1 Tim. 2:4]

EVEN THE WORST SINNERS CAN BE MADE RIGHT WITH GOD

I am now a minister of the gospel though I was a great sinner. God's grace was especially abundant to me, demonstrating God's infinite love and mercy. I was the leading enemy of God, mocking the name of Jesus and persecuting His people. It is an ageless truth that Christ Jesus came into the world for the express purpose of saving sinners. I was the worst one. Since Christ saved me, He will save anyone who believes on Him. For this we give praise, honor and glory forever to the only true God, invisible, immortal, the eternal King, the Savior. [14) 1 Tim 1:17]

A STANDARD OF GODLY LEADERSHIP

Timothy, be enthusiastic in your ministry. Keep both the faith and your conscience pure, for some have not done so and have been ruined. Pray for yourself, for other leaders, and for all in authority. Lead a quiet, peaceful life, clean and pure, pleasing God. Be able when you pray to lift up innocent hands, harboring no malice. [8) 1 Tim. 2:8] Then you will not doubt that God hears you.

A STANDARD FOR A PASTOR

The pastor of a local church is in a good work. He should have a spotless reputation, have one wife, be earnest and moderate, of good character, a good host, able to teach, not a drunkard, not greedy for money, not a brawler, not envious, not naive or gullible, be patient, in control of his own household, and well thought of by unbelievers.

A STANDARD FOR LAY LEADERS

Similarly, church leaders should be serious, not two-faced or talking out of both sides of their mouth, not drunkards, not greedy of wealth, with a pure conscience, the husband of one wife, and in control of their own family.

Their wife should be sincere, not a gossip, sober, and faithful in all she undertakes. In fact, all women should be modest and emphasize inner beauty over outer beauty, being subject to the leadership of their man. Leading in the church is important business.

A SUMMARY OF THE TRUE GOSPEL

Without question, the essence of God and salvation is a great mystery. God became flesh, [14) 1 Tim. 3:16] was proven to be the answer for the problem of sin when He was raised from the dead by the Spirit, was seen alive by men and angels, and again received into glory.

REJECT FALSE GOSPELS

The Spirit has given specific warning that in the latter days some who claim to be saints will depart from the True Faith, listening to deceiving spirits, doctrines from the devil, hypocritical lies. Others will forbid marriage and the eating of meat. As a good minister, warn against these errors and nourish your people in the words of true faith and sound doctrine. Reject irreverent visions supposedly from God. Exercise godliness. Physical exercise has some benefit and developing godliness has eternal benefit. Trust in the living God who has provided salvation for everyone and who will save those who believe.

EXEMPLIFY TRUTH

Teach these truths with authority. Prepare diligently so no one can mock your youth. Be an example in conduct, in the way you talk, in love, in attitude, in faith and purity. Keep on reading and preaching. Do not neglect your spiritual gift and responsibility. <u>Meditate on truth, commit yourself totally to it, and everyone will see in you the good results. Keep yourself and your doctrine pure and unchanged to protect yourself and those you teach</u>. [7] 1 Tim. 4:15,16

EXERCISE GOOD JUDGMENT

Don't be curt with older men, but respectfully reason with them as you would your father. Relate to young men as brothers, young women as sisters, and older women as you would your mother.

It is proper for relatives to provide for the financial needs of those who are destitute in their family. In fact, if anyone does not take care of his own family, then he is by his lack of action denying his faith and is worse than one who verbally denounces God.

Don't have partiality. Don't judge people too hastily. Don't join in mob rule. Use a little wine for your stomach trouble and your frequent illnesses. Remember that it is not always possible to tell in advance who are the winners and who are the losers. With some you have to wait to see by their performance over time.

MONETARY ADVICE

Instruct employees to be effective and loyal to their employer. Those who have a Christian employer should not take advantage of his good nature. Gain is not necessarily godliness, but godliness with contentment is great gain. We came into the world with nothing and we can take nothing out of the world, therefore, we ought to be content if we have the basics of life.

The rich, and those who will do anything to get rich, fall into temptations and snares. The love of money is the root of all evil. Coveting money, many have erred from the faith and brought to themselves many sorrows.

Keep in mind the values and perspective of a dying person toward money. Charge wealthy individuals not to be conceited nor to trust in their riches, but to trust in God who gives generously to us all the things we enjoy. Instruct them to do charitable work, ready to share, laying up for themselves a trust account for the life which is eternal.

<u>**FOLLOW GOD OVER MEN**</u>

Timothy, cling to the doctrine committed to your trust. Ignore irreverent and worthless arguments and opposition from the godless who haughtily call themselves scientists. They like to sound intellectual, but in reality it is themselves they condemn. Some believers have followed their atheistic line of reasoning and have erred from the faith.

But you, as a man of God, <u>run from those things</u> [16) 1 Tim. 6:11] and follow righteousness, godliness, faith, love, patience, humility. Fight a pure fight for the faith and for eternal life. Seek to be unimpeachable until <u>Christ</u> returns, <u>who is the blessed and only Potentate, the King of kings and Lord of lords, who only has inherent immortality dwelling in light no one can approach, whom no one has ever seen nor can see</u>. [14) 1 Tim. 6:15,16] To Him be everlasting honor and power. Amen.

From 2nd Timothy

Timothy, I write this second time to remind you to keep active your spiritual gift. I pray for you night and day. God has not given us a spirit of fear, but of love, strength and intelligence. Don't be ashamed of the gospel of our Lord or of those who do His work. Continue to minister with us in God's work, even though He saved us not based on our work, but only because of His grace through Jesus Christ. <u>I know Him in whom I believe and am convinced He is able to keep through the judgment day and on into His eternal kingdom everything which I have entrusted to Him</u>. [11) 2 Tim. 1:12] Be committed!

<u>**SHARE YOUR COMMITMENT**</u>

Timothy, never let go of the hope and love in Christ Jesus. Be strong in His grace. <u>Take the truth which you have learned from me and teach it to those who will in turn teach others, who will teach others, and so on in endless spiritual reproduction</u>. [12) 2 Tim. 2:2]

PRACTICE WHAT YOU PREACH

Be tough in Christ, like a good solider. A committed soldier does not get enmeshed with the affairs of life, but concentrates on battle preparedness to please his commander. In another figure of speech, no one who strives to be a champion is able to keep the title he attains unless he has won it legally, by the rules. A third illustration is that a gardener eats the produce of his own garden. Think on the meaning of these parables and ask God to give understanding.

CHRIST IS COMMITTED TO US

These truths are ageless: if we died with Christ, we shall also live with Him; if we suffer with Him, we shall also rule with Him; if we withhold from Him, He will withhold from us; <u>if we feel like we have lost the faith, He does not lose faith but remains faithful and will not deny His own commitment to us. He keeps all those whom His love has found</u>. [11] 2 Tim. 2:13

TRUST TRUTH AND TEACH TRUTH

<u>Study to prove yourself approved to God, a student never ashamed, for you understand the word of truth</u>. [7] 2 Tim. 2:15 Don't engage in worthless arguments that only confuse people. Shun irreverent babblings of egotistical intellectuals. Don't get frustrated trying to silence all arguments. Truth is truth. Truth is singular. What is, is, regardless of how erudite some may be who say it is otherwise. The foundation of God is secure and the Lord knows who are His own. Humbly continue to teach truth. Some of those who oppose themselves will come to repentance when they see the light, and will be saved from the intellectual snare of satan, who so easily captures the so-called intelligentsia.

KEEP PURE

In a home, some containers are used for food, some for garbage. Keep pure so you are prepared for good, honorable usefulness. <u>Run from sinful desires</u>. [16] 2 Tim. 2:22 Be able to call on the Lord from a pure heart.

KEEP SCRIPTURE AS YOUR UNCHANGING GUIDE

In the last days, times will be dangerous. People will be overly in love with themselves, covetous, braggarts, proud, jealous, having unnatural affection, will be truce breakers, false accusers, fierce, despisers of those who are good, traitors, willing to do anything for money, lovers of pleasure more than lovers of God, having a form of religion but denying the power of God. Some will be worshipers of education, always learning a new philosophy but never able to be sure about anything or confident of what is truth. Some always resist truth, having unprincipled minds regarding faith. But in time, their folly will become obvious.

Stay away from these. It will cost you something, for all who choose to live godly in Christ Jesus will suffer persecution. But continue in the truth from the Holy Scripture you learned as a child. Truth will make you wise unto salvation. All scripture is given by inspiration of God and is profitable for doctrine, for reproof, for correction, for instruction in righteousness in order that the people of God may be progressing toward perfection, completely prepared to do good. 7) 2 Tim. 3:16,17

A FINAL CHALLENGE

I challenge you before Christ Jesus who will judge the living and the dead at His appearing and at His kingdom, preach the word. Be consistent, when you feel like it and when you don't, when there appears to be results and when there doesn't. Reprove, rebuke, exhort with patience and doctrinal proof. 12) 2 Tim 4:2 People will want to turn from truth to new visions and new doctrines. Some will leave because of love for this present world. Do your evangelistic work and carry your ministry to completion.

A FINAL TESTING

The time of my death is near. I have fought a good fight. I have completed my race. I have kept the faith. The Lord, the righteous Judge, has a crown to give me at the day of judgment, and not to me alone, but also to all those who cherish His return.

The Lord Jesus Christ is with your spirit and His grace is upon you. Amen.

From Titus

TEACH THIS TRUTH

The grace of God which provides salvation to everyone, teaches us to <u>abstain from ungodliness and sinful lusts, to live moderately, righteously and godly in this life,</u> 15) Titus 2:11-13 anticipating with assurance, the glorious appearing of <u>the great God and Savior Jesus Christ, who gave Himself for us</u> 14) Titus 2:13 to redeem us from all sin and to purify us unto Himself a unique people, zealous in good works. Teach this truth with authority, ignoring mockers.

SALVATION IS BY FAITH

The kindness and love of God our Savior which provides salvation for everyone, teaches us that <u>it is not by good works which we do but only because of His mercy that He saves us, cleansing us from sin, giving us a new birth, and indwelling us with the Holy Spirit. By His grace alone He makes us as if we had never sinned, able to inherit eternal life</u>. 6) Titus 3:5,6

GENUINE SALVATION RESULTS IN GODLY LIVING

Nevertheless, it is true and should be taught constantly that <u>those who believe in Jesus should be diligent in good works</u>. 15) Titus 3:8 This is beneficial to all and produces fruitfulness.

<u>Someone who has left the faith and causes divisions among you should be reasoned with a couple of times to see if he can be rescued from his error. If he persists, let him go. He is trapped by sin and is confused, condemning himself</u>. 13) Titus 3:10,11

THE EXAMPLES OF PAUL & CHRIST

Philippians

From Paul and Timothy, servants of Jesus Christ, to the saints in Christ at Philippi. Grace and peace to you from God our Father and from the Lord Jesus Christ.

PRAYER BASED ON LOVE

I thank God for you every time I think of you. In my prayers I am constantly grateful for your friendship based on our common belief in the gospel. I am confident that the Spirit who started the good work in you will finish it, assuring that you will be with Jesus Christ.

It is fitting that I feel so good about you, for God knows how much I love you in Christ. I pray that you will grow in knowledge and discernment, so you will be able to recognize the difference between the acceptable and the best. I pray that you may be genuine in your faith, producing proper living, causing praise and glory to God.

PERSECUTION CAN HAVE A POSITIVE RESULT

Do you realize that my persecution has led to the spreading of the gospel even into the palace and other places? Also, because I am imprisoned, some of the believers have begun speaking out in my stead. Christ is preached, and I am happy. I am not ashamed of imprisonment, because it is benefiting the message of Christ. If I live, it is for Christ; if I am executed, it is my gain. 15) Phil. 1:21-27 I would rather be with Christ, but I stay here to continue to build you in faith and joy.

Be sure that your manner of living is a positive reflection of the gospel, that you work harmoniously for the gospel, and that you are not afraid because of persecutors. For just as with me, so with you, you have the privilege not only to believe on Christ, but also to suffer for Him.

PLACE OTHERS AHEAD OF SELF

But there is consolation in Christ. There is the comfort of His love, the fellowship of His Spirit, the experience of His compassion and mercy. Make me pleased by being harmonious, sharing love, having one purpose and goal. Do nothing out of a jealous spirit or self pride. Be humble, thinking of others before yourself. Advance the other person's well-being, not just your own. 15) Phil. 2:3-8 Think like the example of Christ who is God the

Son, but did not flaunt it [14) Phil. 2:6] and became a working man, and then humbled Himself further to be executed as a criminal. Now God has highly exalted Him and glorified Him above all. Everyone shall bow to Him and confess Him Lord. So, believers, whether I am with you, or in prison unable to observe, let your salvation work out through your actions as God within you causes you not only to want to do, but actually to do His will. Don't complain or argue all the time, but be unique as lights in darkness, offering the message of life.

<u>PARTICIPANTS IN INFINITE LIFE</u>

In conclusion, be happy in the Lord. But still <u>beware of evil workers and those who teach reliance on good works for salvation. I, above all, could have confidence in good works, but all my religious efforts which made me look good to pious leaders I now see as worthless. Everything is worthless compared to knowing Christ Jesus my Lord and being part of Him. I want to be in Him, with His righteousness, not outside of Him with my own supposed righteousness.</u> [6) Phil. 3:7-9] <u>By faith I want to know Him and the power that raised Him from death, and the spiritual fellowship experienced when suffering for Him. I want to vicariously participate in His death so I can also participate in His life. That is my goal. I reach for the reward of the high calling of God in Christ. Let all of us believers think this way. Follow my example.</u> [15) Phil. 3:14-4:1]

There are false leaders, enemies of Christ, who are in religion for ego, or for physical gratification, or for praise of men, or for material possessions. Be observant. Don't follow them. For our life style is dictated from heaven and it's from there Christ will come for us to change us to be like Him, and it's there we shall rule over all things with Him.

<u>PEACE OF MIND CAN BE YOURS</u>

With this in mind, stand solidly in the Lord. Harmoniously help each other. Be happy in the Lord all the time. Yes, choose to be happy. Be known for your moderation. <u>The Lord is at your side so don't worry about anything but instead pray about everything.</u> [8) Phil. 4:6] You may not understand it, but God's peace will calm your mind and emotions through Jesus Christ.

In closing, here's a list for meditation: True things; just things; pure things; lovely things; honest things; things of good reputation; virtuous things; things of praise. Ponder these types of things. Do what you have heard me teach and seen me do, and you will be aware that the God of peace is with you.

PROVISION FOR ALL YOU NEED

As for myself, I appreciate your care for me. I have learned to be content regardless of my circumstances, whether having much or little. I can do anything through Christ who is my strength. Nevertheless, thank you for the gifts you sent me. <u>My God shall take care of all your needs through Christ Jesus in proportion to His riches in glory</u>. 2) Phil 4: 19 To Him be glory forever. The grace of our Lord Jesus Christ be with each of you. Amen.

EXAMPLES OF FAITH

FROM

Hebrews

THE CREATOR HAS COMMUNICATED WITH US

God spoke in the past through the prophets. Now He has spoken to us through His Son. His Son is the creator and owner of the universe, the brightness of God's glory and the exact embodiment of God's essence. The Son's power holds everything together. Now that He has cleansed us from sin, He is at the right hand of the Majesty on high.

A COMPARISON REGARDING ANGELS

The Son is far above the angels. God the Father said to His Son, "Your throne, O God, is eternal. Righteousness is the scepter of Your kingdom. You founded the laws of the universe. You will allow it to disintegrate, but You are eternal. Sit at My right hand. I will make Your enemies Your footstool."

Angels are emissaries to believers. Since God judged angels, it is clear <u>we cannot escape if we neglect God's great salvation</u>. [13) Heb. 2:3] Jesus did not take the form of angels, but was born lower than angels to suffer death for every person. He became flesh and blood to destroy the power of death and satan. <u>He has freed us from the fear of death. As a faithful and merciful high priest, He made reconciliation for the sins of everyone. Since He Himself suffered firsthand temptations, He is able, with full understanding, to help us when we are tempted</u>. [4) Heb. 2:16-18]

A CAUTION

<u>Be on guard, believers! Don't let unbelief creep into your heart, causing you to doubt the living God</u>. [13) Heb. 3:12] Urge each other daily along the right path lest sin deceive you. Because of unbelief, many Israelites under Moses' leadership did not enter the promised land. Don't be like them. Keep the faith!

CONFIDENCE THROUGH FAITH

<u>When the gospel is preached, hearers benefit when they exercise faith and believe</u>. [5) Heb. 4:2] By faith alone one ceases from his own futile efforts to earn salvation and enters into God's promised rest. <u>Be diligent in faith, for the word of God is living, powerful and sharp. It can distinguish soul from spirit and can reveal thoughts and intents of one's mind</u>. [7) Heb. 4:12]

God sees and knows everyone; all are exposed to His eyes. Hold tenaciously to your faith, for our High Priest, <u>Jesus,</u>

though He never once sinned, was tempted in all areas of life just as we are. He understands. Come with confidence to His throne. You will obtain mercy and find sufficient grace no matter what your need. [16) Heb. 4:15,16]

CONFIRMATION OF PRIESTHOOD

No man can confer the priesthood. Only God can. Even Christ did not make Himself our high priest, but was appointed by God the Father. In His priestly position on earth, He, although the only born Son of God, still demonstrated obedience through suffering. Being proven perfect, He was able to provide eternal salvation to all who obey the gospel. [4) Heb. 5:9]

GROW IN MATURITY AND SECURITY

For as long as you have been believers, you ought to be teachers of these truths. But you are still learning basic principles of the gospel. You are feeding on milk when you ought to be feasting on meat. Milk is needful for babies, but adults need to exercise their spiritual minds so that they know the difference between good and evil, and are ready for meat. Progress to the mature aspects of salvation.

Be diligent. Follow the example of those believing Israelites who did inherit the promised land through patience and faith. Because God cannot lie, and it is He who gave the promises in which we trust, we can be sure that our hope in Him will be realized. This hope is a sure anchor of our soul, secure even into the very presence of God, where Jesus our high priest and savior has already gone to prepare to receive us. [11) Heb. 6: 18-20]

THE UNCHANGEABLE CHRIST HAS COMPLETED SALVATION

Jesus, as our high priest, is infinitely better than were the human high priests of Israel. Those priests died and had to be replaced. But Jesus lives forever in an unchangeable priesthood which is not passed from man to man. Therefore, He is able to save to infinity all those who come to God through Him since He lives eternally to intercede for them. He was and is sinless, infinitely pure, different from us sinners, and now rules in heaven. Unlike human priests, He never needed to first offer a sacrifice for His own sin and then for the sins of the people. Because without shedding blood there is no remission of sins, and without the death of the testator a last will and testament is of no effect; He, as perfect priest and pure Lamb of God, offered Himself once for all, once forever, sacrificed on the cross. Salvation is completed for evermore and sin has been erased -- remembered no more. <u>Just as everyone has an appointment to die once and then to stand at the judgment, so Christ died once to pay the penalty for the sin of mankind.</u>[3 & 4) Heb. 9:27,28] For those who look for Him, He will return, with sin eliminated, to take His own into eternal salvation.

CONFIDENCE AND CONSISTENCY IN CHRIST

<u>You may come boldly through Jesus into the very presence of God, confident through faith,</u> [4) Heb. 10:19-25] clean of conscience and pure of body. Hold fast to your profession of faith, knowing that Jesus is faithful. Encourage and challenge each other to love, and to good works in Christ. Get together often to exhort one another as the return of Christ gets closer.

If we willfully sin after being born into God's family, Jesus does not have to be sacrificed again, but we will be afraid and ashamed to see Him when He comes, fearing that the fire which will consume His enemies will judge us also. Since the law of Moses called for the death sentence, we reason that we, when we willfully sin, are subject to similar punishment. We remember that the Lord has said, "Vengeance is mine, I will repay." It is a fearful thing to fall into the hands of the living God! But, remember your early days as a believer. You knew that in heaven you have an enduring inheritance. Jesus keeps those He has found. Do not lose your confidence in Jesus, which has momentous reward. You need patience, that having done the will of God in believing the gospel, you will receive the promised salvation at His return. If you go back to your old ways, I am ashamed of you. But you are not of those who go back to judgment, as Judas. You believe, resulting in salvation. <u>The just will live by faith.</u> [5) Heb. 10:38]

FAITH DEFINED AND ILLUSTRATED

<u>Faith is the visualization of something hoped for, the confirmation of something invisible.</u> [5) Heb. 11:1-6]

<u>Without faith it is impossible to please God. One who comes to God must first believe that He exists and that He responds to those who seek Him with diligence.</u> [5) Heb. 11: 6]

By faith the forefathers did well. It is by faith that we understand the universe was created by the edict of God, making the material world from the immaterial, from nothing.

By faith Abel offered the right offering to God.

By faith Enoch walked with God and was, without dying, transported into the presence of God.

By faith Noah, when he was warned by God of things which had never before been experienced, prepared an ark as God instructed, saving his family and setting an example of righteousness.

By faith Abraham obeyed when God called him to go to a place which he had never seen. By faith he traveled to the land of promise, and, with Isaac and Jacob, expected God to fulfill His promises. Abraham looked for a secure city whose architect and builder was God.

Through faith Sarah conceived and delivered a child when she was past childbearing years, concluding that God would be true to His promise. As a result, there came from Abraham, who was in a sense as good as dead, innumerable descendants.

By faith Abraham, when tested, prepared to offer as a sacrifice Isaac his only son of whom God said, "From Isaac shall your descendants come." Abraham concluded that God would raise Isaac from the dead to fulfill His promise.

By faith Isaac blessed Jacob and Esau concerning future events.

By faith Jacob as he lay dying blessed both sons of Joseph.

By faith Joseph, as he died, talked about the departure of the children of Israel out from Egypt and ordered them not to leave his bones in Egypt.

By faith the parents of Moses were not intimidated by Pharaoh's commandment and hid Moses three months because they believed he was a providential child.

By faith Moses, when he was of age, declined to be made the official adopted son of Pharaoh's daughter, choosing to suffer with the people of God rather than to enjoy the pleasures of sin for life's little while. He considered the disgrace of following God greater riches than all the treasures and power of Egypt, for he had a proper perspective of the true value of the reward of each course of action. By faith he left Egypt behind, not intimidated by the intense anger of Pharaoh, enduring whatever confronted him as one who sees the invisible King of kings. [15) Heb. 11:24-26]

Through faith he observed the instructions of that first Passover so the death angel harmed none of the first-born sons of the Israelites. By faith he led them through the Red Sea as on dry ground, while the pursuing Egyptians were drowned.

By faith, under Joshua, after the people obeyed God's instructions, the walls of Jericho fell down.

By faith the prostitute Rahab did not die with the unbelievers of Jericho.

By faith many more lived and died: Gideon, Barak, Samson, Jephtha, David, Samuel, and the prophets. These through faith subdued kingdoms, lived righteously, obtained promises, were unhurt in dens of lions and furnaces of fire, escaped the sword, were made strong out of weakness, did heroic exploits, overpowered stronger enemies, women received their dead back to life. Others were given strength to accept torture, not accepting offers of mercy, believing that their eternal reward was more precious than this life. Others were mocked, beaten, imprisoned, put into chained labor, stoned, cut in pieces, beheaded. Some wandered destitute in desolate places in animal skins, tortured and tormented.

The world was not a worthy place for these who died in faith, believing promises they had not seen fulfilled but only envisioned. They had opportunity to go back to a life of ease, but they were confident and convinced, holding on to those promises, admitting that they were merely strangers and pilgrims on earth in pursuit of a heavenly city. God has prepared for them that city.

All of these had a godly reputation through faith, yet did not on earth receive the fulfillment of the promises. God had something wonderful in mind for those of us who were to come later, and did not allow these faithful ones to experience the fulfillment of His promises and the completion of His work before we could partake with them.

BE AN EXAMPLE OF FAITH FOR TODAY

Do you realize that we today are surrounded by a number of similar examples of living faith, as well as by a curious crowd of onlookers? Therefore, put aside every hindrance, even favorite sins, and run patiently the race of life, keeping your eyes fixed on Jesus. [15) Heb. 12:1]   He is both starter and winners' judge in the marathon of faith. He, for the living trophies He could obtain, at the end of His perfect earthly race endured death on the cross, even though He despised the shame of it, and is now at the right hand of the throne of God in triumph.

ACCEPT THE DISCIPLINE OF GOD AND BENEFIT FROM IT

When you get weary and faint hearted, think of what Jesus endured, even giving His life's blood. In your struggle against sin, it has not yet cost you your life, as it did Him.

Remember to examine your conduct, for the Lord disciplines those He loves. Perhaps your difficulties are a form of discipline. If you patiently bear up during such training, then you will benefit from it, and have the assurance that you are truly God's children. As a loving father, He corrects His children. It is better to be corrected by the Father, and live eternally, than to be outside His family and not be disciplined. The chastening is not pleasant, but it produces righteousness in us. Don't be discouraged.

SERVE GOD

Walk a straight path. Be peaceable with everyone. Be holy and allow God's grace to govern you. Don't let bitterness take root within you. Don't be a fornicator. Do not be like Esau who mocked spiritual things and lost his birthright. Esau despised the old covenant, but we have a new covenant in Jesus.

Don't reject Jesus, for if you do, there's no escape.   In Jesus, you receive a kingdom which is absolutely secure.   [13) Heb. 12:25-29] Outside Him, you will just as surely receive eternal death. Therefore, accept the grace of God, then serve Him with reverence and godly fear, for God is a consuming fire. [15) Heb. 12:28,29]

BE CONTENT

Marriage is completely honorable and marital sex is pure, but God will judge adulterers, homosexuals, pimps and those who habituate prostitutes.

Live without coveting, and be content with what you have. Don't be jealous. It is enough that God has said He will never leave us or forsake us. You may state with confidence,

"The Lord is my helper. I am not intimidated by threats from men." 11) Heb. 13:5,6

<u>UNCHANGING FAITH</u>

Jesus Christ is the same yesterday, today and forever. Do not be taken in by new or strange doctrines. It is important that you be unchangeable in the faith. 13) Heb. 13:8,9 The sacrifices God wants today are the offerings of praise, doing good, and sharing with the needy.

May the God of peace who raised Jesus from the dead, that great Shepherd of the sheep who with His own blood sealed the everlasting covenant, make you just what He wants you to become in Jesus, performing His will as He works within you that which He desires. To God be glory forever. Amen.

EXAMPLES OF THE APOSTLES

FROM

Acts

The actions of the early Church
through the work of the Holy Spirit
within believers.

Birth Of The Church
And Its Early Days

FROM

Acts 1:1 – 9:31

122

After His death and resurrection, but before He permanently returned to glory, Jesus showed Himself alive to His disciples by many indisputable, infallible proofs over a forty day period. He told them to wait in Jerusalem until the Holy Spirit came to live within them.

The disciples asked if Jesus would set up His earthly kingdom at that time, but Jesus said, "It is not yours to know God's specific times"; then added, "<u>You shall receive power after the Holy Spirit comes upon you, and you shall be My witnesses locally, regionally and throughout the world</u>." [12) Acts 1:8]

As He was saying this, while the disciples watched, He was taken up and clouds enveloped Him. As the disciples searched the sky for another glimpse of Him, two angels appeared who asked, "Why are you staring into the sky? This same Jesus shall return in the same way as you have seen Him go."

THE HOLY SPIRIT LIVES IN BELIEVERS

The disciples returned to Jerusalem where they and about 120 other believers gathered in an upstairs hall to worship and pray. On the day of Pentecost, these were all together, united in purpose, when suddenly there came from heaven a sound like strong wind. Something which resembled flames, or tongues, appeared and paused upon each of them. They all began speaking in languages which they had never learned.

In Jerusalem lived devout men from every nation of that part of the world. These came to the assemble hall and were amazed because each heard in their native tongue the believers speak about the wonderful works of God. "How can you be speaking in our own mother languages when you are all Galilaeans?" they questioned. Some sincerely wondered the cause, some were confused, others mockingly explained the phenomena away as a drunken party.

PETER EXPLAINS

But Peter spoke to them all, "Listen, these are not drunk men. This is a fulfillment of the prophecy by Joel, 'In the last days, I will pour out my Spirit'.

"Jesus Christ, approved of God right before your eyes by miracles and signs, according to the plan of God was taken by you and crucified. But God raised Him from the dead. It's not possible for death to hold Him! David spoke as a prophet when he said that God would not allow His Holy One to decay in death, but would raise Him up to sit on the throne.

"We are eye witnesses that God did raise Him from death and take Him to the exalted place at His right hand. Now as He promised, He has sent the Holy Spirit which you observe, confirming for you that Jesus, whom you crucified, is both The Lord God and The Messiah (Christ)."

A CROWD IS CONVERTED

Hearing that, the crowd asked Peter, "What should we do?" Peter replied, "Repent in the name of Jesus, and your sins will be forgiven. Be baptized, and you will receive the Holy Spirit who is promised to everyone the Lord calls."

Those who believed his message were gladly baptized -- about three thousand that very day.

With great respect, the believers lived by the teaching and example of the apostles who performed many miracles in those days. They were joyous, dedicated to one purpose, and every day the Lord brought new converts into the church.

THE MESSAGE SPREADS

As Peter and John went one day to the temple to pray, a man crippled since birth asked them for money.

Scrutinizing him, Peter said, "Look at us. We have no money, but what we have we'll share. In Jesus' name, stand up and walk on your own."

As Peter took his hand and helped him up, the man's body immediately received strength. Standing upright, he walked and jumped around in delight, praising God. The people saw the commotion, and were amazed because they knew this was the man lame all his life. They each wondered how it could be that he was healed.

Peter spoke, "Why are you shocked? Why stare at us as if we by our own power did this? Jesus whom you denied before Pilate, shouting 'Crucify Him' while asking the release of the murderer Barabbas, that Jesus whom you killed did this miracle. We are eyewitnesses that God raised Him from death. It is faith in His name which has made strong and sound this man, whom you know very well. Repent! Change your minds about Jesus so your sins may be erased. As Moses said, if you don't listen to God's chosen One, you will be destroyed. But God wants to bless you, and has sent His Son to save you from your sins."

The people listened to them until evening, but the religious leaders were upset with them because they taught resurrection from death through Jesus. Since many were believing, the temple rulers took Peter and John into custody and held them over night.

FALSE RELIGIONS CANNOT ULTIMATELY STOP TRUTH

The next day a religious court was held, and the high priest and his counselors questioned them by what authority they taught. Peter said, "By Jesus Christ. You crucified Him but God raised Him from death, and by Him this man stands here well. Jesus is the only name by which one can be saved." [4) Acts 4: 12]

When the court saw the boldness of these unschooled men, they were amazed and recalled among themselves that these had been taught by Jesus.

Since the healed man, whom they knew personally, was right there standing in court, the priests could not deny the miracle. Instead, they ordered that these men not speak at all in the name of Jesus. But Peter and John responded, "If it is right to obey you instead of God you can decide for yourself; but as for us, we must teach the things we have seen and heard." The court further threatened them, but released them because so many people witnessed the miracle for this man over forty years old.

POWERFUL PRAYER

Having been let go, Peter and John returned to the assembly of believers and told of the proceedings.

Upon their report, the group agreed in prayer, asking for courage in the face of the decree of the temple court, and for strength to go on preaching God's word, teaching and working miracles in the name of Jesus. As they prayed, the place was shaken and they were again filled with the Holy Spirit and given great boldness. With power and grace the apostles continued witnessing about Jesus' resurrection.

DEDICATION AND DECEIT AND DISCIPLINE AMONG THE DISCIPLES

The believers were united heart and soul, sharing every necessity with other Christians so that no one had a need unmet. Many who owned valuable possessions, even houses and lands, sold them and put the entire proceeds into the common treasury.

Annanias and his wife Sapphira sold their possessions. The man brought money to the apostles and said it was all the money received from the sale, and it was all a donation. But Peter reacted, "Annanias, why have you lied to the Holy Spirit about the price of the land? The land and the proceeds of the sale were your own. Why have you lied to God to impress men falsely with your charity?" Hearing this, Annanias fell down dead.

About three hours later, his wife, unaware of what had occurred, came to Peter. Peter asked her, "Did you sell your land for the amount your husband contributed?" She answered, "Yes, that was the full amount." Peter replied, "Why did you and Annanias conspire to tempt God? Those who buried your husband have just returned." Hearing that, she too fell down dead. Great fear came upon the believers and all who heard this story, and multitudes continued to believe and join the church.

IMPRISONED FOR PREACHING

Filled with jealousy and indignation, the high priests put the apostles in jail. But an angel opened the doors that night and let them out, instructing them, "Stand in the temple and preach to the people all the truth of eternal life."

Therefore, early the next morning, the apostles were again teaching in the temple. Not yet aware of this event, the temple court convened and sent to the prison for the prisoners to be brought. The temple guards returned and reported, "We found the prison shut, secure and all the guards in place; but no one was inside." The court wondered how fast this story would spread.

Just then, a runner came and informed the court that the apostles who had been imprisoned were in the temple courtyard teaching the people. The temple guard was sent to bring the apostles. In court again, the high priest asked the apostles, "Did we not order you to never again teach in the name of Jesus?! But you are filling the city with your message, and you blame us for the death of Jesus!"

Peter replied, "We must obey God more than man. You killed Jesus, but God raised Him an exalted Savior. We are eyewitnesses of this, and the Holy Spirit within us is further witness."

Hearing this, they were cut to the heart and discussed executing Peter and John. But a Pharisee advised leaving them alone, for if their doctrine were only of men then it would come to an end anyway, but if their doctrine was in fact of God, the authorities would be fighting against God. The council agreed with this line of reasoning. Warning the disciples not to speak in the name of Jesus any more, they beat them and let them go.

The disciples left the courtroom rejoicing that they were able to suffer and be shamed for Jesus. Every day they continued to teach and preach, house to house and in the temple.

LEADERS TO CARE FOR ROUTINE NEEDS

The apostles were so busy teaching that they were unable to look after the day to day needs of the people. Therefore, they chose seven men who were controlled by the Holy Spirit, with good reputation and wisdom, to oversee the mundane needs of the believers. With new freedom to minister, the apostles expanded their work, and the number of believers grew rapidly. Even many of the priests became followers of the way, obeying the faith.

TESTIMONY AND MARTYRDOM OF STEPHEN

Stephen, one of the seven appointed to oversee daily operations, was also gifted by the Holy Spirit to do miracles and preach. Unbelieving religious leaders argued and debated with Stephen but couldn't overcome his logic and fervent spirit. Angered and embarrassed, they stirred up a crowd against him, accusing him of breaking the law of Moses, of blaspheming against the law and Moses and the temple and God himself. Dragging him before the court and restating their accusations, the council saw the glory of God on his face.

Told by the court to defend himself, Stephen reviewed God's workings with Israel through the prophets of the past and concluded, "You are just like your ancestors who killed God's prophets. You murdered the Deliverer and Savior whom they said would come. You are the ones breaking God's law."

The priests were cut to the heart and convicted of conscience. They scowled and ground their teeth as Stephen continued, "I see heaven opened, and Jesus standing on the right hand of God."

The priests shrieked and rushed Stephen, threw him out of the city wall and stoned him. Those who hurled the rocks handed their outer robes to one named Saul, a young Pharisee from Tarsus.

As Stephen died, he kneeled and prayed loudly, "Lord Jesus, receive my Spirit. Don't count this sin against them." And he fell over dead.

GREAT PERSECUTION WREAKED BY SAUL

This Saul, who assisted Stephen's execution, greatly persecuted the believers, throwing men and women alike into prison. Many believers left Jerusalem to escape this suffering, and as they went, they preached the gospel.

BELIEVER REFUGEES SPREAD THE GOOD NEWS

Philip was such a refugee. He escaped to Samaria and there preached Christ and performed miracles, causing great joy in that place and winning many believers.

One powerful leader there, Simon, using magic to fool the people, was highly regarded by his townsmen. Simon, seeing genuine miracles performed in the name of the Lord, professed to be converted and was baptized.

When word of this great Samaritan revival reached Jerusalem, apostles Peter and John were dispatched to help. Upon their arrival, they placed their hands on the believers, praying that the Holy Spirit would infill them.

When Simon saw that the Holy Spirit, with manifestation of power and gifts, came upon the believers through the prayer of Peter and John, he offered to purchase that ability from them.

But Peter corrected him, "You will perish with your money if you believe that the infilling or the gifts of the Holy Spirit can be bought. With that attitude, your heart can't be right with God and you can't be one of us. You need to genuinely repent and accept God's forgiveness, for you are bitter against us for not selling you spirituality, and you are a slave of sin."

THE GOSPEL GOES TO AFRICA

Peter and John returned to Jerusalem, preaching as they went.

Then God told Philip to leave Samaria and go to a desert road which led south from Jerusalem. Philip left, and, as soon as he reached that road, a royal chariot was there. The treasurer of Ethiopia was returning to his country from Jerusalem, reading Isaiah as he journeyed. God told Philip to go to the chariot.

Philip hurried to the chariot and asked the statesman if he understood the prophet. "No," said the man, "would you explain it to me?" Beginning at the text being read, Isaiah 53, Philip taught the Ethiopian about Jesus. (see page 30)

As the journey south continued, they came to a body of water. At the request of the statesman, Philip baptized him.

As the two of them were coming up out of the water, the Spirit of the Lord caught Philip away and the Ethiopian never saw him again. He went on home, rejoicing in the Lord; but Philip found himself at Azotas, where he began preaching in all the cities on his way to Caesarea.

DEADLY PERSECUTION INTERRUPTED

In contrast, Saul, swearing to slaughter believers, asked the high priest for authority to forcefully bring Damascus believers to Jerusalem.

As he approached Damascus to carry out this purge, there suddenly engulfed him a brilliant light from heaven. Stunned, he fell to the ground and heard a voice which said, "Saul! Saul! Why do you persecute Me?"

Saul answered, "Lord, God, who are You that I am persecuting?"

The voice said, "I am Jesus." 14) Acts 9: 5

SAUL LEARNED THAT JEHOVAH AND JESUS ARE IDENTICAL

Saul shook with fear and amazement and said, "Lord, what do You want me to do?"

Jesus said, "Your work against Me is awkward. Go on into the city, and there I will instruct you how to work with Me."

Saul got up, but had been blinded. He was led into Damascus where he lodged three days, refusing food or drink.

In Damascus the Lord said to a disciple, "Ananias, go to the house of Judas on Straight Street and ask for Saul of Tarsus. He is there in prayer. I have shown him that you will come to lay your hands on him to restore his sight."

"But Lord," answered Ananias, "that man has done so much evil to the believers, and has come here to capture us and deliver us to Jerusalem authorities."

The Lord said, "Just go. I have chosen him to be My servant, to preach My message and to suffer for My sake."

So Ananias obeyed, put his hand on Saul, and said, "Brother Saul, the Lord sent me as His instrument to restore your sight and to signal your being filled with the Holy Spirit." At once, Saul could see again and was baptized.

After Saul had eaten for a few days with the believers in Damascus and his strength was restored, he began to preach in the synagogues that Jesus is Christ (Messiah), the Son of God.

Those who heard him were confused and asked, "Isn't this the man who killed believers?"

But Saul grew more eloquent, and with logic and persuasion proved that Jesus is Christ, the Jews' Messiah.

THOSE FOR WHOM SAUL ONCE WORKED NOW WANT HIM DEAD

The Jews, therefore, plotted to kill Saul. But when this plot became known, the disciples hid Saul and one night let him down the outside of the city wall in a basket on ropes.

After about three years alone, Saul returned to Jerusalem and tried to join the disciples there. But they were afraid it was a trick, not being convinced that he truly was converted. However, one of them, Barnabas, befriended Saul, got to know him, and then took him to the other disciples. Barnabas explained how the Lord had changed Saul, and how Saul had preached in Damascus.

So Saul was accepted by believers at Jerusalem, and he began debating and preaching in the name of Jesus. The Jewish leaders of Jerusalem, therefore, determined to kill him. But again the disciples found out about this plan and sent Saul to Tarsus.

THE CHURCH GROWS

With their greatest enemy and persecutor converted, the believers had respite, and the number of believers multiplied.

Primarily Under Peter

FROM

Acts 9:32 – 12:24

Peter was also being used by God. In a town called Lydda, he prayed for a man who had been sick in bed for eight years, and said to him, "Jesus has made you well. In His name, get up and make your bed." Immediately, the sick man was healed. Upon seeing this, it seemed the whole town turned to Jesus.

Dorcas, a generous, helpful woman in the town of Joppa, died, and her body was washed in preparation for burial. The believers sent for Peter, who came at once. Through tears, the mourners told Peter how charitable Dorcas had been.

Peter put them out of the room, turned to the body and prayed. Then he said, "Dorcas, arise." She opened her eyes and sat up. Peter took her hand and presented her alive to her friends. Because of this event, many in Joppa believed in the Lord. Peter stayed in Joppa for some time, lodging with Simon the Tanner.

THE GOSPEL IS FOR GENTILES AS WELL AS JEWS

There was a Centurion in Caesarea named Cornelius, a devout Gentile, revering God, generous in charity, and who prayed often. In a vision, God said to him, "Your prayers are answered. Send men to Joppa, to the house of Simon the Tanner by the sea, and ask for a man called Simon Peter. Peter will have instructions for you." Cornelius immediately sent two servants and a soldier on this mission.

The next day as these three were nearing Joppa, Peter went up to the roof of the house to pray. Becoming hungry, he asked for food, but while it was being prepared, he fell asleep. Dreaming, Peter saw lowered from heaven a great container in which were all sorts of wild animals, reptiles, and birds. A voice said, "Get up. Prepare and eat." But in his dream Peter replied, "No, Lord. I do not eat common or unclean meat." The voice answered, "Do not call common or unclean what God has cleansed." This scene was repeated three times and then Peter awoke, wondering what it all meant.

At that moment, the three men from Cornelius were at the front door inquiring about a man called Peter. As Peter contemplated his vision, the Spirit spoke within him and said, "Three men are at the door looking for you. Go with them without questioning, for I have sent them." Peter went to the men

132

and told them whom he was and asked what they desired of him. They told Peter about Cornelius and his vision, and asked Peter to return with them. Peter boarded the men overnight, then, with a delegation of believers, set out the next day.

At the home of Cornelius were relatives and friends awaiting with him the arrival of Peter. When Peter came in, Cornelius knelt, but Peter pulled him up and said, "I am just a man." Peter continued, "God is not a respecter of persons. Everyone who revers and believes Him is acceptable to God. The message God sends to everyone is peace through Jesus Christ, the Lord of all. You have heard the stories of John the Baptist and Jesus of Nazareth. We are eyewitnesses who corroborate those facts. The Jews crucified Jesus, but God raised Him back to life and showed Him alive to many, including me. He told us to teach that He will one day judge the living and the dead, and that whoever believes in Him shall have remission of sins."

As Peter spoke, the Holy Spirit came upon the hearers. Jewish believers with Peter were amazed that the Holy Spirit had come to Gentiles, but they saw the evidence as these non-Jews began exercising gifts of the Spirit, speaking in languages they had never learned, and worshipping God. Peter commanded that these be baptized with water in the name of the Lord.

In Jerusalem, the main group of apostles soon heard that Gentiles had believed the word of God. When Peter returned to Jerusalem, some of the Jewish believers reprimanded Peter, questioning why he went into the house of a Gentile.

Peter said, "God saved them and gave them spiritual gifts. Who am I that I could stop God?" When the Jerusalem believers heard the full story, they gave glory to God, accepting the fact that Gentiles as well as Jews were intended to be saved.

NEW CONVERTS INSTRUCTED

Those believers who had been scattered to other cities because of the persecution at Jerusalem were making converts wherever they went. The church in Jerusalem sent Barnabas to instruct these new converts and to exhort them to stay faithful to the Lord. Barnabas went as far as Antioch in this work. It was there the nickname "Christian" was first attached to believers. Barnabas arranged for Saul to come assist him in Antioch where the two of them taught one year. Many believed and joined the church. At that time, Barnabas and Saul delivered from the Antioch church to the church at Jerusalem a large gift to assist the impoverished believers there during a great famine.

THE EXECUTION OF CHRISTIANS IS RENEWED

About this time, Herod (Herod Agrippa I) the king decided to kill some in the church. When he killed James the brother of John and saw that it pleased the Jews, he captured Peter during the feast days of Unleavened Bread. In prison, many soldiers were assigned to secure him until after Easter. So Peter was in prison, but the church was in prayer.

GOD CHOOSES TO FREE PETER

The night before his scheduled execution, Peter was chained between two soldiers and extra guards were at the prison door. All security precautions were in place. Nevertheless, an angel of the Lord came to Peter, and awoke him. As Peter got up, his wrist shackles and leg irons fell off. As Peter followed the angel, the doors of the first and second ward and the gate that gave access from the prison to the city opened by themselves. They had walked a couple of streets when the angel vanished.

Peter thought he had been dreaming, but now realized this was reality. He was out of prison -- the Lord had delivered him from Herod. He went to the house of Mary, the mother of John Mark, where believers were still in prayer for him. When Peter knocked at the courtyard gate, a maiden came to the door. Recognizing Peter, she was so overcome with excitement that she didn't open the gate, but rushed back inside to tell the others he was there. They told her she was crazy, but when Peter continued rattling the gate, they finally went to let him in, and were amazed. He quieted them, and told how the angel had set him free. Instructing them to relate the news to those not there, Peter left.

CHRISTIANS CONTINUE TO DUPLICATE

At daybreak, there was a major commotion among the soldiers at the prison. Herod sent for Peter and, when told Peter had escaped, he executed the soldiers.

The next day, as Herod made an awesome political speech, the listeners were so mesmerized that they called him a god. Immediately, Herod fell down dead, slain by the angel of the Lord. But the gospel spread, and the church greatly multiplied.

Primarily Under Paul

FROM

Acts 12:25 – 28:31

SAUL IS NOW CALLED PAUL AND IS ON A MISSION

Barnabas and Saul took John Mark with them in their ministry.

At a place called Paphos, the proconsul named Sergius Paulus asked Barnabas and Saul, now called Paul, to explain the gospel. However, a sorcerer named Elymas didn't want the proconsul to believe. Paul turned to Elymas and said, "You enemy of righteousness. Will you never stop trying to pervert the way of the Lord. You will be blind for a while, because the hand of the Lord is upon you." Immediately, Elymas was blind.

The proconsul, seeing this, believed in the Lord.

JESUS FULFILLS OLD TESTAMENT PROPHESIES

Having left Paphos, the next Sabbath day they were in Antioch of Pisidia and were invited by the ruler of the Synagogue to speak to the people.

Paul first reviewed the history of the Israelites, how God had brought them out of Egypt, spoken through the prophets and judges, and given them King David. He rehearsed the prophecies of a Messiah, and the preaching of John the Baptist. He continued, "Brethren, to you is the promised salvation sent. The Jewish leaders in Jerusalem, though they read the scriptures every Sabbath, don't understand them, for in condemning Jesus, though Pilate found no fault in Him, they fulfilled those very Scriptures. They crucified Him, buried Him and sealed the tomb, but God raised Him from death. He was seen alive by many people from Galilee to Jerusalem who are living eyewitnesses of this truth. We bring you glad news. The scriptures have been fulfilled and through Jesus is forgiveness of sins. By Him, whoever believes is cleansed from all wrong. Be careful, lest you fulfill another prophecy which states that God will do a wonderful work right before your eyes, yet you will not believe, even though it is explained to you."

EVEN THOSE NOT JEWS RESPOND TO THE MESSAGE

The Gentiles, who heard about this message preached in the synagogue, asked Paul to give them the same sermon.

Such a multitude of Jews followed Paul and Barnabas that the Jewish leaders were filled with envy, and spoke against their new Christian doctrine. Therefore, Paul boldly said to the

Jewish authorities, "It was necessary that the word of God be given first to you, but now, we turn to the Gentiles, and they will take salvation to the entire world."

When the Gentiles heard this, they were ecstatic and glorified the Lord. But the Jewish authorities stirred up a persecution against Paul and Barnabas, and expelled them from that area. Despite all this, the believers were filled with the joy of the Holy Spirit.

PREACHING RESULTS IN PERSECUTIONS AND DIVISIONS

Paul and Barnabas traveled to Iconium where they both spoke in the synagogue, resulting in a large number of converts.

But again the Jews stirred up a tumult, spreading false rumor about them. Yet, they stayed and taught there a long time, working miracles. The city was split because of them, some holding with the Jews and some with the believers. When a plan was laid to stone Paul and Barnabas, they were made aware of it and escaped, and began preaching in the cities around Lyconia.

A MIRACLE MISUNDERSTOOD

In one of those cities, a man crippled from birth who had never walked a step in his life was brought to hear Paul.

Sensing that the man had faith to be healed, Paul commanded him, "Stand up and walk."

When the man leaped and walked, the people began worshipping Paul and Barnabas. A pagan priest even prepared to offer sacrifice to them as gods. But Paul and Barnabas emphatically resisted and said, "We are just men like you. It is this very kind of thing that we preach against. Turn to the living God, creator of heaven and earth."

In a dramatic turn of events, Jews from Antioch infiltrated the crowd and convinced the people to stone Paul as an impostor. After the stoning, they drug Paul out of the city, dead.

Presently, as the sorrowing disciples stood helplessly around him, Paul stood up, and they all went into the city.

RETRACING STEPS AND ENCOURAGING BELIEVERS

The next day they went to Derbe, where they preached for some time. Then they returned to Lystra, Iconium and Antioch, confirming the faith of the disciples and exhorting them to continue in faith, assuring them it's not unusual to pass through tribulation entering the kingdom of God.

They continued on to many other cities until they circuitously came back to the church which had sent them on this missionary journey. Home again, they reviewed the happenings of their trip and remained there with the believers a long time.

FAITH IS THE ONLY REQUIREMENT FOR SALVATION

Some of the believing Jews were teaching the believing Gentiles that, in addition to faith in Christ, they must keep the law of Moses to be saved. But at a meeting of the apostles in Jerusalem, it was clarified that God made no difference between races or previous religions. It is by faith alone in Jesus Christ that we shall all be saved. It is pure grace.

OTHER MISSIONARY EXCURSIONS

Some time later, Paul took Silas and began a journey to revisit many of the churches founded on his previous trip. Barnabas took John Mark and went in a different direction to visit other young churches, confirming them in the faith and giving further instruction in the Word of God.

On this trip, Paul met Timothy, a young man of excellent reputation from a good family. Paul took Timothy to Macedonia where they joined in a prayer meeting along a river where several women met. Lydia, who worshipped God, believed Paul's teaching and invited Paul's team to lodge at her home.

OPPOSITION AND CONVERSIONS IN A PRISON

For many days, a fortune teller, who produced a good income for her owners, followed Paul and taunted him, stating the truth in a mocking manner, "These men are servants of the most high God and show the way of salvation." Paul, grieved that satan used her to deride the gospel, turned one day and said, "I command you, evil spirit, come out of her."

When the spirit left, the owners, realizing their means of profit was gone, brought Paul and Silas before the magistrates. "These Jews teach anti-Roman treason," they charged.

To please these wealthy leaders, Paul and Silas were beaten and imprisoned, the jailer being told to be especially careful about their security. With such instructions, he put their feet in stocks in a maximum security cell deep within the prison.

Notwithstanding their shackles and lacerated backs, Paul and Silas sang praises to God -- and the other prisoners heard and were impressed with their musical testimony.

About midnight, a terrific earthquake hit the prison, breaking the foundations, opening all doors and loosening chains and stocks from their pinnings. All the prisoners were freed.

Awakened, the jailer rushed to see the damages. Thinking all the prisoners escaped, he drew his sword to kill himself, since execution would be his punishment. But Paul shouted, "Don't harm yourself! We are all still here."

Trembling, the jailer got lamps, went inside to Paul, and falling on his knees in amazement, asked, "Sirs, what must I do to be saved?" They replied, "<u>Believe on the Lord Jesus Christ and you will be saved,</u>[5) Acts 16: 32] as is true for your family and all in this prison house." Paul and Silas instructed the jailer's family all night in God's truth, and they all believed and were baptized.

PREACHING JESUS FROM THE OLD TESTAMENT

The next stop was Thessalonica. Paul, as accustomed, reasoned with the Jews in the synagogue from their own scriptures, showing how the Messiah needed to die and rise from the dead as prophesied, and proving that Jesus was Messiah. Some Jews believed as did many Greeks and leading women.

THE LIFE OF BELIEVERS WAS NOT EASY

The Jews who would not believe hired ruffians to create a mob and incite a riot. They assaulted the house in which Paul stayed and demanded that the preachers be brought out. When Paul and Silas were not found, they took the homeowner to the magistrates saying, "Those who are turning the world upside down have now come here, teaching that Jesus is the King to be obeyed, not Caesar. This man is harboring them."

The magistrates rescued the man and dispersed the crowd. Paul and Silas left for Berea.

SCRIPTURE IS THE STANDARD FOR TRUTH

The people of Berea were <u>wiser</u> than the Thessalonians, <u>for they received the word with a ready mind, examining the scripture daily to confirm that the doctrine Paul preached was true. Seeing for themselves the congruity of the scripture and the gospel, many believed</u>.[7) Acts 17:11]

But unbelieving Jews, hearing of many converts, came there to stir up the people. Paul and Silas with Timothy, therefore, left for Athens.

THE ANSWER IS NOT IN RELIGION

At Athens, aroused by the numerous idols and shrines, Paul debated with many. Since Paul argued for the resurrection of the dead, he was asked to present his view at the Areopagus.

Paul spoke out, "You men of Athens are too religious. Among your many deities, you even have an altar 'to the unknown god'. I tell you of the God you honor by accident in ignorance. The God who gives life and breath and all things, does not need us to offer Him anything as enticements to mercy. He makes us all of one blood; He sets our times and destiny; He determines our place of habitation; He creates the emptiness within us that causes us to need Him; He is right beside us and by Him we exist. Since we are made in the image of God, we should not think of God as some gold, silver or stone work of art. God commands us to repent before the day of judgment when He will judge each one of us by Jesus, whom He raised from death."

Upon hearing of the resurrection, some jeered, some were curious, others wanted to hear more, and some believed. Paul left for Corinth.

OPPOSING THE GOSPEL IS AGAINST YOUR OWN WELFARE

In Corinth, Paul met Aquilla and Priscilla, working with them to make tents. Sabbath days he preached in the synagogues, logically showing that Jesus is the Messiah of scripture. Paul became more urgent in his message, but when the Jews there continued to oppose themselves by rejecting truth, Paul said, "Your blood is on your own head. I have given you the gospel and warned you. Now I will teach Gentiles."

MANY CONTINUE TO BELIEVE

Paul began lodging with Justice, whose house had a common wall with the synagogue. During that time, the chief ruler of that synagogue believed on Jesus and was baptized. Because of his belief, many other Jews there also were converted. Encouraged by God to remain there, Paul taught in Corinth a year and a half before he went with Aquilla and Priscilla to Ephesus.

In Ephesus, Paul taught for a time, but when asked to remain, he said he must take the gospel to regions beyond and would return in God's time.

THE OLD TESTAMENT AND JOHN THE BAPTIZER POINTED TO JESUS

Apollos, an eloquent Jew, well-versed in the Old Testament and the teaching of John the Baptist, came to Ephesus. There Aquilla and Priscilla instructed him in the fulfillment of John's message, that, in Jesus, Messiah had indeed come as prophesied. Having heard and believed the complete message, Apollos began powerfully persuading Jews to follow Jesus.

OPPOSITION PRODUCES DEDICATION IN BELIEVERS

Paul did return to Ephesus, but, frustrated in trying to preach in the synagogues, he taught in a school for two years.

Certain exorcists tried to imitate Paul in eradicating evil spirits. Seven men attempting to cast out a demon were overpowered by a possessed man. This caused new fear and respect for the name of the Lord. Many who engaged in witchcraft and black magic burned their books, repented of their practices, and followed Jesus. Resiliently, the word of God spread and prevailed.

The silversmiths of Ephesus created a riot against Paul because their business was falling off. The sale of silver shrines of their goddess Diana was a major source of profit. Paul taught that no true God was made by men, which degraded their goddess and her temple. The silversmiths got a crowd together shouting, "Great is Diana. Great is Diana of the Ephesians." The whole town was in uproar for more than two hours. When finally an official was able to get their attention, he warned them that they would have to answer to the Roman authorities for this riot. At last, he was able to calm and disperse the mob.

That riot over, Paul embraced the believers and left for Macedonia where he taught for some time before going on to Greece and then returning to Macedonia. There, Paul spoke to believers through the night. A youth sitting in an upstairs window fell asleep and, dropping to the street below, was killed. But Paul went to the body and brought him back to the group alive. Relieved and delighted, the believers stayed until morning listening to Paul.

SAYING GOOD BYE TO THE FAITHFUL

Paul preached in several cities and arrived back in Ephesus on his way to Jerusalem. To the Ephesian elders he said, "I have served the Lord before you in humility, tears and even temptations when the Jews harassed me. I have taught you the entire gospel, publicly and from house to house. Now I go to Jerusalem, being warned of awaiting persecution. That does not deter me for I do not count my life precious to myself, I only want to finish my assignment with joy -- to complete my ministry. I will not see you again, so I remind you that I am no longer responsible for your salvation, having given you the whole counsel of God. Be careful for yourselves and for the believers under your leadership. Feed them spiritually, for Christ bought them with His own life's blood. The enemy will try to win them back. Even some of your own leaders will turn to false doctrine and get others to follow. Be alert! Remember what I taught. I entrust you to God and to His grace which is able to strengthen you and to give you an inheritance. I have coveted no one's money or possessions, but have worked to support myself, even giving to the needs of others. I have set an example, for it is more satisfying to give than to receive."

Then they prayed together, and with tears and embraces accompanied Paul to the ship.

On his way to Jerusalem, Paul was warned that there he would be bound and turned over to the Romans. The disciples begged Paul to not go, but Paul answered, "Do not weep and break my heart. I am ready to be bound and to die for the Lord in Jerusalem."

TRANSITIONAL DIFFICULTIES IN THE YOUNG CHURCH

Once at Jerusalem, Paul met with the other apostles and related what God had done among the Gentiles through his ministry. The apostles glorified God because of the report, but brought up a troubling issue. They said, "You see the thousands of Jews who believe here at Jerusalem. They have heard that you encourage the Jews living in places to which you have traveled not to keep the traditional law of Moses, not even circumcision. These disciples here need assurance that you condone the keeping of the law by Jewish believers, though we do not expect Gentile converts to keep our traditions. Please join with four men who

142

are purifying themselves in the temple and shaving their heads for a vow. This will comfort our believing Jews." Paul, consenting, entered the temple to solemnize and fulfill the vow.

A RELIGIOUS RIOT OVER A MISUNDERSTANDING

When the seven days of his purification were nearly ended, certain Jews from Asia who were in Jerusalem saw Paul joining in this Jewish custom. They immediately stirred up a riot and manhandled Paul, shouting, "This man has preached all over Asia that the keeping of the law is not necessary, and has even taken Greeks into the temple, profaning it. He teaches that our religion isn't complete without Christ, yet, here he is in the temple participating in our law. He is a hypocrite and traitor."

A mob formed, dragged Paul out of the temple, and set about to kill him.

Someone alerted the military tribune in charge of the cohort, who sent soldiers on the double to stop the riot. Seeing the soldiers, the crowd stopped lashing Paul. The soldiers took him, chained him, and began interrogating him on the spot. But with the crowd shouting accusations, order was impossible, so the soldiers began to take Paul to the castle. Before he was led away, Paul requested, and was granted, permission to speak.

PAUL GIVES HIS PERSONAL TESTIMONY

"Hear my defense," Paul entreated the mob. "I am a Jew from Tarsus, taught in this city by Gamaliel in the Jewish law. I was zealous in my belief, as you are today. I persecuted those who believed in Jesus, throwing both men and women into prison. The High Priest and all the elders of the temple can confirm this. An enemy of Jesus, I was on my way to Damascus with authority from your leaders to bring back all the believers I could to Jerusalem for punishment or death. Near Damascus, God used an intense light to get my attention and a voice from heaven to instruct me. I became a believer in the message which I was persecuting, and started preaching the gospel.

"Converted, I returned to Jerusalem, but God told me to leave because Jews in Jerusalem wouldn't accept my testimony. I argued, 'Lord, they know how I persecuted and imprisoned those who believe on You, and how I aided in the death of Stephen.' But He said to leave and preach in other places."

At this point, the mob raged and shouted for his execution. Therefore, the captain took Paul into the castle and told soldiers to lash him until he told the truth about why the crowd demanded his death. As they bound him, Paul said to a centurion, "Is it lawful for you to whip me, a Roman citizen, without a trial and conviction?" The centurion reported this to the captain, who then questioned Paul, "Are you indeed a Roman?" Paul answered, "Absolutely."

Fearful because he had not followed due process in handling a Roman, the captain exercised care in the proceedings against Paul. Court was held with Paul's accusers confronting him, and Paul was allowed to speak.

"Brethren, I have lived before God with a clear conscience, keeping the Jewish laws. I am in court because I teach the resurrection of the dead."

On the Jewish Counsel that was accusing Paul were both Sadducees, who do not believe in any resurrection, and Pharisees, who do. Therefore, this statement caused a dissension among them. The Pharisees said, "If an angel or spirit has spoken to this man, let us not resist it."

The dissension became so great that the captain took Paul from the court back to the castle. There in prison, God told Paul that he must testify in both Jerusalem and Rome.

More than forty Jews entered a pact that they would not eat until they had killed Paul. Council members among them would request the captain to bring Paul to court for further questioning. Others would lay in wait and ambush the guard as it escorted Paul.

Paul's nephew heard of this plan and gained permission to visit Paul. Paul requested a centurion to take the young man to the captain. The captain instructed two centurions to escort Paul under cover of night to Felix, the governor in Caesarea. He sent a letter reviewing the entire episode. Felix read the letter and agreed to hear the case once Paul's accusers were present. Meanwhile, he ordered Paul kept in the Praetorium.

PAUL ON TRIAL

After five days, Paul's accusers arrived in the persons of the high priest with his elders and an orator. With flattery toward Felix and moving words against Paul, they accused Paul of religious crimes and sedition.

Felix instructed Paul to answer. Said Paul, "These people did not find me inciting riot nor disputing in the temple nor doing anything seditious. I do follow the way which they call heresy, believing in the law and the prophets and in the resurrection of the dead for both the just and the unjust. In bringing my contribution to the temple, I was found by certain Jews from Asia, quietly purified under a vow. Those eyewitnesses should be here if they have anything against me."

Having heard this, and having some knowledge of "The Way", Felix deferred the case until the captain who arrested Paul could be in attendance. He commanded a centurion to hold Paul, letting him have certain liberty, such as the visits and care of his friends.

After several days, Felix and his Jewish wife requested Paul to tell them more about the faith in Christ. As Paul reasoned about faith, a life controlled by God, and judgment, Felix began to tremble and said, "Go for now. When I have a more convenient time I will again ask for you." Hoping that Paul would offer money for his release, he sent often for him and engaged in conversation. Wanting to show the Jews a favor, Felix kept Paul under arrest.

PAUL AND ROMAN JUSTICE

After two years, a high official, Porcius Festus, visited Felix. When Festus came to Jerusalem from Caesarea, the high priest requested that Festus hear Paul in Jerusalem, planning an ambush to kill Paul as he was brought to the city. But Festus replied that he would hear Paul in Caesarea, inviting accusers to be in attendance.

A few days later in Caesarea, Festus had Paul brought before him. The Jews accused Paul of many serious wrongs. Festus, not wanting to offend these Jewish leaders, asked Paul why he shouldn't be tried in Jerusalem by Jewish law. Paul answered, "I haven't wronged the Jews. I'm standing at the proper court. If I've committed a capital offense, I'm willing to die; but I'm not guilty of their charges. As a Roman citizen, I cannot be handed over to them. I appeal to Caesar."

Festus granted that appeal. "To Caesar you shall go."

Some time later, King Agrippa (Herod Agrippa II) came to Caesarea to pay a political visit to Festus. When the story of Paul came into their conversations, King Agrippa said he would like to hear Paul. The next day, with ceremony and pomp, court was set up for Agrippa, and Paul was brought in.

Festus began the proceedings saying, "King Agrippa, here's a man the chief Jews from Jerusalem say is not fit to live. Their accusations are not civil or criminal in nature, but religious, and specifically relate to the belief of Paul that a man called Jesus, who died by crucifixion, is now alive again. I found that he had done no capital offense, yet am holding him to send to Caesar, as he himself has requested. I have no intelligent charges against him, and it seems unreasonable to send a man for trial without stating his alleged crimes. Therefore, Agrippa, I bring him before you to determine how to charge him."

PAUL AGAIN SHARES HIS FAITH IN COURT

Agrippa told Paul to speak.

Paul began, "I am pleased to speak before you, Agrippa, because I know you are familiar with Jews and their customs. I grew up in the Jewish religion, and lived much of my early life at Jerusalem acquainted with these accusers. They know that I lived the most strict sect of our religion, a Pharisee. I am now judged because of my faith in the promises made by God to our forefathers. Why should you or anyone think it incredible that God should raise the dead?

"In truth, I convinced myself that it was my duty to oppose the name of Jesus. With permission of the chief priests, I put many believers in prison. When they were put to death, I mocked. I punished believers from every synagogue in Jerusalem, forcing them to blaspheme against God on fear of death. In my vendetta against that way, I pursued them into other cities to persecute them. As I went to Damascus with authority from the chief priests against them, about midday, a light from heaven brighter than the sun hit me, knocking me to the ground. A voice said, 'Saul, why do you persecute Me? It is troublesome for you to do this.' I said, 'Who are You, Lord, that I am persecuting?' And the voice said, 'I am Jesus! Get up. I am making you a minister for Me, a witness to the world. I will especially send you to Gentiles, to show them the truth, to turn them from darkness to the light, from the power of satan to God, in order that they may be forgiven of their sins and may have an eternal inheritance by faith in Me'."

Paul continued, "King Agrippa, I obeyed the heavenly vision. Starting there at Damascus, then at Jerusalem, then throughout Judaea and other places, I have taken God's message of repentance and a changed life. Because of this, the Jews took me from the temple to kill me. But by God's plan, I am alive today and share with dignitaries and common people the message of Scripture, how the promises about the Messiah were fulfilled by Jesus when He suffered, died and rose from the dead."

Festus interrupted at this point and shouted, "You've gone crazy. Too much education has cost you your mind."

Paul replied, "No, I have not lost my mind, but am stating truth. You yourself, honorable Festus, know these facts are true, for they were done openly. And you, King Agrippa, I know that you believe the prophets."

Then said Agrippa, "Paul, you have almost convinced me to be a Christian." To which Paul responded, "I wish that you were not almost, but altogether just like me, except my chains."

At that, the king and the governor went into private chambers, agreeing that Paul had done nothing worthy of death. Agrippa said to Festus, "I would set Paul free if he had not made a formal appeal to Caesar."

PAUL SENT TO STAND TRIAL IN ROME

For the sail to Rome, Paul, with other prisoners, was put under the charge of a centurion. Along the way, Paul was given permission to visit his friends at ports where the ship docked for supplies. After sailing many weeks in unfavorable winds and making slow progress, the season of storms arrived. Paul advised that if the voyage continued at this time, the ship with its cargo would be lost. But the owner of the ship disagreed, and the voyage continued.

Not long thereafter, a tremendous storm overtook them. The sailors, unable to control the ship, lowered the sails, letting the ship go with the wind. The next day, orders were given to throw freight overboard. Sea anchors were put out but helped little during several days when neither stars nor the sun could be seen. Everyone believed they would be drowned.

Days later, Paul stood and said, "Remember I advised not to sail. But, be encouraged. An angel told me we will lose the ship but not any lives when we are wrecked upon an island. I believe God that it will be just that way."

During the fourteenth night of the storm, the sailors determined that the ship was approaching a shore. Fearing breaking up on rocks, they cast four anchors out the stern and hoped for daylight. Suddenly, the sailors decided to make a run for it in a lifeboat, leaving the others to perish with the ship. But Paul warned the centurion, "Unless these men stay with the ship, all is lost."

The centurion ordered, "Cut the ropes holding the lifeboat;" and it fell away empty into the raging sea.

As the skies became lighter at dawn, Paul encouraged everyone to eat, for they had not had food in several days. Said Paul, "No one shall be hurt in this catastrophe." When all 276 people on board had eaten, they cast overboard the rest of the supplies to lighten the ship.

At daybreak, they could see land but couldn't determine what land it was. When a river was spotted, the captain decided to try to run the ship into its channel. The sailors unleashed the rudder, lifted the anchors, hoisted the mainsail, and tried for the inlet. As the ship approached land, it got caught in a cross current and ran aground. The bow stuck fast while the stern was broken apart. The soldiers intended to kill all the prisoners so that none of them could escape, but the centurion, wanting to save Paul, prevented it.

SHIPWRECKED ON AN ISLAND

The command was issued to abandon ship. Strong swimmers made for the beach while the others grabbed broken parts of the hull for floatation. All got safely to shore.

PAUL MINISTERS IN ADVERSE CIRCUMSTANCES

The primitive people there welcomed them with a fire to warm them from the rain and cold. As Paul was laying wood on the fire, a viper bit him and fastened on his hand.

The natives saw the venomous snake on him, and whispered among themselves that this man must be a murderer whom fate was determined to kill though he had escaped the sea.

But Paul shook off the snake into the fire. The natives, looking for Paul to swell up and die but seeing no ill effects, decided that he was some kind of god. Thereafter, the head man of the island took in the shipwrecked people and cared for them three days.

At that time, the head man's father was very sick. Paul laid hands on him and healed him. After this, a wave of island sick folk came to see Paul, and were healed. Therefore the natives honored Paul, and, when the centurion was ready to leave on another ship, the islanders gave them many provisions.

IN ROME

At last arriving in Rome, the centurion delivered the prisoners to the captain of the guard, but Paul was given house arrest and his own guard soldier.

On his third day in Rome, Paul called for the chief Jewish leaders, and said, "Brethren, I have done nothing against our people or the customs of our fathers. I was taken as prisoner in Jerusalem and turned over to the Roman authorities. After they had tried me and found no evidence of crimes, they would have released me, but the chief Jews of Jerusalem continued to accuse me and to provoke trouble. I was forced in self defense to appeal to Caesar, even though I have nothing against my nation. That is why I asked you here. It is for my belief in the true Hope of Israel that I am bound with this chain."

These Jewish leaders in Rome replied, "We've received no letters from Jerusalem nor any witnesses against you. But we do want to hear your thoughts about 'The Way', for we know it is spoken against everywhere."

On a set day, a large group came to where he was under house arrest. Paul gave his own personal testimony, and from the Old Testament Law and Prophets taught Jesus as the Christ -- Messiah. Some believed, but others would not, creating a dissension.

Paul left them with a probing quote and commentary by saying, "The prophet Isaiah was correct when he said, 'This people shall hear but not understand, and see but not perceive.' Let me advise you that the salvation of God is being sent to the Gentiles, and they will receive it."

With this, the Jews, still arguing, left Paul.

Paul lived two years there under house arrest, wrote letters to the young churches, and visited with all who came to see him. Guarded by a solider, he preached the kingdom of God and taught the doctrine of the Lord Jesus Christ with boldness and confidence. No one prevented him. In this way, the gospel penetrated into homes, synagogues and temples under Paul's work, and also into Roman legions, courts and to the highest rulers of the day.

THE GREATEST LIFE
EVER LIVED

THE GREATEST STORY
EVER TOLD

THE BEST NEWS
EVER WITNESSED

JESUS THE CHRIST

A BIOGRAPHY

LIFE AND EVENTS OF MESSIAH

The Combined Gospels of the New Testament

from

MATTHEW, Mark, Luke, John

SOMEONE TO ANNOUNCE THE ARRIVAL OF MESSIAH

When Herod the Great was king of Judea, there was a priest named Zacharias whose wife was Elizabeth. They were old and childless. As Zacharias burned incense in the temple, the angel Gabriel appeared to him. Fearing for his life, Zacharias heard the angel say, "Don't be afraid. Your prayers are answered. You and Elizabeth will have a son whom you are to name John. Dedicate him to the Lord, for he shall be filled with the Holy Spirit from the day of his birth. He will prepare the way for the Messiah to come and he will turn many people to the Lord."

Zacharias said, "How can I know this is true?"

Replied the angel, "As confirmation, you will not be able to talk until John is born and named."

The people waiting outside the sanctuary of the temple wondered why Zacharias was so long completing the ceremony. When he came out, he was unable to speak, but communicated using sign language.

To her delight, Elizabeth soon knew she was pregnant.

THE MESSIAH WILL BE BORN TO A VIRGIN

Six months later, the angel went to Nazareth and appeared to a young virgin named Mary who was engaged to a man named Joseph. She had never had sexual relations. Said Gabriel to Mary, "Don't be afraid. You are highly favored and God is with you. You are going to have a Baby whom you will name Jesus. He will be the Son of God and will rule forever over Israel in the throne line of King David."

Said Mary, "How can this be? I am truly a virgin."

THE MESSIAH IS THE ONLY BORN SON OF GOD

Replied Gabriel, "The Holy Spirit is the Father of your Child who will be the only begotten Son of God. Elizabeth and Zacharias are having a son in their old age, demonstrating the power of God. She is six months along. Her son will be called John, and he will announce Jesus as the Messiah. With God, nothing is impossible."

THE COMMITMENT OF MARY

Mary said, "I'm ready -- willing to serve God in this way."

Mary immediately left to visit her cousin Elizabeth.

When Elizabeth saw Mary she said, "You are the most honored of women, and holy is your Baby, my Messiah."

Mary responded, "My soul magnifies the Lord and my spirit rejoices in God my Savior. Because of this miracle, all generations will call me blessed. God is fulfilling His promise to our forefathers."

Mary stayed three months.

JOHN THE BAPTIZER IS BORN

After Elizabeth delivered her baby, friends and neighbors gathered the eighth day for the circumcision and naming ceremony. Everyone expected him to be called Zacharias, but Elizabeth told them he was John. To silence the objections, Zacharias wrote on a tablet that John was his name. As soon as this was done, Zacharias was able to speak again. Everyone knew then that this baby was a miracle child with a special mission. Zacharias began to praise God and to prophesy about the soon coming of Messiah.

THE STRUGGLE AND FAITH OF JOSEPH

About six months later, the time came when Jesus would soon be born. Joseph had been shocked when Mary first told him she was pregnant. He loved her, wanted to believe her story, and decided to keep her out of public view until the baby was born. Afterward, he would marry her.

While he had struggled with this plan, an angel appeared to Joseph and confirmed what Mary had said: the Baby was virgin born, was the Son of God, His name was Jesus, and He was the promised Messiah come to save the people from their sins in fulfillment of Old Testament prophecies. Joseph married Mary, taking care of her without sexual relations until Jesus was born.

GOD USED CAESAR TO GET MARY TO BETHLEHEM FOR THE BIRTH OF MESSIAH

Caesar Augustus declared from Rome that all in his empire were to be counted in a census and assessed a tax. Each one was to report to their family's home town for this purpose. Joseph, being in King David's line, had to go to Bethlehem. Bethlehem was full of travelers and no accommodation was

available. Shelter could only be found in a stable. It was there
Jesus was born.

THE ANNOUNCEMENT TO SHEPHERDS

Near Bethlehem, shepherds were caring for their flocks
when suddenly an angel appeared. Heavenly glory permeated
everywhere and the shepherds were extremely frightened. Said
the angel, "Don't be afraid. I've good news. Today, in the city of
David, the Savior has been born, Messiah, the Lord. You'll find
Him wrapped in swaddling cloth and lying in a manger." All at
once an entire heavenly army of angels joined the first angel,
chanting, "Glory to God in the highest and Peace on earth to men
who please Him."

As soon as the angels left, the shepherds went into
Bethlehem to find the One whom the Lord had announced. They
searched for the Baby and found Him in a manger in the shed
where Mary and Joseph had taken shelter. While searching, the
shepherds had told people about the angels and what they had
said. All who heard the story were amazed, but Mary continued
to quietly contemplate all this within her heart. The shepherds
returned to their fields, singing and praising God for all they had
seen and heard.

JESUS CIRCUMCISED AND NAMED

When Mary's Child was eight days old, He was taken
to the Jerusalem temple for circumcision and was named Jesus, as
the angel instructed. An old man named Simion took Jesus into
his arms, blessed Him, worshipped God and said, "I can die in
peace, for I have seen the promised Messiah, the Savior."

An aged woman named Anna, who lived at the temple
and spent all her time in worship, took Jesus and said similar
things. These confirmations of the identity of Jesus deeply moved
Mary and Joseph.

THE VISIT OF THE WISEMEN

Joseph established a home in Bethlehem.

Several months after Jesus' birth, travelers from the
east arrived in Jerusalem inquiring at the palace where a new King
of the Jews had been born, saying they had seen His birth star and
had come to worship Him. Enraged, King Herod gathered
scholars with the chief priests and scribes and demanded to know

where scripture said Messiah would be born. Quoting prophecy, they said, "In Bethlehem of Judea".

Herod met with the Wisemen, questioning them until he knew exactly when they had initially seen the birth star. Then he sent them on to Bethlehem with explicit instructions, "Search and find the Child, and return to me with directions, so I may pay homage also."

The Wisemen left Jerusalem and were ecstatic to see again a star-like sign directing their journey until it indicated the house where Jesus was. In the house they worshipped Jesus and presented gifts of gold, frankincense and myrrh. Then, they departed. But, warned by God not to return to Herod, they went home another way.

ESCAPING TO EGYPT WITH JESUS

That same day, an angel instructed Joseph to leave at once for Egypt with Mary and Jesus, because Herod would try to find and kill the Baby. Joseph left that night and stayed in Egypt for some time.

HEROD TRIES TO ELIMINATE THE KING OF THE JEWS

Meanwhile, realizing the Wisemen had made a fool of him, Herod was outraged. He sent soldiers to Bethlehem and the surrounding area to kill every male child two years old and younger, based on the time the Wisemen said they had first seen the star, and allowing for error. Sadly this fulfilled the prophecy which said that in this place there would be a great wailing, mothers weeping for their babies who were slaughtered.

OUT OF EGYPT TO NAZARETH

When Herod the Great* was dead, an angel advised Joseph to return out of Egypt. In this way another prophecy was fulfilled, "Out of Egypt will I call My Son." Joseph moved his family to Nazareth, fulfilling another prophecy that Messiah would be a Nazarene. Jesus grew and became both strong and intelligent, and liked by everyone. And God was within Him.

(* Herod the Great's three sons, Herod Archelaus, Herod Antipas, Herod Phillip, inherited their father's divided kingdom. In the Herod family was also Herod Agrippa I & II. Several Herods are mentioned in the gospel story playing their sordid parts.)

JESUS IN THE TEMPLE DEBATING WITH LAWYERS

When Jesus was twelve, His parents took Him to the Feast of Passover in Jerusalem. Leaving to return home, they discovered Jesus was not with them. Searching, they found Him in the temple with the doctors of law, questioning, reasoning and debating. All were astonished at His wisdom and knowledge. When Mary asked Him why He had not stayed close to His family, Jesus said, "I must be engaged in My Father's business." They didn't understand that statement, but Jesus left to go with them and was subordinate to them in honor and obedience.

CHILDHOOD AND GROWTH OF JESUS

In favor with God and with the people, Jesus developed physically, preparing Himself for the time when His earthly ministry would begin.

THE MINISTRY OF JOHN THE BAPTIZER

When Jesus was about thirty years of age, John the Baptist, the son of Zacharias, began preaching "Repent, for the kingdom of Heaven is near."

This fulfilled what Isaiah had said, "There shall come in the wilderness the voice of one to prepare the way for the Lord." John wore camel's skin and lived off the land. He spoke of repentance for remission of sin, and baptized in the Jordan river. Multitudes came to hear him preach, including tax collectors, soldiers and religious leaders. John said, "There is One coming who is mightier than I. I'm not worthy to carry His sandals. He will baptize with the Holy Spirit and with fiery judgment. He is the Messiah, the Promised One of Israel."

JESUS BAPTIZED BY JOHN

Jesus of Nazareth came to John to be baptized. John said, "I need to be baptized by You." But Jesus replied, "This is necessary to fulfill the Father's plan." As John baptized Jesus, as Jesus was coming up out of the water, the heavens opened and the Spirit of God came on Jesus as a dove, and a voice from heaven said, "This is My beloved Son in whom I am well pleased."

JESUS TESTED

Immediately after the public baptism, Jesus was led by the Holy Spirit deep into the wilderness where He was tested by satan for forty days and nights. Refuting satan with Scripture,

Jesus was victor over every test. Defeated, the devil left Jesus, and angels ministered to His needs.

JOHN THE BAPTIZER CONFRONTS THE SINS OF HEROD

John publicly condemned Herod for adultery with the wife of Herod's brother. In anger, Herod had John put in prison.

JESUS BEGINS TO PREACH

Jesus went to Galilee through Samaria and began preaching and teaching. "Repent, for the kingdom of heaven is here. The time is fulfilled. Believe the good news." One of John the Baptizer's disciples, Andrew, brought his brother Simon Peter to listen to Jesus, and they spent some time with Him.

JESUS ANNOUNCES HIS MESSIAHSHIP AND IS REJECTED IN NAZARETH

In a synagogue in Nazareth where He grew up, Jesus read one Sabbath day from the scripture in Isaiah, "The Spirit of the Lord is upon Me, anointing Me to preach good news to the poor, freedom to prisoners, sight for the blind and liberty to slaves." Closing the book, He said, "This scripture is fulfilled today before you." But the crowd said, "Is not this the son of Joseph?" Jesus responded, "No prophet has honor in his own hometown." Angered, the people ran Him out of the city, wanting to kill Him, but He walked through the middle of the mob and went His way to Capernaum.

THE FIRST MIRACLE OF JESUS

Jesus and His mother attended a marriage feast in Cana of Galilee. During the celebration, Mary said to Jesus, "They are out of wine." She said in turn to the servants, "Do whatever Jesus tells you."

Soon thereafter Jesus spoke to the servants, "Fill those large water jars with water." They had no sooner filled them to the brim when Jesus said, "Take a drink to the host." When the host tasted from the cup brought to him, he said, "This is the finest wine. Why was it not served first?" This was the first miracle Jesus performed.

JESUS INVESTIGATED BY THE PHARISEE NICODEMUS

In Jerusalem during Passover, a Pharisee named Nicodemus came to Jesus under the cover of night for fear of his colleagues. He said, "Teacher, I know You are from God."

Jesus replied, "Unless you are born again you will never see God or enter His kingdom." Nicodemus asked, "How can an adult be reborn?" Jesus said, "I am speaking of a spiritual rebirth. You must be born in the spirit to enter the kingdom of God." "How?" asked Nicodemus.

Jesus said, "I am God the Son. I will be lifted up in death in order to give eternal life. God loves everyone so much that He sent Me, His only born Son, into the world, so that everyone who believes Me should not suffer eternal death, but instead have eternal life. One who believes on Me will not be condemned, but one who does not believe Me is judged already. I do not wish that anyone be condemned, but that all be saved."

JESUS MAKES DISCIPLES OF PREVIOUS SEEKERS

By the sea of Galilee, two former disciples of John the Baptist, brothers whom Jesus knew, were going about their fishing business. Jesus said to Simon Peter and Andrew, "Follow Me, and you will catch men." They immediately went with Him. Soon they came upon two other fisher brothers, James and John. When Jesus called them, they also left their boat and their father Zebedee, and took up with Jesus.

JESUS GIVES LIVING WATER TO A LOOSE WOMAN

As He traveled, Jesus made a point of passing through Samaria and a city named Sycar. Jesus was sitting on a well when a woman came to draw water. Jesus said, "Please give Me a drink." The woman replied, "Why would You, a Jew, ask me, a Samaritan and a woman, for anything?" Jesus said, "I want you to know who it is with whom you are speaking. I am able to give you living water so that you never thirst again. I am able to give you everlasting life." The woman said, "Give me that water." Jesus said, "Go call your husband." The woman replied, "I have no husband." Jesus said, "I know that you have had five husbands and are now living with a man not your husband." The woman said, "You must be a prophet. Do You think we should worship here in Samaria or in Jerusalem?" Jesus answered, "God is interested not in the location but in the attitude of worship. God is Spirit, and those who genuinely worship Him must worship in spirit and in truth." The woman said, "I believe that Messiah is coming." Jesus said, "I am Messiah."

JESUS EXERCISES POWER OVER DEMONS

One Sabbath in synagogue, Jesus was teaching when a man possessed with demons began crying out, "Jesus, are You come to destroy us? I know You! You are the Holy One of God!" Jesus said, "Evil spirits, be quiet. Come out of this man." At once the demons left the man. The crowd was amazed and said among themselves, "What kind of authority does He hold, that even demons obey Him?" The reputation of Jesus spread quickly.

JESUS HEALS MANY

Jesus and his small group of followers went to the home of Simon Peter and found Peter's mother very ill. But as Jesus took her hand and helped her out of bed, the fever left her.

Soon, people in the area were bringing to Jesus all their sick and those possessed with demons. Jesus healed them all as Isaiah said, "He took our infirmities and bare our diseases."

JESUS TAKES TIME FOR SOLITUDE

Early next morning, long before dawn, Jesus went to a solitary place to pray. Later His disciples told Him that throngs of sick were looking for Him to be healed. But Jesus said, "We will leave for the next town. I must preach there also. That's why I came."

So it went throughout Galilee. Jesus preached in synagogues, taught people everywhere and healed the sick.

A FISHING LESSON

As He preached on the sea shore, the crowd got so compressed Jesus stood in a boat to speak. After the teaching, His disciples went fishing. They fished all night but caught nothing. In the morning, Jesus said, "Throw out the nets once more." When they did this, the take was so great the fish filled two boats. Peter fell at the feet of Jesus saying, "I'm not worthy to be in Your presence." Jesus replied, "Now, let's fish for souls of living individuals."

MORE MIRACLES AND MORE QUIET TIMES

A leper said to Jesus, "If You want to, You can make me well." Jesus reached out, touched this incurable, outcast man, and said, "I want to. Be clean." Immediately, the leprosy left the man, and he began to excitedly tell everyone how Jesus had healed him. As a result, more throngs sought Jesus. But often Jesus made time to be alone to pray.

One day Jesus was teaching surrounded by Pharisees, Scribes and Doctors of Law from several cities. The large house in which He taught was so jammed that no one else could get in. Friends of a man sick with palsy wanted Jesus to heal him. Going onto the roof, they removed tiles and by using ropes let him down on a stretcher .

When Jesus saw the faith of these men, He said to the sick man, "Your sins are forgiven."

The religious leaders were furious and said, "Only God can forgive sins! This Jesus is a blasphemer!"

Knowing their thoughts, Jesus said, "Is it easier to forgive sins or to heal sickness? So you will understand that the Son of God has authority on earth to forgive sins, I will heal this man." He then said to the palsied man, "Get up. Gather the stretcher and leave." Immediately the man was totally healed. He took his cot and left in front of them all.

The people were amazed and terrified. They glorified God and said, "We have seen strange things today. When has God ever given such power and authority to anyone before? This Jesus is not like the religious leaders."

JESUS MAKES DISCIPLES OF THOSE WHO REALIZE THEY ARE SINNERS

One day as Jesus passed by Matthew, a tax collector, He said, "Follow Me". Leaving everything, Matthew followed Him. Later, Matthew put on a feast for Jesus. When the Scribes and Pharisees heard of it, they said to the disciples, "Why does your Master eat with sinners?" When Jesus perceived the question, He said, "I am here to help those in need. A physician does not visit those who think they are well, but those who realize they are sick. Similarly, I came to call to repentance those who admit they are sinners, not those who think they are righteous."

GOD IS INTERESTED IN THE SPIRIT OF THE LAW AND THE INTENT OF THE HEART

One Sabbath day, His disciples, walking next to a grain field, stripped some of the grain, rubbed off the husks with their hands, and ate the kernels. Observing this, the Pharisees questioned, "Why do You let Your disciples work on the Sabbath day against the Mosaic law?"

Jesus answered, "Remember how David and his men, when starving, ate the temple cerimonial bread? It was lawful for only the priests to eat that bread. Even the priests, in the duties they perform each Sabbath, are working, technically breaking the law of the Sabbath, yet are not sinning. God is interested in showing mercy, not in forcing technical compliance with rituals. Don't you understand that I am greater than the temple and Sabbath rituals?!"

The Pharisees followed as He entered a synagogue. There He came face to face with a man with a spastic hand. The leaders asked Him, "Is it lawful to heal on the Sabbath day?" They wanted to accuse Him of willfully breaking the Sabbath traditions.

Jesus said, "If one of your sheep falls into a pit on the Sabbath day, you pull it out to save its life. Are not men worth more than sheep?" The leaders would not answer His question. Grieving for their stubborn rejection of truth Jesus turned to the man with the withered hand and said, "Stretch out your arm and spread your fingers." The man did, and his hand became normal in sight of everyone. The infuriated Pharisees discussed how to destroy Jesus, but He was thronged by crowds seeking a miracle, and many were healed.

HOW TO BE HAPPY AND EFFECTIVE

Jesus got alone with His disciples, instructing them: "Happy are those who are humble of spirit, for they will be in Heaven. Happy are mourners, for they shall be comforted. Happy are gentle people, for they shall do well in this life. Happy are those who desire righteousness, for they shall have it. Happy are those who show mercy, for they shall be shown mercy. Happy are those with pure hearts, for they shall see God. Happy are those who make peace, for they shall be known as children of God. Happy are those who suffer because they do right, for they will enjoy Heaven. Happy are you if men falsely accuse you for My name's sake, for you will be rewarded. You are the salt of the earth, to add flavor and to preserve. Don't lose your saltiness even when it hurts open wounds. You are the light of the world and will stand out in the darkness. Do not lose your glow even though the light reveals problems that need to be corrected and sins that need to be cleansed. Let your light radiate truth, so that people will see your good deeds and give praise to God."

THE PURE STANDARD OF JESUS

"Don't misunderstand and think I came to destroy the Mosaic Law. I came to fulfill it. I will complete all it requires. Unless your righteousness is purer than that of the Pharisees, who try so hard to keep the letter of the traditional Mosaic Law, you can never get into heaven.

"The law says, Do not murder. I say, Do not even be angry with someone. The law says, Do not commit adultery. I say, If you even lust after a woman, you are an adulterer. It would be better to be blind than to see and sin because of sight. It would be better to be disfigured than to sin because of your physique. The law says, If you are tired of your wife, divorce her legally. I say, Do not divorce unless for unfaithfulness. The law says, An eye for an eye and a tooth for a tooth. I say, If you are slapped on one check, turn the other cheek. If you are robbed for your coat, give your scarf also. If you are forced to go one mile for someone, voluntarily go the second mile. Give without a grudge. The law says, Love your neighbor, hate your enemy. I say, Love your enemy and pray for those who mistreat you. Be like your heavenly Father who is kind and merciful, and who sends sunshine and rain to both the just and the unjust."

LESSONS ON PRAYER AND GIVING

"When you give to God, don't do it to get praise of men. If you do that, then the praise of men is your total reward. Instead, give secretly. Then your reward will be from God.

"When you pray, don't pray to show off to those around you. Let your prayers be private between you and God. Don't pray with much repetition. God hears you and knows what you need.

"Here's an example of prayer: 'Father in heaven, Your name is holy. May Your kingdom come quickly. Help us accomplish Your will on earth. Please provide our daily nourishment. Cleanse us and forgive us of our sins, and help us to forgive those who sin against us. Don't allow us to be trapped by temptation, but deliver us from satan's grasp. Amen'."

LESSON ON WORSHIP

"When you fast to draw closer to God, don't let others know you are doing it. If you fast to please men or to get honor from men, then that is your full reward. But if you fast secretly, unto God, He will reward you."

LESSON ON RICHES

"Don't horde riches on earth. It will be stolen or lose value or not satisfy. If your wealth is on earth, earth is where your love and attention will be. Stockpile riches in heaven. Heavenly wealth increases in value, can't be stolen, and satisfies. If your treasure is in heaven, then your love and attention will also be there. You can't serve God while being wholly consumed with wealth. Seek God's kingdom and His righteousness, and He will provide your needs."

LESSON ON JUDGING AND CONDUCT

"Don't judge others, for you'll be judged by as strict a standard as you apply to them. First, take care of your own shortcomings, and then, when you have a more full understanding, help your brother with his.

"Ask, and you will receive. Seek, and you will find. Knock, and the door will open. Do unto others as you would have others do unto you. Good men produce good, evil men produce evil. What men say reveals the contents of their inner self, for out of the heart comes one's conversation. Just as you identify a tree by its fruit, you can discern people by the life that is their habit."

LESSON ON RELIGIONS VS TRUTH

"Look for the narrow gate and enter it. There's a wide and convenient gate, a lenient way which everyone starts on, but it leads to eternal destruction. Search for the narrow gate and the true way to eternal life, for few find it.

"Be alert for false prophets, pseudo guides, who are wolves dressed as sheep. Not everyone who uses My name will enter heaven. Many will say at the judgment, 'Lord, didn't we call ourselves by Your name, prophesy in Your name, and do many good deeds in Your name'. But I'll say to them, 'Be gone, this isn't your home. I don't know you. Your good-works-religion is sin because it's a lie.'

"Whoever obeys what I teach is like a wise man who chooses a solid rock foundation on which to build his home. It will stand against storms and tests of time. Whoever doesn't obey what I teach is like a foolish man who builds his house on sand. The storms destroy that house in total destruction."

THE VOICE OF AUTHORITY

When Jesus finished teaching on the mountain, He descended and a great crowd continued to follow Him because they recognized the voice of authority, so different from the religious leaders of the day.

AN EXAMPLE OF FAITH

Soon He started toward Capernaum. On the way, a centurion asked Him to heal his servant who was near death. Jesus assured him that He would.

The centurion said, "I'm not worthy for You to enter my house. I understand authority, for I have those under me who do what I say. If You only speak the word, I know my servant will be healed."

Jesus said, "Yours is the clearest faith I have yet witnessed. Your servant is well. Go home contented."

Arriving home, the centurion found his servant healed.

INTERRUPTING A FUNERAL

Soon afterward, Jesus and the crowd came to a city called Nain. A funeral procession was leaving the city to bury a young man who had been the only son of his widowed mother.

Seeing the grieving mother, Jesus took pity on her, and said, "Don't cry." Then, He stopped those who carried the bier, and spoke to the body, "Young man, get up." Life came back to the boy, and Jesus presented him to his amazed mother.

Everyone in the crowd shook with fear, and then praised God, saying, "God is here with us." This story spread rapidly.

REASSURING THE FAITH OF JOHN

John the Baptist sent a messenger from prison to Jesus asking, "Are You truly Messiah?"

Jesus sent the emissary back to report Jesus' preaching and teaching; and that the blind, deaf, dumb, crippled, and lepers were being healed; the poor were being given the gospel; and the dead were being raised from death. Jesus told John, "Be happy, for you have no reason to doubt Me."

Then Jesus turned to the crowd and said, "When John was preaching, many went out in the desert to see and hear that prophet. I am greater than John, for I am the One of whom he prophesied. Many of you rejected John, saying he was too strict. Many of you reject Me saying I am too lenient. I tell you, if the people in Sodom had seen the miracles you have seen, they would have repented. I will, therefore, be more lenient with them in the day of judgment than with you."

TAKING TIME WITH THE FATHER

Jesus prayed, "I thank You My Father, Lord of the universe, that You have hidden these truths from the worldly wise and arrogant, but have made them plain to the humble and believing. You know Me, Father, and I know You, and I reveal You to those I choose."

PARTNERS WITH JESUS

Then Jesus said to the crowd, "Come to Me, you who are tired and weighted down, and I will give you rest. Join Me in My work, learning from Me, for I am willing to work with you, and you will find contentment in your souls. When we labor together, you will find your part of the work is easy."

GRATITUDE IN ACTION

Jesus accepted a Pharisee's invitation to dine at his house. As He reclined at the table, a prostitute from the city streets gained entrance and stood behind Jesus where she began to weep. With tears she washed Jesus' feet and then soothed them with ointment from a flask.

The Pharisee who hosted the dinner thought, If Jesus were truly divine, He would know what kind of woman this is, and stop her.

Just then Jesus spoke to the Pharisee, "If two men were forgiven a debt by the same lender, one being forgiven five dollars and the other five thousand dollars, which would be more appreciative?" Answered the Pharisee, "The one forgiven the largest debt." Jesus went on, "When I came in, you didn't give Me water to wash the dust off My feet, but this woman has washed them in her tears. You didn't even hug Me in greeting, but this woman has been kissing My feet. You gave Me no hair oil with which to freshen up, but she has anointed My feet with fine ointment. While you didn't do even the customary courtesies of a host, she has gone over and beyond to show her affection. She has shown much love because her sins which are many, and which you classify as especially heinous, are forgiven. Those who think they have little of which to be forgiven, unfortunately often experience little love."

He turned and said to the woman, "Your sins are forgiven. Your faith has saved you. Go in peace." Those at the dinner questioned among each other how Jesus could authoritatively forgive sins.

WOMEN IN THE WORK WITH JESUS

As Jesus and His disciples went about preaching the gospel, Mary Magdalene, from whom He had cast seven demons; Joanna, the wife of one of Herod's stewards; Susanna; and several other wealthy women went with Him, contributing financially to the ministry. Against the custom of the times, Jesus respected and honored women.

THE UNPARDONABLE SIN

Brought to Jesus was a man possessed with a demon which made him blind and dumb. Jesus exorcised the demon and the man could see and speak. The crowd expressed amazement, saying, "Surely, this miracle worker is more than just a man. Remember, He is a descendant of King David."

The envious Pharisees said, "He casts out demons by the power of satan." But Jesus said, "If satan casts out his own demons, he is warring against himself. To cast out demons, one must first bind the power of satan. Listen, all sins can be forgiven except this sin of calling the work of God through the Holy Spirit the work of satan. One who says The Spirit of God is satan will not be forgiven."

JESUS SAYS HIS RESURRECTION IS PROOF OF HIS AUTHORITY

The religious leaders then asked Jesus to give them a visible sign evidencing His authority -- to do some miracle to please their curiosity. Jesus replied, "As Jonah was three days and three nights in the stomach of the big fish, so shall I be three days and three nights in the grave. That is the only sign you need if you are sincere. The people of Ninevah repented when they heard the message of Jonah, and One greater than Jonah is among you. The Ninevites put you to shame and will fare better than you in the judgment."

JESUS TELLS ABOUT THE SEED

One day, as had occurred before, a great crowd nearly pushed Jesus into the water as He taught them by a seaside. Jesus got in a boat to lecture the people thronging the beach. "A sower broadcast seed. Some seed fell on the pathway where it was walked on and birds ate it. Some seed fell on rocks where it sprouted quickly in the cracks. Under the heat of the sun, with no moisture in the shallow earth there, the young plants wilted and died. Some seed fell among weeds which overpowered the plants, rendering them unproductive. But some seed fell on fertile ground and produced a good crop, some thirty, some sixty, and some a one hundred-fold yield."

THE MEANING EXPLAINED

The disciples asked Jesus in private to explain this parable. Jesus elaborated, "The seed is the word of God. The seed on the path is like people who hear God's message and debate it within themselves. But before they absorb it through belief, satan removes it from their mind. The seed on the rocks is like folks who quickly believe God's message, getting excited about their salvation, but when temptations and trials come, they turn away from their faith. The seed among the weeds is like those who believe God's word, but inordinate time committed to careers, or the deceitfulness and temptation of accumulating excessive wealth, or the worries of this life, or the pursuit of pleasure, distract them from serving and fellowshipping with God, and they are unproductive in their spiritual life. The seed on good ground is like those who believe the message and develop spiritual understanding, eternal priorities, and an accurate concept of themselves and others. These reproduce spiritually, with endurance and patience. These become sowers."

COUNTERFEITS

Jesus continued with another similarity of farming and His kingdom. "A sower broadcast good seed in his fields, but his competitor came and in the same fields sowed darnel (which looks like wheat but has bad tasting grain). When the seeds grew, the help reported to the owner, 'Darnel is throughout your wheat field. Shall we weed it out?' The owner said, 'Wait until the harvest. At that time, reap the entire field, separating the darnel for burning, but keeping the true wheat for my grain'."

THE MEANING EXPLAINED

Later, the disciples asked Jesus to explain the meaning of the story about the darnel. Jesus said, "I sow good seed in the world. The genuine wheat represents the true believers, My faithful followers. Satan sows bad seed. The darnel represents those who follow him. The harvest is the end of the world, and the reapers are the angels. At the last judgment, I shall identify the true believers and take them into My everlasting kingdom, but those who followed false religions will be destroyed."

LIGHT REPELS DARKNESS WHILE ILLUMINATING REALITY AND TRUTH

Jesus taught a story of a lamp. "When one buys a lamp, he doesn't cover its light but puts it on a lamp stand for illumination. So it is that everything done in secret shall be revealed, hidden things will be exposed."

SIMILES OF THE KINGDOM OF GOD

"The kingdom of God is similar to the tiny mustard seed which grows into a large plant that birds can sit in. It is like a little leaven which permeates all the dough. It is like a man finding a treasure buried in a field, who sells all he has to buy that field and claim the treasure. It is like a collector who finds the perfect pearl with a high price, and sells everything he has to acquire that one superlative pearl. It is like a net pulled in by a fisherman who keeps the good fish and throws away the bad."

JESUS CALMS A STORM

Jesus and His disciples got into a boat to cross a large lake. An intense storm washed waves over the boat, swamping it so that it was in danger of sinking. But Jesus peacefully slept in a sheltered place in the stern. His frantic disciples awoke Him, "Don't You care that we are going to drown?!"

Jesus got up and spoke to the wind. The storm not only quit blowing, but also the waves were instantly calm. Jesus asked, "What happened to your faith?" Terrified by such power, the disciples asked among themselves, "What is the extent of His power, that even the wind and sea instantly obey Him?"

TWO MEN POSSESSED BY DEMONS ARE HEALED

Arriving at their destination, they were met by two men possessed with demons. These men had often been chained but with satanic strength they broke any fetters man could put on them. They were wild and dangerous and lived naked in a cemetery, cutting themselves with stones and frightening any one who passed that way. Seeing Jesus they said, "We know You are the Son of God. Have You come here to torment us?"

Nearby was a herd of swine, and the many demons in these two deranged men asked, "If You cast us out of these men, will You allow us to inhabit those swine?" Jesus commanded, "Go!" They left the men and entered the pigs, which ran down a cliff and drowned in the lake.

When this was reported in the nearby city, the people came out and saw the crazy men quietly sitting clothed at the feet of Jesus. Nevertheless, the citizens, because of losing their investment in the pigs, asked Jesus to leave their community. The healed men asked if they could follow Jesus, but He told them to go back to their families and tell the good things God had done for them. They spread the good news throughout the entire city. But Jesus got back into the boat and left for the other side.

THE CROWDS WANTED THE ATTENTION OF JESUS

Upon arriving at His destination, a crowd immediately thronged Him. As Jesus began to teach them, a ruler of the synagogue asked Jesus to come to his home to heal his only daughter, about twelve years old, who was at the point of death. Jesus went with him.

A TOUCH OF FAITH

On the way, the crowd so bunched around Him that progress was slow. There was a chronically sick woman in the crowd who had spent her life savings trying everything the doctors had to offer, but for years had not been cured of her plague but instead had gotten worse. She told herself that Jesus could heal her if she could only touch Him.

As the throng pressed about Jesus, she worked her way toward Him and in her weakness and determination made a desperate effort to reach out. She was able to grab only the hem of His garment, and was immediately made well. Jesus turned to her, singling her out of the mob, and said, "It is your faith which has made you whole. Be at peace."

KEEP ON BELIEVING

Just then a runner came and advised the synagogue ruler that his child had died. The man turned to Jesus and said, "Don't trouble Yourself any more to help me. My daughter is dead." Jesus looked at him and said, "Don't be saddened or afraid. Don't give up hope, just keep on believing."

When Jesus came to the house, the mourners met them. Jesus assured them, "The little girl is only asleep." But they laughed and jeered for they knew she was dead. Jesus put them out and took the parents to the child. Taking her hand, He said, "Little girl, wake up." At once the daughter got up and walked to her parents. The report of this miracle spread like wildfire.

THE BLIND AND DUMB ARE HEALED

Shortly thereafter, there met Jesus along the road two blind men who cried out, "Jesus, take pity on us." Jesus answered, "Do you believe I can help?" They said, "Yes, Lord." Jesus replied, "As you believe, let it be." He touched their eyes, producing instant sight. These men went everywhere telling all who would listen how Jesus had given them sight.

About that time, a dumb man was led to Jesus and He cured him. As the healed man went away speaking, the crowd said among themselves, "We have never seen anything like this before."

REJECTED AGAIN AT NAZARETH

Coming again to Nazareth where He grew up, Jesus taught in the synagogue and performed a few miracles there.

But the home folks said, "How can He do and say these things? He's the son of Mary and Joseph the carpenter, and His brothers and sisters live here among us." They were confused and could not believe He was Messiah. Therefore, Jesus did not perform many miracles among them. Because of their unbelief, Jesus said as before, "A prophet is honored except in his hometown."

SHEEP WITH NO SHEPHERD

Jesus went to cities and villages teaching in synagogues, preaching outdoors, and healing sick. Seeing the hearts and minds of the crowds and their lack of direction, He was stirred with compassion because they reminded Him of sheep with no shepherd. Jesus continued His work in the larger cities.

TIME OUT

About this time Herod Antipas beheaded John the Baptizer. Jesus told His disciples, "Come with Me to a quiet place for rest."

JESUS MASTERS THE ELEMENTS AS WELL AS TIME AND SPACE

Later, Jesus sent His disciples across the lake in a boat so He could be alone to pray. When the boat carrying the disciples was near the middle of the lake, a violent storm began to blow. In the darkness, the disciples saw a figure coming toward them, walking on the water. They were weak with fright and gasped in fear, "It's a ghost!" But Jesus sang out, "Cheer up! It is I! Don't be afraid." Peter got excited and said, "Lord, since it is You, let me come out there with You on the water!" Jesus replied, "Come." With his eyes on Jesus, Peter jumped out of the boat and walked on the surface of the raging lake toward Jesus.

But suddenly realizing where he was and seeing the waves, in panic he began to go down. Peter cried out, "Lord, save me!"

Instantly, Jesus grabbed his hand, put His arm around him on the water, and said, "You had a little faith. Why did you let doubts take over?" As they climbed in the boat, the wind quit, the waves calmed, and the boat was instantly at its destination.

Those in the boat were amazed and worshipped Jesus, saying, "Truly, You are God the Son."

OVER FIVE THOUSAND FED

However, the group was seen departing, and soon a crowd followed to find them. When the multitude overtook Jesus and His disciples, Jesus had pity on them and taught them until late in the day. Seeing the hour, the disciples said, "Send the people home; it's past time to eat." But Jesus said, "Why don't you feed them." Philip said, "We can't afford to buy enough to feed this crowd." Andrew suggested, "There's a boy here with five loaves and two fish."

Jesus had everyone sit down in groups of about fifty each. He took the loaves and fishes, blessed them, and began breaking them into pieces, filling baskets to be distributed to the crowd. When everyone had eaten his fill, there were twelve baskets full of food left over. Jesus instructed His disciples to gather up the baskets and not to waste any food. About five thousand men had eaten plus women and children.

THE HEALING TOUCH

Now, at Gennesaret, news that Jesus was there spread quickly. The populace began to bring Jesus the sick from the entire region. Wherever He went people thronged Him, trying even to just touch His garment, that in so doing they would be healed. Many were laid on pallets in His pathway so they could reach up to touch His robe, and all who touched were healed.

WORTHLESS WORSHIP

But Pharisees from Jerusalem came and questioned Jesus, "Before they eat, why don't Your disciples follow the ceremonial washings dictated by Moses in the law?"

Jesus responded, "You honor God with your lips, but your heart is far from Him. You are hypocrites, for you pretend to follow the law of Moses, but have set up traditions which invalidate his instructions. You honor the doctrines of men more than the truth of God. Therefore, your worship of God is worthless."

POLLUTION FROM WITHIN

Then Jesus spoke to the crowd, "It isn't that which you eat but that which you say that pollutes you. The food you eat passes out into waste, but what you say demonstrates what is in your heart. Your conduct and conversations of greed, pride, murder, adultery, lying, dishonesty, gossiping and evil thoughts, these pollute you."

BLIND FOLLOWERS OF BLIND RELIGIOUS LEADERS

The disciples whispered to Jesus, "Do You realize that You offended the Pharisees?" Jesus said, "Be careful not to be blind followers of the blind. These religious leaders will be exposed by My father. Do not follow them! Beware of the way their teachings permeate those around them."

FAITH WITH HUMILITY

In His travels, Jesus was worshipped by a Gentile woman who asked, "Please heal my little daughter." Jesus said, "Shouldn't Israel have first the bread of life?" The lady replied, "Even dogs eat what the children will not eat." Jesus said, "You have great faith. Your daughter is well. Go in peace."

OVER FOUR THOUSAND FED

On one occasion, Jesus was teaching and healing the lame, blind, disfigured, dumb and all who were brought to Him. The people ran out of food, having stayed with Jesus three days. Some were faint from fasting.

Jesus took seven loaves and a few fish, tore them in small pieces, and had His disciples distribute them to the crowd, much as they had done on a previous occasion. This time there were about four thousand men plus women and children and there were seven baskets of food left over when all had eaten their fill.

WHO JESUS REALLY IS

Jesus asked the disciples, "Whom do people say I am?"

They gave several answers, "John the Baptist, Elijah, Jeremiah or other of the prophets."

Jesus asked, "Whom do you say I am?"

Peter replied, "You are the Christ, Messiah, the Son of God."

Jesus said, "You are correct. It is My Father in heaven who enables you to understand. Peter, your name means *little rock*. Upon the foundational rock of the truth you just stated I will build My church, and governmental and other powers in hell together with religious authorities there shall not overpower it."

THINKING LIKE MEN INSTEAD OF LIKE GOD

Beginning at this time, Jesus began to teach them about His atonement and how He would suffer at the hands of the religious leaders and die for the sins of mankind, rising again after three days. Peter disputed Jesus, saying, "This will never happen to You." But Jesus turned to him and said, "Satan, get out of My face. You are thinking like men, not like God."

Jesus said, "If one wants to be like Me, let him take his own cross and follow My example, denying himself every day. If one tries to save his own life, he will lose it, but if one will lose his life for My sake and for the work of the gospel, that one will find real life. What would be the profit to spend your life gaining the whole world, if in doing so you condemn yourself? What could one give in trade to reclaim his life? No amount of wealth can buy back a soul.

"When I return in glory, I will reward everyone according to the life they lived. Whoever is ashamed of Me before this sinful world will find Me ashamed of him in that great day. Some of you here will preview My glory and the power of My eternal kingdom."

A GLIMPSE OF THE GLORY OF JESUS

Six days later, Jesus took Peter, James and John with Him up into a high mountain where they prayed. There Jesus was changed before their eyes. His face radiated like the brilliance of the sun and His garments glistened a dazzling white. Moses and Elijah appeared with Him and they discussed His impending death in Jerusalem.

The disciples were in a kind of trance, but when they regained their composure, Peter said, "Lord, let us build here three memorials -- one each for You, Elijah and Moses." But a dark cloud enveloped them and a voice interrupted him, saying, "This is My beloved Son, listen to Him."

The disciples fell on their faces as dead. Jesus reached out and touched them and said, "You need not be afraid. Get up."

Looking up, the disciples saw only Jesus, and they kept their silence.

AGAIN TEACHING THE ATONEMENT

Leaving the mountain, Jesus instructed the disciples not to tell this incident to anyone until after He had risen from death. They questioned among themselves why He would have to rise from death. They asked, "Why do the Pharisees teach that Elijah must return before Messiah comes?"

Jesus replied, "Elijah has already come back in the power and spirit of John the Baptist, and the leaders did not believe him. But the scriptures also teach that Messiah must suffer and be rejected by His people."

NOTHING IS IMPOSSIBLE WITH GOD

As they approached a crowd, a man emerged, came to Jesus and said, "O, Lord, have mercy on my son. He cannot hear or speak and he has epilepsy. He is wasting away. Your disciples were not able to help him."

When Jesus saw the crowd of curiosity seekers, He immediately healed the boy and gave him to his father.

The crowd was aghast.

The disciples asked Jesus privately, "Why could we not help the lad."

Jesus said, "You need to pray and believe. If your faith is only as big as a mustard seed, you can move mountains. With God, nothing is impossible."

FORETELLING HIS ATONEMENT AGAIN

In Galilee, Jesus began again to prepare His disciple for His sacrificial death. "The Messiah must surrender to the power of men who will kill Him, but after three days, He will come back to life." The disciples did not understand this teaching, but were too timid to ask for clarification.

GOD THE SON SUBMITS TO THE GOVERNMENT

In Capernaum, Peter was approached by those who collected the Temple Tax. They asked, "Does your Master pay the half-shekel Temple Tax? It is due." Evasively, Peter said, "I think so." When he saw Jesus, Jesus said, "Peter, do kings of earth charge their sons tax?" Peter said, "No." Jesus went on, "Then the sons are free of that obligation. But lest we stir up trouble by claiming exemption as God's Son, we will pay. Go to the sea and catch a fish. It will have a shekel in its mouth to pay both our Temple Tax."

GREATNESS IN HUMILITY

As the disciples were debating which of them would be greatest in heaven, they saw Jesus coming, and changed the subject. "What were you arguing about?" He said. But they didn't answer.

Jesus called a little child and set him on His knee. "Whoever seeks to be first shall be last", He said. "Whoever humbles himself as a little child shall be first in the kingdom of heaven. Whoever receives a little child in My name, receives Me. Whoever receives Me, receives My Father. Whoever shall cause a child who believes on Me to fall away from Me would have been better off if he had first been drowned. Do not despise My little children. If a shepherd loses one little lamb, he leaves the flock and goes to find the one lamb that strayed. When he finds it, he gets more joy over that lamb than over all the others in the fold. Similarly, the Father in heaven does not want one little child to perish."

UNITED IN PURPOSE

On one occasion John said to Jesus, "We saw a man casting out demons in Your name, but he is not one of us. We told him to stop." Jesus said, "Don't stop him. He was not speaking evil of Me. One who is not against us is for us. If someone merely gives you a drink of water because you are Mine, he shall have a reward."

HANDLING SERIOUS WRONGS

"If your brother sins against you, go talk to him. If he listens, you have saved your relationship. If he will not listen, then go again to him with two witnesses so the conversation can be documented. If he will not listen to the three of you, take the problem up before the church. If he will not listen to counsel from the church, excommunicate him. When two or three of you gather in My name, I will be with you, and if those two or three of you agree on a thing you ask of Me, it will be done for you."

INFINITELY FORGIVING SERIOUS WRONGS

Peter said, "Lord, how many times shall I forgive my brother? Is seven adequate?"

Jesus assured him, "More than seventy times seven!"

Then He illustrated with a story.

"A king was balancing his accounts and found a servant hopelessly behind in paying a million dollar debt to the king. The king ordered that he and his wife and children be sold as slaves, and their personal belongings auctioned to reduce the debt. But that servant fell down before the king and pleaded for his family and honored the king so much that the king was stirred with pity and forgave him the entire debt.

"In turn, that servant found a man who owed him a thousand dollars. He grabbed him, physically apprehending him by the throat, demanding full payment immediately. This fellow-servant kneeled and assured him that while he couldn't pay him at once, the debt would definitely be paid if he would only allow reasonable time. But the man was unwilling, and had the poor man thrown into debtors' prison.

"The other servants, seeing the incongruity and shame of what was done, reported the incident to the king.

The king was furious. He said to his servant, 'I forgave you a million dollars as you begged. Should you not have forgiven your fellow servant a thousand dollars? I acted in mercy toward you, shouldn't you have done the same?' Then the king cast this man into prison.

"That is My Father's attitude toward you. That is why you should go on forgiving indefinitely with sincerity."

JESUS IS IN FULL CONTROL

The Feast of Tabernacles was at hand. His natural half brothers, who did not at this time believe that Jesus was Messiah, challenged Jesus to go to the feast and there to demonstrate before the masses His powers.

Jesus replied, "The time is not yet right for Me to go to the feast, but you go ahead. I am aware the world hates Me for making them conscious of the evil they do."

THE CHALLENGE AND COST OF DISCIPLESHIP

Later, Jesus quietly left to attend the feast.

Along the way, someone said, "Jesus, I want to follow You wherever You go." Jesus responded, "Do you? Foxes have dens and birds have nests, but I have no place to call home."

To another, Jesus commanded, "You follow Me." But the man replied, "Let me first wait until my aged father dies, then I will go with You." Jesus said, "Let the spiritually dead care for the physical needs of the physically dying. You fulfill My mission for you."

A third man said, "I do want to follow You, Lord, but let me have a farewell party for my family and friends." Jesus said, "One who decides to follow Me, but keeps his eyes longingly on his past life, is not fit to be My disciple."

SURMISINGS ABOUT JESUS

Meanwhile, Jesus was a topic of gossip at the Feast in Jerusalem. Many questioned why He was not there. Some affirmed He was a good man, but others said He was a deceiver leading people astray. However, fear of the temple authorities kept the talk from becoming public debate.

IMPRESSED BY JESUS

During the Feast days, Jesus taught openly in the temple with a knowledge and authority that caused the Jews to question how He was so accomplished having never had school.

THOSE TESTING JESUS CONVICTED THEMSELVES

One morning at the temple, the Scribes and Pharisees brought to Jesus a woman actually caught in the act of adultery. They said, "The law requires this woman be stoned to death. What is Your teaching?"

Jesus said, "Let the stoning begin by the one of you who has not sinned casting the first stone."

The accusers, convicted by their conscious, began to leave until they had all left. Jesus said to the woman, "I do not condemn you. Go, and stop living in adultery."

TO RECOGNIZE TRUTH AND BE FREE

Jesus taught, "I am the light of the world. My followers will live in the light of life. One who lives in Me will know truth and be set free."

FROM DEATH TO LIFE

About this time, Jesus brought Lazarus back to life after he had died from an illness and been buried four days. Jesus, said, "I am the resurrection and the life. One who believes in Me may die physically but will live again because one who believes in Me will never really die."

SENT ON A MISSION

After these events, Jesus selected seventy disciples and placed them in pairs. He said, "The harvest is plentiful, but laborers are few. Pray that the Lord will send laborers to bring in the harvest, and go yourself into that harvest. I send you as lambs among wolves. Take no extra provisions, but allow those to whom you minister to care for your needs. Peace shall rest upon those households. The laborer is worthy of his hire. In each city, stay in one house and eat whatever they offer. Heal the sick and preach that the kingdom of God is near. When no one in a city will receive you, wipe the dust of that city off your shoes as a sign against them, and say, 'Be warned, even though you have rejected us, the kingdom of God is near.' One who listens to you, listens to Me. One who rejects you, rejects Me and the One who sent Me."

THE GREATEST DELIGHT

When their mission was complete, the seventy were delighted that God's power had been evidenced through them. Jesus said, "Be happy, not so much for this power that worked through you, but, more importantly, that your names are written in heaven. Many prophets and kings desired in vain to see and hear the things which you have seen and heard. You are privileged."

WHO IS MY NEIGHBOR

A lawyer, trying to trip up Jesus, asked, "Teacher, what shall I do to inherit eternal life?"

Jesus asked him, "What do you read in the law of Moses?" The lawyer replied, "Love the Lord God with all your heart, soul, and strength, and love your neighbor as yourself."

Jesus said, "You have answered correctly. Now do it, and you shall live." But the lawyer, to excuse his failures, said, "Who is meant by 'my neighbor'?"

Jesus answered with a story. "A man traveled from Jerusalem to Jericho. On the way, he was accosted by robbers who stripped him and beat him, leaving him nearly dead. A priest happened along that road, but seeing the desperate man, he crossed over to the other side and went on. Later, a Levite did the same. Then came a Samaritan, who upon seeing him, was compassionate to him, dressed his wounds, placed him upon his own horse and carried him to the nearest inn, where he further aided him. The next day he had to leave but he paid the inn keeper an advance and said, 'Take care of this injured man. When I return, I will pay any balance due.'

"Now, which of these three was neighbor to the man who was robbed?"

The attorney said, "The Samaritan who showed mercy."

Jesus said, "Your answer is correct. Go live similarly."

THE HIGHEST CHOICE

There came a time when Jesus went to the home of Mary and Martha for a rest. Martha was distracted by caring for the needs of the home, and by hostessing for the others and Jesus. But Mary sat at Jesus' feet listening to Him.

After a while, Martha asked the Lord, "Don't You care that Mary just sits there when she should be helping me serve You and the others. Please tell her to help me."

Jesus said, "Martha, you are worried and stress-filled over many things. Only one thing is truly needful. Mary has chosen it. Let's not deprive her of it."

A LESSON IN PRAYING

Once after the Lord had finished praying, His disciples requested, "Lord, teach us to pray." Jesus said, "When you pray, follow this example, 'Father, we reverence Your name. We await the coming of Your kingdom. Meanwhile, may Your will be done on Earth as it is in heaven. Please provide our day to day necessities. Forgive our sins and help us to forgive those who sin against us. Give us victory over sin and satan. We glorify You'."

PRAYERS ARE ANSWERED

Jesus said, "If one were to go to a friend's house at midnight and say to him, 'Friend, please lend me three loaves of bread, for another friend has just arrived from a long journey and I have nothing to serve him'; will your friend say, 'Don't bother me; I and my children are asleep'? No, even though it's inconvenient, he will give the requested bread to help his friend out of a problem.

"Similarly, you should ask and it will be given; seek and you will find; knock and it shall be opened. You who are imperfect give good things to your children, how much more does your perfect heavenly Father want to give the Holy Spirit to those who ask Him."

THE HIGHEST BLESSING

After the healing of a dumb man, a woman in the crowd shouted, "Blessed is Your mother." "Yes," responded Jesus, "and blessed are all who, like her, hear the word of God and keep it."

PROJECT AND PROTECT THE LIGHT

"No one lights a lamp to put it under a basket, but to sit it up where it will throw light all around so he can see. The lamp of the body is the eye. If you allow only light into your eye, then you live in light. If you allow darkness in your eye, then you are full of darkness and the light is gone. Be careful, lest that which you think is light is darkness."

INWARD MORE IMPORTANT THAN OUTWARD

A Pharisee invited Jesus to dinner. The Pharisee was amazed that Jesus ate without the customary Jewish religious washings.

Jesus said, "You Pharisees wash the outside of a cup while the inside is diseased. You perform ceremonial washings, but inside you are full of extortion and wickedness. You pay tithes on the smallest values, but you overlook being fair and just in your dealings, and you forget the love of God. You love prominent positions and to be publicly called by religious titles. You are like an open grave into which someone falls in the dark, or like an unmarked grave over which people walk unaware that death and decay are there."

A lawyer responded, "Teacher, You are not being kind."

Jesus replied, "You godless, greedy lawyers place heavy loads on the back of men, a load you would not want to bear. You build the arguments under which true prophets are killed. You have removed from those who follow you the key of honest knowledge. You do not recognize truth and you prevent others from following truth who otherwise would do so."

These words caused the Pharisees and lawyers to set themselves adamantly against Him and to seek to trap Him in His words, repeatedly asking Him loaded questions.

RELIGIOUS LEADERS ARE LIMITED IN AUTHORITY

Jesus said to His disciples in the hearing of the crowd, "Beware of the hypocrisy of the Pharisees. It permeates like leaven. But every hidden thing shall be revealed. Don't be afraid of the Pharisees. They are able to have you killed but that is the end of their power. Fear Him whose power extends to heaven and hell and eternity. We think sparrows worthless, but the omniscient, omnipotent God remembers each of them. And you -- He even knows the number of hairs on your head.

"Whoever admits publicly to being My disciple, I will publicly admit that one is Mine in heaven. But whoever publicly denies Me, I will deny that one is Mine in heaven. Whoever speaks against Me can be forgiven, but whoever speaks against the Holy Spirit can not be forgiven.

"When the Pharisees drag you before the religious authorities, don't be afraid. The all-wise Holy Spirit will be with you and give you words to say."

EMPHASIZE GODLINESS AND ETERNAL VALUES

A voice in the crowd yelled out, "Teacher, make my brother split the inheritance with me." Jesus said, "I'm not here to judge between brothers."

Then He said to them all, "Don't covet. A man's life is not made up of the number of things he can accumulate. Listen to this example:

"A man's ground produced very well for several years so that the man had no more room to store his grain or house his possessions. He decided to build bigger barns to hold the overflow. He said to himself, 'You have financial security. Relax. Eat, drink and be merry.' But God said, 'You fool. Tonight you will die. Then who will get all your accumulations?' So it is with anyone who only hoards for himself but is not rich toward God and eternal life.

"Don't be overly concerned about necessities of life. Life is more than food, clothing and shelter. Can you live longer by worrying about it? Consider the birds. God feeds them all. Consider the flowers. God cloths them. Even Solomon in his glory was not as free as a bird nor as dazzling as a lily.

"Have more faith. Don't be stressful on the one hand over providing your basic needs or certainly not on the other hand of hoarding wealth like the godless. Remember, your Father knows your needs. Make it your first priority to seek the kingdom of God, then your basic needs will be supplied. "

KEEP YOUR TREASURE IN HEAVEN

"Don't fear want. Your Father enjoys giving to you. You can sell your earthly hoardings and give to charity. Store your treasure in heaven where it is imperishable and secure. Where your treasure is, there also is your love and concern."

THE TEST OF ETERNAL RESPONSIBILITY

"Keep in a state of readiness for the Lord to return. Be prepared to welcome Him back at any time. When you least expect, the Lord will return. At that day, the ones to whom much was given will be required to show more results. The ones to whom little was given shall be required to show less results. Each must be faithful according to his ability, for according to ability and opportunity shall each be accountable."

JESUS DIVIDES OPINIONS

Jesus taught, "I bring a cleansing fire to earth. How wonderful if it were not needed. But I have a job to do and I am committed to fulfill it.

"In a sense I came to bring peace on earth and in another sense I came to bring division. In some families, the parents will be divided from their children, or one spouse from the other over Me. In other families, in-laws will be divided from in-laws because of Me."

TRAGIC EVENTS ARE NOT DIVINE RETRIBUTION

At that time, Pilate had some Galilaeans slaughtered while they were performing religious sacrifices. Some of the Jews said that God allowed these to be slain because of some terrible secret sins. About the same time, a tower fell and killed eighteen men in Jerusalem. The Jewish leaders were teaching that these, also, were killed because of especially heinous sins.

But Jesus said, "The Galilaeans who were slaughtered and the men killed in Jerusalem by the tower were no more sinful than anyone else. Catastrophes are not necessarily divine judgment on specific sins. All have sinned. All of you will perish eternally unless you repent."

MAKE CERTAIN YOUR FAITH IS IN THE GOOD SHEPHERD

As Jesus traveled in the cities and villages teaching, someone asked, "Lord, are only a few going to be saved?"

Jesus answered, "Be sure to walk through the narrow door while you have opportunity. Many will want to enter after God has shut the door. They will pound on the door for admittance, but it will be too late. Many tears will flow when some find themselves outside but see in the kingdom of God Abraham, Isaac and Jacob along with the prophets. Many inside will be from all areas of the globe, while many here today, who had the best opportunities, will be shut out. In that day, many who seemed first shall be last, and many who seemed last shall be first. Be sure of your own salvation."

Jesus taught, "I am the Good Shepherd who gives His life for the sheep and then reclaims His life. I know My sheep. Not all of them are yet in My fold. I am the door of the sheep fold. My sheep hear My voice and follow Me. I know them and give them eternal life. No one is able to snatch them from Me. They are given to Me by My Father, and no one could take them from My Father. I and My Father are One."

THE CONFIDENCE AND COMPASSION OF JESUS

At that time, some sympathetic Pharisees warned Jesus to run, for Herod had said he would kill Him.

Jesus said, "Go tell that fox that I will be working here for three days. He can not touch Me at this time."

Then Jesus said, "Oh, Jerusalem, Jerusalem. You have a history of killing prophets and stoning messengers of God. I want to gather you as a hen protects her chicks under her wings, but you refuse. Therefore, even your homes will be destroyed. Ironically, the next time you see Me, you will shout, 'Blessed is He who comes in the name of the Lord'."

LEADERS WITH MISPLACED ALLEGIANCE

One of the Pharisees asked Jesus to his home for the Sabbath meal.

As He was there, the religious rulers watched Him suspiciously. A man was brought who had epilepsy, and Jesus healed him -- an act which the religious leaders said constituted unlawfully working on the Sabbath.

Jesus looked squarely at the lawyers and Pharisees and asked, "Do you agree that I have done right under the law of Moses?" Though they hated what Jesus had done, no one answered. Jesus went on, "As I have asked you before, I ask you again, if one of your sons, or even your animals, fell into a hole on the Sabbath, would you rescue him, or let him die?" They still would not answer.

A LESSON ON PRIDE AND HUMILITY

Jesus then taught another lesson from His observations of their conduct and attitudes as they came to the dinner table. Each one had taken the most prestigious place he could.

"When you are invited to a feast, don't grab the seats of honor at the head table. What if someone of higher rank is intended for the chair you commandeered? The host will ask you to sit elsewhere, and you will be embarrassed before all. Instead, choose a place in the back of the room. How wonderful if the host asks you to take a place at the head table. You will then be honored by all. One who exalts himself will be humbled, but one who humbles himself will be exalted."

PROPER MOTIVATION AND PRIORITIES

Jesus spoke to the host who had invited him, "When you put on a feast like this, why ask politicians, or rich friends, or others who will return the favor? Then you will be further in their debt, or at best, you have gotten your reward for your kindness. It is better to invite the poor and needy to enjoy your generosity. They cannot repay you, but you will be rewarded in eternity.

"A certain man prepared a great feast and invited many important people. But each one had an excuse. One said he had contracted for some real estate which he needed to inspect. Another said he had bought some business equipment which he needed to try out. Another said he had gotten married and just couldn't get to the feast. All the invited sent their regrets. The host was angry and said to his employees, 'Go out and get the street people and those at the poor house. Go to the ordinary folks and encourage them to come enjoy the feast. My house will be full at dinner time, but I assure you, none of those who were first invited shall taste one bite.'

"So shall be the kingdom of heaven."

THOUGHTFUL DISCIPLESHIP

One day Jesus said to a crowd following him, "One who follows Me must be willing to forsake his family, to leave his possessions or even to lose his life for Me. Such a one is truly My disciple. You must be willing to bear your cross to follow Me.

"Consider this before you say you want to be My disciple. If a man starts to build a palatial estate, but runs out of money before he can finish it, people will mock and call him foolish. Salt is good, but if it has lost its saltiness it is worthless and housewives toss it out. These examples are similar to ones who start to follow Me but lose conviction. Count the cost; calculate the benefits; and be a consistent disciple. Are you listening?!"

SEEKING THE LOST

Jesus had become friends with many tax collectors and adulterers. These types of persons were often around Him, listening to His teachings. The religious leaders whispered, "Jesus befriends sinners and eats with them."

AS A LOST SHEEP

In response to this, Jesus spoke a parable. "If one of you had one hundred sheep, and one sheep got lost, would you not leave the ninety-nine and go after the one lost sheep until you had found it? And when you did find it, would you not be delighted? When you came in from the mountains, would you not tell the story to your friends and rejoice together because of finding one lost sheep? So those in heaven celebrate when one sinner repents."

AS A LOST COIN

"Similarly, if a woman losses one of a collection of ten valuable coins, doesn't she light all the lights, sweep the whole house and look diligently until she finds it? And when it's found, doesn't she call her friends and neighbors to share her delight? Much the same, there is joy among the angels when one sinner repents."

AS A LOST SON

"A man had two sons. The younger said, 'Father, give me now my share of the inheritance.' The father complied and gave him in cash his total inheritance. A few days later, the son took all his wealth and left for the city. There, he enjoyed fast living. When he had spent his entire fortune, he realized he would have to take a job. But the area was now in a recession and the only job he could find was feeding pigs. Friendless, he was so desperate that he ate the feed he gave the pigs. No one pitied him or offered assistance.

"One day he came to his senses and thought, 'Even the servants of my father have plenty to eat, and extra to give away. Yet I am dying of hunger. I will go to my father and confess, *I have sinned against heaven and against you. I am not worthy to be called your son. But please let me work for you as a servant.*' With this plan in mind, the fellow left the pigs and traveled home.

"When he was still a long way off, his father saw him and was overcome with love and pity, and ran to him and hugged and kissed him.

"The son said to his father, '*I have sinned against you and against heaven! I am not worthy to be called your son.*' But the father interrupted him and ordered servants, 'Bring my best clothes and dress my son. Put shoes on his feet and a ring on his finger. Break out the best steaks and prime rib and set a feast and prepare to celebrate. For this my son was dead and is alive again, he was lost but now is found.' And the festivities began.

"The older son had been working in the fields. As he came toward the house he heard all the commotion and saw dancing. He inquired of a servant what was going on. When the servant told of the celebration for his returned brother, the older son was furious and refused to join in the festivities. His father came out and asked him to be part of the occasion. But this eldest son said, 'All these years I have worked faithfully for you and have not disobeyed or dishonored you. Yet, never did you throw a party for me and my friends. But, as soon as my brother comes back home, who has wasted your wealth with gamblers and prostitutes, you put on a festival.' The father said, 'Son, you have always been here with me. Everything I have is yours. It is fitting to be happy and to celebrate, for your brother was as dead and is now alive, he was lost and is found.'

"So the Father in heaven rejoices over one soul who repents."

BE WISE AND HONEST IN MONETARY MATTERS

Jesus taught His disciples with another parable. "The accountant of a rich man was accused of wasting the rich man's money, perhaps skimming. The wealthy man called the accountant and said, 'Your honesty is questionable and I must terminate your employment. We will meet to review the books.'

"The accountant realized that an accountant terminated for dishonesty is unemployable as an accountant, and he was not capable of doing other types of work. Quickly he put a plan in action to endear himself to both his employer and to those who were indebted to his boss.

"He called the bad-risk creditors with past due accounts and negotiated a discount for immediate cash payment. One owed a hundred measures of oil, but the accountant told him fifty today would be full payment. Another owed one hundred measures of wheat, but the accountant accepted eighty today as payment in full. In similar fashion, he brought in all bad debts.

"The employer commended the accountant whom he had thought dishonest for bringing in the uncollectible debts at a discount instead of the whole amount being lost.

"Believers should take instruction from those wise in business. Use money wisely. It shall fail you on earth, but there are methods by which money can be sent on ahead to welcome you into eternal mansions.

"One faithful in tiny things will be faithful in important things; one dishonest in small things will be dishonest in big things. If you are dishonest over money, who will trust you for the welfare of their soul? You cannot serve two masters. You will always favor one. You cannot serve God and riches."

TO WHOM ARE YOU LOOKING GOOD

The Pharisees, hearing this teaching, laughed, because they loved money. Jesus said to them, "You look good to men but to God you look abominable. God sees your motives and knows what you love."

WHAT ABOUT DIVORCE

To change the subject, the Pharisees asked, "Can a man leave his wife for any justifiable reason?" Jesus said, "Scripture says that when a man leaves his mother and father to join his wife, they are made one; they are no longer separate. What God has made one, man should not divide."

A Pharisee responded, "But Moses provided for giving a divorce." Jesus said, "He accommodated your stubbornness, but that's not God's ideal. Some of you divorce and remarry as a kind of legalized adultery."

Jesus brought the subject back to the identity of true wealth. "There was a rich man who dressed lavishly, who lived in luxury, who entertained with levity and the finest libations. At his gate every day lay a beggar named Lazarus, covered with sores, hoping only to get some crumbs from the scraps that the rich man's servants threw to the dogs which licked his sores.

"In that condition, Lazarus died and was carried by angels to Abraham's bosom. The rich man also died and was buried.

"In the place of the dead, the rich man found himself in torment, but far off, he saw Abraham embracing Lazarus. He cried out, 'Pity me, Father Abraham, and send Lazarus that he might dip his finger in water and place one drop on my tongue, for I am tortured in flames.'

"But Abraham replied, 'Remember the many good things you enjoyed in your lifetime while you watched Lazarus suffer. Now it has changed, and he is in comfort while you are in anguish. There is a great barrier fixed between you and us. Those here who wish to help you cannot, and those there who wish to come here cannot.' The rich man continued, 'Please send Lazarus back to earth to warn my brothers, or they will come also to this place of torment.' But Abraham said, 'They have the scriptures. Let them listen to God's written word and heed that message.' But the rich man pleaded, 'No, Abraham. If one goes to them from the dead, then they will repent.' But Abraham assured him, 'If they do not obey the Bible they will not listen even though one is resurrected from the dead'." *(One has been permanently resurrected from death -- **Jesus**)*

GRATITUDE EXPRESSED OR NEGLECTED

On the way to Jerusalem by way of Samaria and Galilee, in a certain village Jesus was met by ten lepers who from a distance shouted, "Jesus, Master, have pity on us." Seeing them, Jesus ordered, "Go and show yourselves to the priest, as a healed leper is required to do." Though still covered with leprosy, they started in the direction of a priest, and as they went, they were healed. One of them, as soon as he noticed he was healed, turned back to Jesus and began with a loud voice to praise God. He bowed his face at the feet of Jesus and thanked Him. This man was a Samaritan.

Jesus asked, "Where are the other nine who were healed? Do they not give glory to God?" Then He spoke to the grateful man, "Stand up and go on your way in health and peace. Your faith is making you a whole man."

THE SECOND COMING OF JESUS WILL BE AWESOME AND PUBLIC

Some Pharisees taunted Jesus, "Your Kingdom, when is it coming?"

Jesus said, "You can't see God's kingdom, nor can you say it is here or there. It is within a person." Then He said to His disciples, "There is a time coming when you will want to see Me again. Some will say, 'Look, He has come back and is secretly with this group or in that place.' Do not believe such teachings. When I return, it will be as public as lightning that fills the sky. But before that occurs, I must suffer and be rejected by this generation. Then, as it was in the time of Noah, so will it be when I return. People ate, worked, partied, condoned sin, married and carried on as usual, until Noah went into the ark and the flood came and destroyed them all.

"Similarly in Lot's day, the people of Sodom, with no regard for God, took care of everyday needs, did normal business, invested, and reveled in life. But as Lot left Sodom, God in an instant destroyed that city and everyone in it.

"Before I return, people will be doing the ordinary things of life with no thought of Me. In that day, one who is relaxing in the yard should not go into the house to get belongings, or one who is at work should not go back home as Lot's wife tried. Whoever tries to save his wealth shall lose his life, but whoever sacrifices his life's gains shall save his life. That night, two shall be in one bed. One will be taken, the other left. Two will be working together. One will be taken, the other left. Everyone will be drawn to where this takes place as vultures attracted to a carcass -- the entire world will focus on the event."

HAVE PATIENCE REGARDING ANSWERS TO PRAYER

With another story Jesus encouraged His followers not to be weary in praying. "There was a crooked judge to whom a widow pleaded time and again, 'Do me justice with the one who hurts me.' The judge was indifferent a long time. However, the woman persisted and finally the judge reasoned, 'Though I do not care about justice, I will help this woman and rid her of her adversary in order to rid myself of her as a nuisance.' If such an unjust judge will care for a widow, surely a just God will care for His own. God is patient and hears your prayers. Nevertheless, when I return to earth, will I find anyone with faith in prayer?"

THE FAILURE OF SELF RIGHTEOUSNESS

Jesus gave another parable to a group who thought they were special, that their self-righteousness would save them, and that all who disagreed with their particular doctrines were wrong and inferior.

"Two men prayed at the temple. One was a very pious religious leader, and one a despised tax collector. The respected elder stood where he'd easily be seen and prayed proudly and loudly, 'God, I thank You that I am not like others, extortioners, unjust, adulterers, or even as this tax collector. I observe the required fasts, I fulfill required temple rituals, I give the required tithes, I wear the proper garments, I am a very religious man.'

"But the tax collector, stood in a corner, bowed his head and beat his fist on his chest as a sign of contrition, and quietly said, 'God, have mercy on me, the sinner.'

"I assure you," said Jesus, "this man went home forgiven and justified before God, but not the Pharisee. He who exalts himself shall be humbled, and he who humbles himself shall be exalted."

JESUS HUGS LITTLE CHILDREN

Families were bringing little children to Jesus for Him to touch them and pray. But the disciples tried to stop them.

Jesus, disappointed with His disciples at this, said, "Allow little children to come to Me. Do not prevent them. To such as these belongs the kingdom of God, for only those who receive Me with the attitude of a little child shall gain entrance." Then He held the girls and boys, praying with each one.

CHOOSING WEALTH ABOVE GOD

A young man of the ruling class kneeled and asked Jesus, "Good Teacher, what must I do to inherit eternal life?" Jesus said, "You called Me good, realizing that only God is truly good. The commandments are familiar to you -- Do not kill, or commit adultery, or steal, or lie about others, and do honor your father and mother, and love your neighbor the same as you love yourself." The man replied, "I have kept these truths since I was a child." Jesus was drawn to the man and said, "You lack one thing to have complete understanding. Sell all you own, give the proceeds to the poor, and come follow Me. You will have treasure in heaven." When the young man heard that, he left with a sad heart, for it was his wealth with which he was in love.

ETERNAL PRIORITIES AND REWARDS

Jesus looked at His disciples, "It is difficult for a rich person, or anyone who finds security in riches, to enter the kingdom of heaven. With man it is impossible, but with God everything is possible."

Peter said, "We have left it all to follow You."

Jesus responded, "One who leaves a business, investments, position, home or loved ones for Me shall be repaid many times over in this life and in the life to come. But many who think they are first shall be last, and many thought last shall be placed first.

"For the kingdom of heaven is like a farmer who early in the morning hires laborers to work his field all day for a set wage. At midday the farmer finds unemployed workers whom he also sends to work the same field. Late in the afternoon, he finds still other idle workers whom he also puts to work in the same field, agreeing to pay them a fair wage at the end of the day.

"At sundown, the farmer calls in all the workers and pays them all the same wage that he had agreed upon with the first ones whom he had hired and set to work just after sunrise. Those who worked all day began to complain to the farmer, 'You paid those who worked just a short time the same as you paid us who worked through the heat and dust of the entire day. It's not fair.' But the farmer said, 'Friend, did I not pay you the wage to which we had agreed? Take what you have earned, but do not be angry with me if I choose to be generous to the others. May I not do what I choose with my own money? Don't let my goodness to others cause jealousy in your heart?' This is another example of how the first shall be last and the last shall be first."

JESUS PREPARES HIS FOLLOWERS FOR HIS SUFFERING AND DEATH AND RESURRECTION

Continuing to Jerusalem, Jesus told His disciples, "I will be given over to the chief priests and scribes. They shall condemn Me to death and deliver Me to the Romans to carry out the sentence. I shall be mocked, beaten, shamefully treated, spit upon, and crucified. The third day I shall rise to life again."

The disciples didn't understand what Jesus was saying.

IMPROPER PRAYER REQUEST DENIED

James and John, the sons of Zebedee, came with their mother to Jesus and worshipped Him. They said, "You have told us that whatever we ask, You will give us." Jesus said, "State your wish." The mother said, "Grant that my sons will set on Your right and left hands in Your kingdom." "Yes," said the men, "Let us sit in the seats of honor with You in Your glory."

THE HONOR OF SERVING

Jesus said, "You don't know what you ask. Those seats are for whom My Father has prepared that honor." The other disciples were angry with James and John for making this request.

Jesus said, "Rulers of earth lord it over their subjects and relish their authority over others. It is not to be so among you. Whoever desires to be great among you must be your servant, and one desiring to be first must serve many. I did not come to be served but to serve and to give My life as a ransom."

A BLIND MAN HEALED

Near Jericho, as they went along the road, a blind man asked what the commotion was about. He was told that Jesus of Nazareth was passing by. The blind man got excited and began to yell out, shouting at the top of his voice, "Jesus, Son of David, have mercy on me! Jesus, take pity on me!"

Those near him ordered him to be quiet, but he only screamed louder. Jesus stopped and called for the man to be brought. "State what you want," said Jesus.

Said the blind man, "Lord, that I may see."

Jesus said to him, "Receive your sight, your faith has made you whole." Immediately the man could see. He began to praise God and, when the people around saw him, they joined in his praise of God. The man followed Jesus.

A NOTORIOUS SINNER CONVERTED

In Jericho lived a very rich chief tax collector. This Zacchaeus wanted to see Jesus, but because he was short, could not see over the crowd. He went ahead of the masses and climbed a sycamore tree under which Jesus must pass. When Jesus got to the place, He looked up and said, "Hurry and come down, Zacchaeus. I'd like to stay at your house today." The tax collector got down and with joy invited Jesus to his home.

When the religious leaders saw this, they said, "Look! He has gone to lodge with a major sinner."

In contrast to their holier-than-thou attitude, Zacchaeus committed to Jesus, "To make restitution for cheating, half of all I have I will give to the poor. To those I have wrongfully taxed, I will repay four hundred percent."

Jesus said, "This household has experienced salvation. I am come to find and to save those who know they are lost."

USE WELL WHAT YOU HAVE WHILE JESUS IS GONE

Getting near Jerusalem, because the people still expected Jesus to introduce immediately the visible kingdom of God on earth, Jesus gave them another parable.

"A Nobleman went to a distant country to receive to himself a kingdom and to return. Before leaving, he met with ten servants, giving to each one a thousand dollars with instructions to invest it in enterprise until his return. When he came back from his journey, the master called his servants for an accounting. The first one had earned $10,000 dollars. The master said, 'Well done. You were faithful in small things, you will rule ten cities in my new kingdom.' Another came who had earned $5000 dollars. 'Very well done,' said the master, 'be ruler over five cities.' As the accounting continued, one came who reported, 'Here is your $1000 safely returned. I feared to do anything with the money. I know you are demanding, so I hid your money and kept it safe.' The master said, 'Your own words are that I am a demanding person. You should have at least put my money where it would have earned interest.' Then he said to a supervisor, 'Take the $1000 from this fellow and give it to the man who earned $10,000.' 'But master,' the supervisor questioned, 'that fellow already has $10,000.' 'Yes,' said the master, 'to the one who has used his talents shall more be given, and from the one who does nothing with the talent he was given shall be taken away even the little that he has'."

In the city of Bethany, where Jesus had raised Lazarus from the tomb, Jesus was invited to dinner in the home of Simon the Leper. Lazarus and his sisters were with Jesus at this meal. Martha helped serve, but Mary took some expensive oil and anointed the head and feet of Jesus, similar to what she had done before in her own home. A magnificent aroma filled the whole house. Some in attendance were indignant and said among themselves, "What a waste of money". As before, Judas Iscariot said, "I still think this type of fine oil should be sold and the money given to the poor?" (He wanted this as treasurer, for he skimmed from the funds. He didn't really care about the poor.)

Jesus said, "This woman anoints My body for burial. The poor will always be among you but I will soon be gone. What she has done should be told everywhere for she does it as a memorial to Me."

BELIEVING IN JESUS BECAUSE OF LAZARUS

When the crowds heard Jesus was with Lazarus, they came to see Jesus and the man raised from the dead. Because of Lazarus, many believed on Jesus. Therefore, the jealous chief priests took counsel to kill Lazarus as well as Jesus.

TRIUMPHANT ENTRY

Jesus selected two disciples and instructed them, "Go into that village and as you enter you will find a donkey with a colt on which no one has ever sat. Bring the colt to Me."

When the unbroken colt was brought to Jesus, they placed a coat on it and Jesus sat on him. People began to spread palm branches and garments in the road, and began shouting, "Blessed is the King who comes in the name of the Lord. Hosanna to the Son of David, Hosanna in the highest."

The Pharisees said, "Teacher, rebuke Your followers."

Jesus said, "If these are quiet, the stones will shout."

JESUS WAS SAD OF HEART FOR THE PEOPLE

Approaching Jerusalem, Jesus wept and said, "If you knew today who could give you peace...! But your eyes are blind. Your enemies will conquer you and shall destroy you with your children. Because you do not recognize your Savior, not one stone of the temple will be left standing on another."

As the procession entered the city, bystanders asked, "For whom is the parade?" The marchers said, "It's the Prophet, Jesus from Nazareth of Galilee."

To onlookers, it seemed as if the whole world were crusading for Jesus.

DISRUPTING DISHONEST BUSINESS IN THE HOUSE OF GOD

Jesus went into the temple, and, observing the greedy merchandising going on there, He threw out those who were profiting by the sale of animals for sacrifice, or by changing money to facilitate the payment of the temple tax, or by buying and selling other religious commodities. He scolded them, "The scripture says, 'My house shall be a place of prayer, but you have made it a haven for charlatans and dishonest business'."

For this costly and embarrassing action, the scribes and other temple leaders resolved to destroy Him, but were not willing to take action at that time because the worshippers respected His teaching and were enamored with Him.

THE BUSINESS OF GOD IN THE HOUSE OF GOD

As the lame and blind came to Jesus in the temple courtyard and were healed, children were shouting, "Praise to the Son of David!" The chief priests and scribes, watching, were overcome with anger and jealousy, and said to Jesus, "Don't You hear the adulation these are giving You?" Jesus, ignoring the implied accusation that worship of Him was improper, said, "The scripture says, 'Perfect praise shall come from the mouths of children and babies'."

MOVING MOUNTAINS AND REMOVING JUDGMENTS

That evening, as they walked along, returning to lodge at Bethany, Jesus taught, "If you have faith in God and say to a mountain, 'Move out of the way' it will obey. Whatever you ask in prayer, with belief, you will have. Remember to forgive others when you prayer just as you desire My Father to forgive you."

INSINCERE RELIGIOUS LEADERS

As He walked in the temple one day thereafter, a delegation of chief priests, scribes and elders accosted Him and asked, "Who gives You the authority to teach as You do and to remove businesses from the temple steps?"

Jesus responded, "Tell Me who was the authority for the ministry of John the Baptist and I will tell you who is Mine."

The leaders felt trapped, for if they said John's message was authorized from heaven, Jesus would ask why they did not follow it, for John testified that Jesus was the Messiah; but if they said John was only a deranged preacher, then they would alienate the people, for the people believed John was a prophet of God. Therefore, they said, "We haven't researched that question adequately, and do not wish to answer."

LEADERS WHO LEAD AWAY FROM GOD

Jesus said, "Neither will I answer you. But let Me tell you a story. A man had two sons. He told both to go work in his fields. The one said, 'No, I do not want to work today', but later he was ashamed of himself and went to work. The other said, 'I'll go to work right away', but he never went. Which of the two sons did as the father asked?"

They replied, "The one who actually went to work."

Jesus said, "Yes, and you're like the one who did no work though you profess to serve God. You say you are leaders for God, you have a beautiful temple for your religion, but you rejected God's man, John. When common sinners accepted him, and you saw their renewed lives, you still would not change your attitude. The common sinners who believe will go into the kingdom of heaven without you."

DISHONEST AND MURDEROUS LEADERS

"Listen to another illustration. A businessman moved to a different city leaving his business in the management of others. At proper times, he sent assistants to collect a distribution of the profits from the managers. The managers embarrassed his assistants and sent them away empty. The owner sent other representatives and they also were treated shamefully and sent away with nothing. Then the owner sent his own son, expecting the managers to respect his offspring. But the managers said, 'This is the only son, the sole heir. Let's kill him and perhaps we will inherit the business.'

"What actions will the business owner take? He will have those murdering managers executed, and will hire other management who will distribute the profits to the owner."

The religious leaders realized these stories were about them, and they were irate. They rededicated themselves to destroy Jesus whenever they could sway the people against Him.

MANY ARE SOLICITED BUT FEW ARE SELECTED

Jesus told another parable. "The kingdom of heaven has similarity to a king, who after preparing a marriage feast for his son, sent his servants to bring those who had been invited. But the invited guests would not come, giving various excuses. The king's servants were treated shamefully and some even murdered. The king was incensed and sent his army to destroy those killers and their city. Then he ordered his servants to go out and bring to the wedding feast anyone they saw, rich or poor, friend or stranger. The servants brought in many and provided a wedding garment for all to put on.

"The tables were filled with guests when the king came in, but he saw one who was not wearing the wedding garment provided. When he asked the man why he did not have on the garment given him, the man was speechless. The king ordered his servants to throw him out and said, 'Many are solicited, but only a few are selected'."

BALANCE EARTHLY AND HEAVENLY OBLIGATIONS

The Pharisees, intending to cause Jesus to break a Roman law, tried to ensnare Him with this question, "Is it right to pay taxes to Caesar?"

Jesus said, "Show me a coin."   Looking at the coin, Jesus asked, "Whose image is on this coin?"

They replied, "Caesar's."

Said Jesus, "Give to Caesar the things that belong to Caesar, and give to God the things that belong to God."

Hearing this, the Pharisees were dumbfounded and went away.

EARTHLY REASONING VS HEAVENLY REALITY

The Sadduccees, who do not believe that the dead will be resurrected, once approached Jesus and asked, "A woman died who had been the wife of seven husbands. If there is a resurrection, whose wife will she be?"

Replied Jesus, "You err because you do not understand the scripture nor God's power to give everlasting life. In resurrection life there is no marriage, but all will live as do the angels in heaven. Be assured, God is the God of the living, not of the dead; and scripture says that God is the God of your forefathers who long since were buried. These all are alive with Him." This silenced the insincere questioners.

THE ESSENCE OF THE ENTIRE LAW OF GOD

A lawyer asked, "Which commandment is greatest?"

Jesus said, "You shall love the Lord God with all your heart, soul and mind. And the second is, You shall love your neighbor as you love yourself. Within these two commands lies the intent of the entire law as it relates to both God and man."

MESSIAH IS ETERNAL

In the debate, Jesus asked the questioners, "Who's Son is the Messiah?" The religious leaders answered, "He is the Son of King David." (i.e.: a descendant -- heir to the throne)

Jesus asked, "Why then did David call Messiah Lord? Since David clearly calls Messiah his Lord, how could King David be father (i.e.: forebear) of Messiah?"

BEWARE FALSE RELIGIOUS LEADERS

Jesus turned to the crowd, "Beware of religious leaders who like to label themselves counselors, prophets, elders and priests. They like to dress in symbols of their position, to be publicly called an authority, and to be assigned prestigious places. They give themselves exclusive signs and passes into secret chambers. They set up priesthoods and call themselves prophets. They do good deeds to be praised by men. They demand to be given the estates of widows even while for a pretense they make pious prayers. These are destined for the worst kind of condemnation, for in the name of religion they make people worse off spiritually than they were before. These are hypocrites, setting up rules, doctrines and covenants that supposedly came from God, while they call God a liar. They are blind leaders of the blind, while they and their fathers are full of sin. They will not escape the judgment of hell."

<u>GODLY GIVING</u>

Jesus sat down near the treasury box and noticed those putting in contributions. Many wealthy men put in large amounts out of their riches. And a poor widow put in two dollars. Jesus said to his disciples, "That poor woman has just given to God more than all the others combined. They gave a small portion of their excess affluence, but she gave all she had to live on today."

<u>THE DESTRUCTION OF THE TEMPLE PREDICTED</u>

As Jesus left the temple, the disciples remarked at how elegant and excellent was the structure, even being made of special stones that were memorials of personal contributions.

Jesus warned, "Yes, look at it. But there will one day not be two stones left together. It will be entirely destroyed."

<u>JUDAS AGREES TO ENTRAP JESUS</u>

By night Jesus went to the mount of Olives, and by day He taught in the temple where the people arrived early to listen.

Jesus said to His disciples, "In two days begins the Passover Feast. I will be turned over to the authorities to be crucified."

The chief priests were plotting to kill Jesus, but did not want to take Him during the Feast because of the potential for a riot.

Judas Iscariot, however, one of the disciples, went to the religious authorities and told them that, for the right price, he could deliver Jesus to them without a public display. When offered thirty pieces of silver, Judas agreed to lead them to Jesus in a quiet, out of the way place. He began watching for the right occasion in a secluded setting.

<u>PREPARING FOR THE PASSOVER FEAST</u>

On the day in which the Passover lamb was sacrificed, some of the disciples asked Jesus where He would like for them to prepare to observe the Passover Feast.

Jesus instructed, "Go into the city and follow a man carrying a water pitcher. Say to the owner of the house into which he enters, 'The Teacher is inquiring about the room in which He will eat the Passover with His followers.' The owner will show you an upstairs room furnished for the occasion. Prepare it for our Feast together."

The disciples, following directions and finding everything just as Jesus said, prepared for the Passover.

THE GREATNESS OF SERVICE EXEMPLIFIED BY JESUS

That evening, Jesus was aware that the time of His sacrificial execution was at hand. Sitting at the table with His twelve followers, He heard them begin again to argue who among them would be greatest in heaven.

Jesus wrapped a towel around Himself and washed His disciples' feet. When He was through, He taught, "It is natural to want to be lord over others. But among you, greater is the one who serves than the one who is served. I, the Lord, have washed your feet to set an example for you to follow. You will be happy if you live this way."

JUDAS LEAVES

"One among us will betray Me," said Jesus.

John was very close to Jesus, so Peter motioned for him to ask Jesus whom He meant. Each disciple wondered if it would somehow be him.

Judas asked, "Is it I?"

Jesus replied, "What you must do, do now."

After Judas left, Jesus said, "It's now time for My glorification."

SHARING BREAD AND WINE

Jesus took a loaf of bread, blessed it, broke it in pieces, gave it to them, and said, "This is My body. Remember Me."

Then He took a goblet and said, "This is the new promise, sealed by My blood which I will shed to remit sin."

JESUS SHARES INTIMATELY WITH HIS DISCIPLES

Jesus continued, "I will be with you only a little while longer. Continue to love each other in such a way that everyone will know that you are My followers. Tonight, all of you will be embarrassed over Me and will run from Me. After I am raised from the dead, I will go ahead of you into Galilee. Meet me there."

But Peter said, "Lord, I will never desert You."

Jesus said, "Peter, before the rooster crows three times in the morning you will have denied Me three time."

Peter and the others assured Jesus they would never desert Him, and showed Him that they had two swords among them.

Jesus said, "Don't live in doubt. Believe in Me as you believe in God. I will prepare a place for you in heaven."

Thomas asked, "Where is heaven and how can we get there?"

Jesus said, "I am the way, the truth and the life. No one gets to My Father's house except by Me. Because you know Me, you know My Father. One who has seen Me, has seen My Father. I and My Father are One. If you love Me, you will obey Me. To those who obey Me, I will reveal Myself. I will live within you by My Spirit."

Singing a hymn, they went, as had become routine, to the mount of Olives.

Jesus said as they walked, "I am like a vine and you are like branches. You get your life and fruitfulness from Me. Live in My love. Love each other as I have loved you. Pray in My name and your joy will be complete."

JESUS PRAYS IN GETHSEMANE

In the garden, Gethsemane, Jesus said to His disciples, "Sit here while I go on ahead to pray alone."

But Peter, James and John He took a little farther with Him and said to them, "My soul is deeply disturbed looking forward to My death. Stay here and pray with Me."

Then Jesus went on a few steps and prayed, "Father, if there is any other way, release Me from this mission. I have finished My task on Earth except for this hour. I will bring glory to You as You have given glory to Me. I have given eternal life to those You gave Me. Eternal life is knowing You, the only true God, through Jesus Christ whom You sent. "

He looked back and saw the three disciples asleep. He awoke them and said, "Could you not pray with Me a short time? Be alert and pray that you not yield to the coming temptation. I know your spirit is willing, it's your bodies that are weak."

He went back to pray a second time, "Father, since My sacrifice is the only means of salvation, let Your will be done. I pray for those who believe in Me. I have given them Your word and the world hates them for it. I do not ask that You take My own out of the world, but that You keep them from its evil. Keep them set apart through Your word of truth. I send them into the world as you sent Me. I pray for them who will believe on Me through their work. I want those who believe in Me to be with Me, to see My glory which I had with You before the world was created. I want to give them My glory."

He turned to His disciples, and again they were asleep.

He prayed on alone, agonizing over the prospect of becoming sin for mankind. Then He said to the disciples, "You can't sleep now, I'm being betrayed to My executioners."

THE BETRAYAL

Judas appeared at that moment with armed guards, approached Jesus, and greeted Him with a kiss.

Jesus said, "Judas, would you use the kiss of friendship to betray Me? Don't waste time, finish your task."

Judas stepped aside and soldiers seized Jesus.

Peter reacted by slashing out with a short sword, severing an ear of one of the servants to the high priest. Jesus instructed Peter to put away his weapon, and healed the amputated ear with a touch.

Jesus said to the guards, "It's out of the ordinary that you didn't take Me when I was teaching at the temple, but you have fulfilled scripture by using clandestine tactics."

At that, all the disciples ran for their lives.

JESUS ARRAIGNED BEFORE THE HIGH PRIEST

Jesus was brought before high priest Caiaphas. Being unsuccessful in seeking witnesses to testify something against Jesus for which He could be executed, Caiaphas asked Jesus, "Are you the Messiah, the Son of God?"

Jesus responded, "Yes, I am. One day you will see Me sitting at the right hand of God and coming back to earth with the armies of heaven."

The high priest raved, "We need no other witness. We have heard His blasphemy. He should be put to death."

The temple guards began to spit on Jesus, to hit Him with weapons, and to mock Him.

Peter had secretly followed those who kidnapped Jesus and was warming himself by a fire in the temple courtyard with some officers. A temple housekeeper asked him, "Are you not one of the followers of Jesus?"

Peter denied it in front of all those staring at him.

Peter left to find refuge in an entry way. But presently the maid followed him and seeing him in the entry, said, "Certainly you are one of the disciples."

Peter denied it vehemently.

After a while, those around Peter said, "We think you are one of them because you speak with the accent of a Galilean."

Peter began to curse and to swear by oaths that he never ever knew Jesus.

At that instant Jesus was able to see Peter, and their eyes met. Peter, remembering how Jesus had said he would deny Him three times, rushed out in bitter tears, and, as he was leaving, he heard the roosters crowing. Deep was his remorse.

JESUS BEFORE THE COUNCIL

At daylight assembled the ruling elders of the people with the chief priest and scribes and the entire council. They asked Jesus, "Did You claim to be the Messiah, the Son of God?"

Jesus said, "You have said the truth."

This combined group of leaders confirmed that Jesus should be executed on the charge of claiming to be Son of God.

SUICIDE OF JUDAS

Judas, upon seeing the condemnation of Jesus, regretted his own participation in this treachery. But instead of going to Jesus for forgiveness, he took the thirty pieces of silver to the chief priests. "Take back your money", he said, "I betrayed an innocent Man."

Having flung the money at their feet, he went out and hanged himself, and in the hanging was disemboweled.

The chief priests agreed that blood money could not be put into the temple treasury, so with it they purchased from a potter a field in which to bury strangers. They unwittingly in this way fulfilled another prophecy which said, "They shall take His price, thirty pieces of silver, and buy a potter's field."

JESUS BEFORE PILATE

To obtain a sentence of crucifixion, the Jewish rulers took Jesus to Pilate, the Roman governor. Accusers said, "This man told us not to pay tribute to Caesar, and claimed to be Himself our King."

Pilate asked Jesus, "Are you the King of the Jews?"

Jesus said, "Yes, that is truth."

Pilate said, "What is truth?" And not waiting for an answer, he left the courtroom.

Upon returning Pilate asked Jesus more questions, but Jesus no longer answered.

Pilate went out again to the mob and said, "I find no fault in this Man." But the Jews became outraged, saying, "He caused trouble all over Judea and Galilee and here."

JESUS BEFORE HEROD

Learning Jesus was Galilean, Pilate sent Him to Herod Antipas, ruler of Galilee visiting Jerusalem.

Herod was delighted to hear Jesus, hoping to see a miracle. But as Herod questioned Him, Jesus never responded. Herod and his soldiers, therefore, put a royal robe on Him and began to deride and mock Him.

When their game grew boring, Herod sent Jesus back to Pilate.

TO PILATE AGAIN

Pilate called the Jewish officials into conference and said, "Neither Herod nor I find any guilt in this Man. I should let Him go. Besides, it is the custom at the feast of Passover that I release for you one prisoner. I suggest we release Jesus."

But the Jewish officials responded, "Release the zealot Barabbas."

JESUS OR BARABBAS

Pilate, realizing it was envy which made the rulers hate Jesus, wanted to let Him go. But the chief priests and elders incited the crowd to riot, chanting "Release Barabbas. Release Barabbas."

Pilate said, "Barabbas is a murderer. What evil has Jesus ever done?" But the crowd went wild and in a frenzy shouted, "Crucify Jesus!"

Seeing he couldn't prevail, Pilate took a bowl of water, washed his hands before them and said, "I am innocent of the death of this righteous Man. It is your responsibility."

The people said, "Let His blood be on us and on our posterity."

Then Pilate sentenced Jesus to be beaten and crucified, and ordered Barabbas to be released.

The soldiers took Jesus into the Praetorium. Stripping Him naked, they put a royal robe on Him, pressed a crown of thorns on His head and put a reed in His hand. Then they mockingly said, "Hail, King of the Jews", and bowed to Him. Simultaneously, they spit on Him and beat Him.

When they tired of this derision, they took off the purple robe, put His own clothing on Him, and led Him out to be crucified.

ANOTHER GOOD SAMARITAN

They laid a cross on Jesus' back and made for Golgotha. When Jesus fell along the way, a man identified as Simon of Cyrene was ordered to carry the cross for Jesus.

THE CRUCIFIXION

With His crime written on a sign over His head, "Jesus of Nazareth, The King of the Jews", Jesus was crucified between two criminals.

The soldiers had again stripped Jesus, and now they tore His garments at the seams, each taking part of the cloth. But His robe being seamless, they gambled for it in one piece, fulfilling another prophecy by these actions.

Jesus was heard to say, "Father, forgive them; they do not realize what they are doing."

Many passersby and onlookers, as well as the soldiers, taunted Jesus, "You saved others. Save Yourself!" And the scoffing continued.

The religious leaders laughed at Him and joked, "You are the King of Israel, save Yourself! You are the Son of God, won't Your Father deliver You?"

Even the criminals being crucified with Him derided Him, "Save Yourself, and us!"

CONVERSION ON A CROSS

One of the dying criminals changed his mind and said, "I am justly being crucified for a crime I committed, but Jesus is wholly innocent."

Then speaking directly to Jesus he said, "Jesus, please think of me someday when You arrive in Your heavenly kingdom."

Jesus said, "I assure you, this day you will be with Me in Paradise."

SALVATION IS COMPLETED

At this time, it became completely dark for three hours.

When it began to be light again, Jesus said, "My God, My God, why have You forsaken Me?" Then, knowing He had fulfilled His mission, Jesus said, "**It is finished**. Father, into Your hands I send My spirit." At that instant, He voluntarily died.

CONVERTED CENTURION

At the moment of His death, the veil of the temple was torn without hands from the top to the bottom and there were great earthquakes.

The centurion who stood nearby Him heard Jesus dismiss His Spirit and die, and then immediately felt the earthquakes, and remembering the earlier darkness, he said, "Truly this is the Son of God."

Among the women at the crucifixion were Mary the mother of Jesus, Mary Magdalene, Mary the mother of James and Joses, and Salome.

MORE PROPHESIES FULFILLED

The Jews did not want the bodies left on the crosses through a Sabbath, especially during Passover. They asked Pilate to order the legs of those crucified to be broken, thus hastening their deaths.

As the soldiers broke legs, they did not break the legs of Jesus for He was already dead. A soldier instead ran a spear into His side, which released from Jesus' abdominal cavity a buildup of blood mixed with watery fluids.

This fulfilled prophecies of Messiah that none of His bones would be broken and that He would be pierced.

THE BURIAL

On the council that had condemned Jesus, sat Joseph of Arimathaea, a Pharisee. He had dissented in the council's decisions against Jesus, for he was a secret disciple of Jesus and a good man. Joseph asked Pilate for the body of Jesus, to bury it.

After Pilate checked with the centurion to confirm Jesus' death, it was so ordered.

Joseph, with Nicodemus, lowered the corpse from the cross, hurriedly prepared it for burial and laid it in a tomb owned by Joseph. The tomb had been cut out of solid rock, and after the body was interred, a huge rock was rolled against the opening.

Mary Magdalene and Mary the mother of James and Joses, lingering near the tomb, were there and observed all this. After the tomb was shut, these women went home to prepare ointment and spices to further anoint the body after Sabbath.

THE TOMB SECURED

The chief priests approached Pilate and said, "Sir, Jesus said He would rise from death after three days. Please order a guard at the tomb to prevent His disciples from taking the body and claiming that He rose from the dead."

After confirming Jesus' death and place of interment, Pilate said, "Take guards. Seal the stone closure with my seal. Secure the tomb."

So the tomb was inspected, the stone was sealed and the guard was set.

LIFE OVERCOMES DEATH

Early in the morning, while still dark as Sabbath was ending, Mary Magdalene prepared to go the short distance to the tomb. As Sunday was dawning, she and Mary the mother of James and Joses, with Salome and Joanna took to the grave the spices which they had prepared to finish anointing Jesus' body.

Suddenly there was a great earthquake and an angel rolled away the rock at the door of the tomb, and sat on it. He was as bright as lightning and his robe was brilliant white. In terror, the guards fell down as dead.

With the guards disposed, the women, after regaining some composure, timidly approached the tomb. They now saw a young man sitting inside in a white robe. They were again overcome. But the man stood and said, "Don't be shocked. Jesus who was crucified has risen from the dead. Look here where He had been laid."

Outside, an angel said, "Don't look for the Living among the dead. Jesus is alive. Remember He said He would go ahead of you to Galilee after He was crucified, for He'd rise again on the third day. Go and tell His disciples."

<u>CONFIRMING THE RESURRECTION</u>

The women ran from the tomb, hardly able to speak from amazement and terror. To report the empty grave, Mary Magdalene ran to Peter and John; and the other women hurried to the other disciples. None believed them, but Peter and John ran to see for themselves. In the tomb they saw empty but undisturbed grave clothes with the folded face napkin, and they believed. *(Note: no natural body could vacate still-wound grave linen; and thieves, even if friends of Jesus, would in their frightened rush have taken the body wrapped. The disciples would later die terrible deaths to verify their testimony that Jesus was alive.)*

Mary Magdalene had returned alone to the grave site and was crying. Jesus appeared to her and said, "Mary." She turned and said, "Teacher!" Jesus said, "Tell My disciples." Mary ran and told a group of disciples, "Now I have seen the Lord alive." Again they would not believe her.

Jesus appeared to the other women, who worshipped Him. He sent them to tell the remaining disciples that they had now seen Him alive.

About this time Jesus showed Himself alive to Peter.

<u>A COVERUP PLOT</u>

During the time the women were breaking their news to the disciples, the tomb guards reported the resurrection to the chief priests. The priests consulted among themselves and paid these guards a large bribe in exchange for their agreement to say the disciples stole Jesus' body while the guards slept. The priests assured the guards that disciplinary action taken due to negligence would be bought off through the guards' superiors and no penalty would be carried out. With that assurance, the guards took the money and agreed to the fabrication. *(Note: How could sleeping guards identify alleged grave robbers?!)*

WALKING AND TALKING WITH THE LIVING LORD

Later, while two of Jesus' disciples walked to Emmaus, they talked about the death and burial of Jesus, and the story of the women. Jesus appeared to them, but in such a way that they did not know who He was. He asked what it was they were discussing. They said, "You must be the only one in the area who doesn't know these events. A Prophet of God, a miracle worker, Jesus of Nazareth was crucified. We hoped He was the Messiah. Today is the third day since His burial, and some of the women who also believed in Him said that when they visited His tomb this morning, it was empty, except for an angel who told them Jesus was alive from the dead. Two of our men went immediately to the tomb and confirmed it empty except for undisturbed grave clothes and a folded face napkin."

Jesus said to them, "It was right for the Messiah to suffer and die and then to be glorified. That is what all the prophets said." Then He explained to them the scriptures concerning Messiah, the promised redeemer.

When the travelers arrived home, not realizing who it was, but wanting more of this stranger's teaching, they invited Him to dine with them. At the table, Jesus broke bread, blessed it and passed it to them. At that moment, they were able to recognize who He was, but He vanished from the room.

They said, "No wonder our hearts were on fire as He taught scripture."

PHYSICAL EVIDENCES

These two rushed back to Jerusalem that same evening to tell the other disciples their experience of seeing Jesus alive. But the others found it impossible to believe. Just then, even though the place was secured, Jesus appeared to them. They were scared to death, thinking Him an apparition.

Jesus said, "Don't be terrified. Be at peace. I am Jesus. You should be ashamed that you have not believed the others who have told you they have <u>seen Me alive. Look here at My hands and feet and side. Go ahead, touch Me. I have flesh and bone. I am no ghost</u>." 17) Luke 24: 36-43; John 20: 19-29

Having seen and touched Him, the disciples were overcome with joy, but still afraid this was a dream.

Jesus said, "Look, I am eating fish and honey. It is really I." Seeing the fish that had been on the table consumed by Jesus, these disciples were convinced they were not dreaming, but that this in fact was the Lord, and not just a vision. [17] Jesus said, "Yes, enjoy My peace. Now, much as the Father sent Me, I am sending you, in the power of the Holy Spirit."

A LINGERING DOUBT

The disciple Thomas was not at this gathering. When he was told of it by the others, he said, "Unless I myself see Him and feel His wounds, I will not believe He is alive."

FROM DOUBT TO BELIEF

Eight days later, Thomas was there when Jesus again appeared to the group. "Be at peace", He said. "Thomas, touch My wounds and put your doubts aside. Be a believer."

Thomas, doing as commanded, said, "You are my Lord and my God." Jesus said, "Thomas, you believe because you have physically seen and touched Me. Happy indeed are those who are not able to see or touch Me, but still believe."

OTHER RESURRECTION EVIDENCES

Jesus showed Himself alive from the dead to over five hundred people at once, and at another time to His brother James. Jesus appeared to many followers on a mountain in Galilee where they worshipped Him. During appearances over forty days, He reviewed with His followers His life with them, reminded them of His teachings, renewed His commandments to them, and ate together with them as friend with friend.

Many other indisputable proofs were done by Jesus for the benefit of His followers. These which have been recorded are for the benefit of the reader, to enable the reader to believe that Jesus is in fact the Messiah, the Savior, the Son of God, and by this belief, to have eternal life.

POWER AND PEACE

Jesus said to His disciples, "All the power in heaven and earth is Mine. Therefore, go in My infinite power and make disciples of all nations. Preach the gospel throughout the world. 12) Mat. 28: 19, 20 Those who believe shall be saved. Those who will not believe shall be judged. As My witnesses, you will be given authority from heaven." He lifted His hands and blessed them.

As He was blessing them, He was lifted into the clouds and was taken to the throne of God.

As the disciples searched the sky for Him, two angels appeared and said, "Be calm and unafraid. You need not gaze longingly into the heavens. This same Jesus shall return in a similar fashion as you saw Him depart. Until He returns, live in the power of His Holy Spirit, whom Jesus promised to you."

The disciples fell down in worship of Jesus.

After a time, with great inner peace and joy they returned to Jerusalem where they constantly praised God together.

A MESSAGE
OF WARNING

FROM

Jude

Jude, servant of Christ, brother of James, to those in Christ where they are set apart and secured by God the Father.

Fight for the faith! Certain men have crept in catching many off guard, proselytizing by using half truths. These deny the true deity of the Lord Jesus Christ, and their doctrines teach sexual perverseness for godliness. As God judged the fallen angels and Sodom and Gomorra, he will judge these who make sexual sins a part of their religion, who call their dreams new revelations from God, and who speak evil of God's leaders.

Their proud missionaries are counterfeits. Their fabulous temples house clandestine rites and convey false hopes. Their priesthood is ordained of men, not of God. Their instructors use flowery speeches to lead astray the unaware. They are arrogant toward the genuine supernatural. These false teachers speak evil against truths they do not understand, and incorporate the animal desires of their body into their false doctrine. They, like Cain, kill good people; like Balaam, they get wealth from prophesying; and like Core, they turn many away from God's real servants. These are those who flaunt men in powerful positions because of advantages it gives them; they mock true religion; they have secret organizations; they practice intimate and sensual rituals; but they do not have the Holy Spirit. To them is reserved the empty, lonely blackness of darkness forever.

Keep yourselves in God's love and mercy, enjoying even now true eternal life in Christ. Have compassion on those deceived by the above described false prophets and their counselors, but use discretion. Some will never be rescued, but some can be saved with fear, snatching them from eternal fire, even though you detest the garments they wear.

Now unto Him who is able to keep you from deserting the true gospel and to joyfully present you without fault to His holy Father, to the only God, our Savior, [14) vs. 25] be glory, majesty, dominion and power, now and forever. Amen.

PREVIEW
OF THE FUTURE

FROM

Revelation

I, John, was meditating and worshipping, when a voice like a trumpet flourish said, "I am first and last, the beginning and the ending."

Turning to look, I saw the glorified Jesus. His attire was golden. His hair was as white as snow. His eyes were like laser beams. His feet like fine brass still gleaming from the furnace. His voice was strong as the oceans. His right hand held seven stars. The words of His mouth were like weapons of war. His face was shining brighter than the sun in its strength. When I saw Him, I fell at His feet as dead. Fear, weakness and worship gripped me. [14) Rev. 1: 17]

He laid His hand upon me and said, "Don't be afraid. I am the One who lived, died and rose again for you. I have the power over death and the keys of hell. Tell believers the following messages:

MESSAGES STRAIGHT FROM GOD THE SON

"Some of you are demonstrating Christianity in your walk. You are patient and do not fellowship with evil doers. You have examined those who give themselves the title of apostles when they are not apostles, and you have found them and their counselors liars. I commend you for all this. But I am disappointed that you have lost the initial fervency of love which you had for Me. Repent and rekindle your first love.

"Some of you are suffering and living in poverty. In truth you are eternally rich. You have investigated those who say they are Jews but are not. You realize these pseudo-Hebrews are of the synagogue of satan. But you, after you suffer for My name sake a little while, shall have a crown of eternal life.

"Some of you are holding securely to true doctrine, but are also using religion to dishonestly enrich yourself. Repent.

"Some of you have a reputation for being alive to God, but you are fooling yourself and others, for you are spiritually dead.

"Some of you are neither cold nor hot in your faith, but are lukewarm. That makes Me sick. Get hot or get cold. You may think you are rich and need nothing, but you are really poor, miserable, blind and naked. Come to Me for pure gold that is worth something in heaven, and for eternally lasting garments of purity, and for clarity of vision."

AN INVITATION FROM JESUS -- RSVP ASAP

"I am standing just outside your door, knocking. If you hear Me, open the door and ask Me in. I will enter and fellowship with you. [4) Rev. 3: 20] To those will I give the right to rule with Me forever. If you are hearing this message, you better listen to what the Spirit is saying."

JESUS THE CONQUEROR

After the passage of time and learning many things about the future, I saw heaven open and there was One on a white horse whose name is Faithful and True. He is the Judge and the Victor because of righteousness. His eyes were as fire, on His head were many crowns, His clothing was stained with blood, and His name is The Word of God. The armies of heaven follow Him, and He wields the fierceness and wrath of Almighty God. He crushes the nations, and rules with absolute authority and unimaginable power. He is King of kings and Lord of lords. [14) Rev. 19: 11-16]

When the armies of earth gathered to fight Him, led by the false prophet who had deceived millions and by satan's strongest political forces, they were defeated *en masse* and cast into the lake of fire. The devil himself was cast for a time into a bottomless pit like a black hole and then into the lake of fire where he and his cohorts shall be tormented day and night forever.

JESUS AS JUDGE

Then I saw a Great White Throne and the One sitting on it. In His presence the entire universe looked for a place to hide from His power and purity. But there is no place to escape. [14) Rev.20:11] I saw the dead, the insignificant and the powerful (those who thought they were great along with those who thought they were nothing; those who thought they were self-righteous along with those who thought they were worthless) all stand before God, to be judged according to the record of time. Everyone was there to be judged, even those who had been buried at sea and those who had already been cast into hell. After the formal judgment, they were all summarily cast into hell unless their name was written in the Book Of Life. <u>Without exception, whoever's name was not found in the Book Of Life was cast into the lake of fire. This is the second death -- eternal death</u>. 3) Rev. 21: 8, 27

LIVING WITH GOD

Then I saw a new heaven and new earth to replace the old galaxies which had evaporated. A new city, New Jerusalem, prepared as if for a bride, came from the hand of God. A great voice said, "<u>The home of God is now with men. He shall live among them and be their personal God. He shall wipe away all tears from their eyes. There shall be no more death or sorrow or pain, for all evil is past.</u>" 17) Rev. 21: 22 - 22: 5

NO ONE NEED BE LEFT OUT

The One on the throne said, "I have made everything new. I am the beginning and the end. To the thirsty, I will freely give water from the fountain of life. The overcomers shall be My children and I will be their God. But <u>the fearful and unbelieving and homosexuals and murderers and pimps and those who practice witchcraft and black magic, and those with false gods, and all liars shall have their place in the lake of fire, which is the second death. Only those can dwell with Me whose names are written in the Lamb's Book Of Life.</u>" 3) Rev. 20: 15 & 21: 8

WHERE GOLD IS PAVING MATERIAL

That great city, the New Jerusalem which descended out of heaven from God, vibrated with the glory of God. The city was pure gold and like clear diamonds, even the streets were pure gold, transparent as glass. There was no temple there, for the Lord God Almighty and the Lamb are the temple there. <u>The people who are saved shall walk in the light of it, and the gates shall not be shut at all in the daytime, and there is no night there. There shall never enter into it any sin or imperfection, but only those whose names are written in the Lamb's Book Of Life.</u> 17) Rev. 21: 22 - 22: 5

WORSHIP ONLY GOD

Then I saw a river as clear as pure crystal flowing from the throne of God and the Lamb of God. <u>There is no more curse</u>

for God is with His people and they see His face. There is no darkness [17] and no need for any other light source for the light emanates from God, who is Light.

I fell at the feet of the angel who showed me all this, and he said, "Do not worship me. Worship God and God only." [14]
Rev. 22: 9

BE PREPARED

Then Jesus said, "I come suddenly, bringing rewards to give to every believer according to their works."

A FINAL INVITATION

The Holy Spirit and the believers invite you to come to Jesus. You who are hearing this message, let your response be, "I am coming to Jesus." Whoever thirsts within the soul needs to come to Jesus. Whoever will, drink of the water of life by putting your faith and trust in Jesus only, and your name will be entered in His book. Remember, He has said, "I will come suddenly." Our response is, "Yes, come, Lord Jesus. I am ready and waiting."

May the grace of our Lord Jesus Christ be yours. Amen.

A PHILOSOPHICAL MESSAGE

FROM

Ecclesiastes

WISDOM OF A KING

Emptiness! All is emptiness. What does a man gain for all his effort in life? Generations come and go. The earth continues and the cycles of nature. Man works more than words can express, still he is not satisfied with the things he sees and hears and experiences. Everyone wants more, no matter how much he has. Neither does he accomplish anything truly new. Life is basically the same as it always has been. The living do not much remember or appreciate those who lived before, and when those now alive pass on, the next generation will forget them. It is emptiness.

I, the writer, am king of the land. I set my goal on wisdom and understanding. In all that I have observed among the human race, it is emptiness. The things that are wrong cannot be made permanently right, and the poor are always innumerable.

I achieved great power, wealth and wisdom. I also allowed myself to experience all the foolish pleasures and every entertainment. It is all emptiness.

I gained more power and wealth than any other alive in the world at my time. I bought every sort of entertainment and diversion. I tried wine, women and song at their best. I had many, many children. I built great financial enterprises. I traveled, studied, worked, played. Anything I ever wanted, I got. It was all worthless and emptiness.

The wise and the fool, the rich and the poor, the famous and the hermit, the old and the young, all die and turn to dust. There is no difference. The poor may be better off than the rich. The rich never have enough to satisfy, and to some the stress of their wealth prevents restful sleep. Meanwhile, a contented working man sleeps well. It is all emptiness.

To everything there is a time and season: A time to be born and a time to die; a time to plant and a time to root up; a time to kill and a time to heal; a time to humiliate and a time to honor; a time to weep and a time to laugh; a time to be distraught and a time to dance; a time to embrace and a time not to embrace; a time to accumulate and a time to give away; a time to tear apart and a time to bring together; a time to be quiet and a time to speak out; a time to love and a time to hate; a time to make war and a time for peace. There is a time for every purpose and every work. Yet, it all is emptiness.

God has made everything beautiful in His own time and place and way. God has placed the instinct of eternity within the heart of men so that men can recognize God by His creation.

Whatever God does is good and eternal, nothing can be added to it or taken from it. Individuals should fear God. Everything else is worthless and emptiness.

Young man, live it up in your youth; laugh until your heart is content; do whatever your glands desire; follow your animal instincts. If you desire something you see, just take it. But know this certainty -- for all this God will judge you.

Now is the time to consider your Creator -- now while you are young, before you scar your life with evil, before you amass a life of regrets, before you inflict yourself with the consequences of sin. Turn to God early while you still have good eyesight, good health, energy, strength, strong voice and time to live for eternal values, amassing an everlasting treasure that is truly worthwhile. Do not waste your life, planning to turn to God when death is at the door. There is no guarantee that you will have that chance, and such a life is worthless -- emptiness.

God will judge every person and every work. In summary, the duty of a man is to fear God and keep His commandments. Only then will one's life be eternally meaningful and worthwhile.

SELECTED PSALMS

Psalm 1

Favored is the man who does not follow ungodly counselors, nor fellowship with wrongdoers, nor fraternize with unbelievers. Instead, he delights in the word of God and meditates in it constantly. He shall be like a well watered tree that bears fruit plentifully and regularly. He shall not dry up, and whatever he does is worthwhile.

Psalm 2

Why do nations flaunt themselves? Why do people arrogantly think of themselves as super-intelligent, important or powerful? Finding support in numbers, they agree together that the Lord and Christ are nothing, and can be dismissed from their lives and overthrown from eternal sovereignty.

The Lord laughs at them. He holds them in derision for they are more ludicrous than an ant challenging a freight train. The day is coming when He will deal with them in holy anger and eternal justice. He will give the entire earth to Christ as a birthday present, and all the rulers and their nations as a toy. He will crush the belligerent as a child smashes clay after molding it.

Wise up, earthlings! Submit to God with fear and reverence, then rejoice in His favor. Worship Christ before you perish forever. Favored are those who acknowledge and trust Him.

Psalm 14

It is a fool who tells himself there is no God.

Mankind is scrutinized by God. God finds none who are pure and perfect, who measure up to His holy standard. None comprehend God, or seek totally after Him. They all get distracted. They all get tainted and corrupted. No one does only good, no not anyone. Those who delight in evil have lost their mind.

Psalm 15

Lord, who can please You and live with You?

One who lives with a pure conscience, who does right and tells the truth to himself and others. One who does not talk behind another's back, who does not stab others in the back or do evil of any kind, nor seeks to take advantage of another. One who despises evildoers but respects and supports those who fear God and do good. One who keeps his word even if it costs him money. One who does not overcharge, nor accept a bribe. This kind of individual is a stable person, a rock.

Psalm 16

Save me, O God, for I am trusting only You. You are my Lord. I can not equal Your holy standard, but I reach out to help Your people and those who do good. I have set You in front of me as my goal and standard. You are always the One to whom I look. You are at my right hand. I need not back down. While I live, You show me the way of true life. In fellowship with You I find complete joy, contentment and satisfaction. My heart is happy in You. I know that when I die, I will be raised to eternal life.

Psalm 19

The galaxies parade the glory of God. The universe shouts that He is its Craftsman. Day after day they prove this concept. Night after night they display this insight. Season following season, and all the harmony of the cosmos, illustrates His intelligence. There is no language that does not understand this message which permeates the entire earth and penetrates the remotest places on the globe. Everyone in every nation and every age can understand the significance of creation -- that God exists and is in control.

As God's law is in nature, so it is in spirit. The law of the Lord is perfect, renewing the soul. The promise of the Lord is reliable, making wise those who simply believe. The requirements of the Lord are needful, making the obedient joyful. The commands of the Lord are pure, giving insight to His followers. Fear of the Lord is appropriate, and forever will be.

The judgments of the Lord are true and absolutely right. All these together are of more value than monetary wealth and sweeter than the finest honey. The obedient are warned by them and given great reward.

Lord, I can not be aware of all my mistakes. Who can see all his own faults? Cleanse me and clear me of inadvertent errors. Please prevent me from rebellious sinning and don't let me become addicted to it. Help me live innocently and not commit grievous sins. May the words I speak and the thoughts I think be pleasing to You, O Lord, my strength, my shelter and my savior.

Psalm 23

The Lord is my shepherd. I am content. He enables me to rest with nourishment and comfort. He leads me, supplying my needs in quiet and peace. He renews my soul. He guides me in the way of righteousness to honor His name. Even though I walk where the threat of death stalks me, I do not fear, for He is with me. His power and faithfulness comfort me. He prepares a feast for me in spite of those who are against me. He heals my wounds and cares for me in love. I am full of joy and contentment -- more than satisfied. I am confident that His goodness and mercy will attend me throughout my life, and I will live with Him forever.

Psalm 27

The Lord is my light and my salvation. Whom should I fear? The Lord strengthens me in life. Of whom should I be afraid?

One thing I desire and pursue: to live in the presence of the Lord all during this life and then to see the glory of the Lord in the presence of His eternal throne.

When the Lord said to seek His face, my soul resolved to seek His face. Even if my father and mother forsake me, the Lord will parent me. Teach me Your way, O Lord, and lead me plainly, so I am not confused. I would be discouraged if not for Your guidance and if I did not believe I will see the holiness of the Lord in His eternal home.

Rely on the Lord. Be courageous and He will give you strength. Take heart and rely patiently on the Lord.

Psalm 32

Favored is one whose transgressions are forgiven and whose sin is pardoned. Happy is one whom God does not hold responsible for his sins.

When I would not admit my sins, guilt ate me up and crushed my spirit. My conscience was heavy and dried me up.

Then I admitted my sin unto the Lord and confessed my transgressions. He forgave me. He is my Savior, my refuge and my deliverer. He has said He will teach me and guide me with His eye.

Do not be stubborn like the mule but be happy in the Lord.

Psalm 33

The universe was created when the Lord spoke the word, all the galaxies were made when He breathed the command. All the inhabitants of earth should be in awe of Him and fear Him, for He spoke and it was completed, He issued the order and it was accomplished.

The Lord reduces the intelligence of unbelievers to less than nothing. He renders their false theories useless. But the Lord's truth is unchanged forever, to all generations. Favored is the nation which makes the only true and living God, the Creator, their Lord. Happy are the people who recognize, and submit to, the Almighty. The Lord observes mankind from heaven. He made them all from the same mold. He understands their minds and realizes the reason for their efforts. No earthly ruler can be saved by an army, or delivered by tanks, missiles and planes. Man's greatest strength is nothing to God, but He looks with favor on those who fear Him and rely on mercy.

Our soul relies fully on the Lord. He is our only hope and defense. Our heart rejoices in Him, for we have trusted in His holy name.

Psalm 34

My desire is to extol the Lord continuously, to praise Him constantly. I desire to brag on the Lord. Glorify the Lord with me. Let's exalt Him together.

Those who look to the Lord have a radiance about them. They will never be ultimately ashamed. When this poor man cried out to God, the Lord heard and preserved me through my troubled times.

Give God a chance. Sample His goodness and you'll be blessed. The Lord keeps watch over His own and listens to their call. The righteous may live with many difficulties, but the Lord will enable them to overcome each one. The Lord saves His servants; no one will be lost who trusts the Lord.

Psalm 37

Don't get upset or envious when evil doers prosper. As grass that grows in the morning is cut down in the afternoon, they will soon be gone. They will wilt like the flowers on that grass and melt like dew in the sunshine.

Do what is right, then trust the Lord for the outcome and your income. He will take care of you and bless your activity. Delight in the Lord, commit your actions to Him, rely on Him for the result and He will give you what your heart truly desires.

Rest in the Lord and wait patiently for Him to act. Do not get frustrated or bitter because the evil doer is getting ahead. Don't try to get even and don't consider doing the kinds of things he has done. After life's little time, the wicked will be forever gone. Even if you were to search for him, you would not find him. But the meek have an eternal inheritance. They will have abundance in peace.

When the wicked plot against the just, the Lord laughs at them for He sees the time of judgment. There is eternal justice. The progress of a godly man is directed by the Lord and He delights in his life. Though he trips up, he will not be completely ruined, for the Lord holds him by the hand. I have seen the wicked build great empires and vast fortunes. Yet they pass away and no one cares or misses them. Their life has little rest and death is their undoing forever. But the godly shall live in inner peace, and in the end the Lord is their eternal salvation because they trust in Him.

Psalm 40

I waited patiently for the Lord, and He responded in His own good timing. He lifted me from failure and despair, and put me on solid ground with a purpose in life. He put a song in my heart and in my mouth. Many shall see my transformation and give honor and praise to God.

Favored is the one who trusts in God, who does not take the credit for his success and who does not deceive to get ahead.

Wonderful are Your works, O Lord, and Your relationships to mankind. You do not desire sacrifices and offerings, but You desire us to delight in obedience and to meditate on Your words.

I have not concealed Your goodness, but have openly spoken Your salvation, Your faithfulness, Your loving kindness, and Your truth. Do not withhold from me Your mercy, for I look to You to preserve me. Let all who seek You and trust in You be glad and rejoice in You. Let all who rely on Your salvation be filled with praise for the Lord. I am poor and needy, but You are my helper and deliverer.

Psalm 42

As a deer seeks a water brook, so my soul seeks for You, O God. My soul thirsts for God, the only true and living God. When shall I see You face to face? O my soul, why are you so discouraged and afraid? Trust in God! I shall yet praise Him, for He shall make me healthy and happy again. Trust in God.

Psalm 43

O God, set me free of the hold of the dishonest and from those who use the law to unjust advantage. You alone are my strength. Send Your light and truth to lead me. In Your presence I find ultimate joy, and I can't help but sing praise to You, my personal God. Why do I get so discouraged and my soul so agitated when my hope is in God? I will overcome, and with a smile on my face I will again praise You.

Psalm 46

The Lord is our refuge and our strength. He is there to help in times of need. We need not be afraid even if earthquakes move mountains into the sea. God has a sure, unmovable heavenly city for us. God is there and His City cannot be touched by earthquake or any other force. God is our help. Be silent and realize that the Lord is God. He will be exalted. He is with us.

Psalm 51

Have mercy on me, O God, according to Your infinite loving kindness. Erase my transgressions according to Your tender mercy. Wash me thoroughly from my iniquity and cleanse me completely from my sins. I admit my transgressions and the guilt of my sin is continually in my thoughts. I confess that I have sinned against You, and done this evil right before Your eyes. I deserve Your judgment. I have been a sinner since birth, and have sinned all my life. I am spilling my guts to You in truthfulness, so You can replace this guilt with new insight. Disinfect me, and I will truly be pure. Sanitize me, and I shall be whiter than snow. Allow me to be joyful and glad once again. Release this burning, crushing burden within me, and replace it with Your peace. Expunge all my sins. Create within me a new heart and renew within me a right attitude. Let me be aware of Your presence within me. Let me again feel the joy of my salvation and experience a willing and obedient spirit free from sin. Then I will be able, without hypocrisy, to teach others Your way, and some will be converted to trust in You. I would bring some sacrifice and give some offering if that were what You want. But all You ask is a humble attitude, a broken and contrite spirit. These are the true sacrifices of God.

Psalm 62

My soul, rely only upon God. God is the only hope. He alone is a rock, a sure defense, a refuge and salvation. I will not be moved from my trust in Him at all times.

Men of poverty and weakness are nothing, and men of wealth, fame and power are nothing but a delusion. Put them all on a scale, and the result is a negative value. Oppressing, or cheating, or taking advantage of others may produce riches on earth, but do not seek that kind of wealth. Both retribution and mercy belong to God, and He will balance the scales.

Psalm 63

O God, You are my God. Early each morning will I seek You out. My soul longs for Your fellowship like one thirsts for water in a desert. I want to see Your power and glory face to face, as I have seen it within when I worship in quiet during the day. Your love and kindness are better than life itself. When I meditate on You before I go to sleep or when I awake during the night, I am filled with joyful praise. I honor You. I praise You. I worship You. I lift up my hands to Your name.

Psalm 84

How friendly is Your presence, O Lord. My soul longs to be with You, to fellowship with the living God. Favored are those who spend time in Your house. Happy is the man who makes You his strength. A day with You is better than a thousand without You. It is better to be a servant in the Lord's house than a ruler in a palace of satan. The Lord is like the sun and a shield from the sun -- glory and grace. No good thing will You withhold from one who walks with You. Happy is one who trusts the Lord.

Psalm 90

Lord, You are our refuge in all generations. Before You formed the earth and the universe, from eternity past to eternity future You alone are God. You designed that man should return to dust, but You have the power to call him back again to life. A thousand years to You are less than the passing of a day. But mankind are as subject to death as to sleep. Or like grass, they grow up in a morning and are cut down that evening. Our iniquities are evident to You, even our secret sins are visible to You, so we are under Your righteous judgment. Our life to You is no more than a sigh. To us, even though we live seventy or eighty or more years, it is filled with sorrow and difficulties, it passes quickly and we are gone. Therefore, teach us to recognize the shortness of our life here and to live according to Your wisdom. How long will it be before You return? Until then, may we find contentment in Your mercy so that we can be happy during life. Let us see Your work in our lives and in the lives of our children, and let us reflect Your glory. May the things we accomplish be that which has eternal value, yes, may we live for eternal values.

Psalm 100

Raise a happy cheer to the Lord all across the land. Serve the Lord with gladness. Come into His presence with singing. Be aware that there is but one God, the Lord who has made us, and we are the sheep in His pasture. Enter into His presence with thankfulness and with praise. Be grateful to Him and honor His name. For the lord is good, His mercy is everlasting, and His truth is unchanged to all generations.

Psalm 103

Bless the Lord, O my soul, and all that is within me, honor His holy name. Bless the Lord, not forgetting His benefits.

He forgives all our sins; He heals our diseases; He redeems us from eternal death; He rewards us with loving kindness and tender mercy; He satisfies us with good things and enables us to endure.

The Lord will execute fairness and justice for all who are oppressed. He is full of mercy and grace, patient, but He will not always resort merely to scoldings, nor forever hold back His judgment. He has not required us to pay for our sins and injustices, because His mercy is so great for them who fear Him. His mercy is greater than the distance between the stars or planets. As infinitely far as east is from west, that is the distance He has removed our sins from us. He is like a father to us who takes pity on His children. He understands our frailties and the temporary nature of our lives. But the mercy of the Lord is eternal to all who reverence Him and keep His commandments. The Lord has placed His throne where it is untouchable and unmovable, and from it He rules over all. Bless the Lord, angels; all the hosts of them, bless the Lord. Bless the Lord, all His creation. Bless the Lord, O my soul.

Psalm 118

Give thanks to the Lord, for His mercy endures forever. The Lord is on my side, I need not fear what man can do to me. It is better to put trust in the Lord than in men. The Lord is my strength, my song and my salvation. This is a day which the Lord has made. I will be delighted and contented in it.

Psalm 119

How can a young man keep his life pure? By guiding his actions according to the word of God! He should be able to say: I have sought You with my whole being, keep me from straying away from Your commandments. I have stored Your words in my mind that I may call upon them to keep me from sinning. I will meditate on Your precepts and respect Your will. I will delight in Your commands. I will not forget Your word.

Your word is forever settled in heaven. It's light on my path, a beacon for right living, illumination for correct decisions.

I despise egotistical thinking but I love Your word. You are my shelter and my defense. I trust Your word. Evildoers, keep away from me, do not try to be my companion, for I want to obey the word of the Lord.

Hang on to me, Lord, as You promised in Your word, that I might live a full life. Never let my hope in You be disappointed nor let me be ashamed of my trust in You. Hold me up, Lord, and I will be safe. You have rejected all those who do not believe Your word, for they rely on deceit and lies. You think of them as the scum of the earth. But I love Your word. I reverence and respect You, and would be afraid to fall under Your condemnation. The infusion of Your word brings insight, understanding and light.

Psalm 121

Why would I look to the hills or to other religions for assistance?! My help comes from the Lord who made not only the hills, but also the world and the entire universe. The Lord shall preserve me in my day to days activities. He shall preserve my soul both today and throughout eternity.

Psalm 126

The Lord has done great things for us and we rejoice. May those who have sown tears of sorrow reap with tears of celebration. Those who go out with compassion spreading the seed of the gospel, shall return with shouts of joy bringing their harvest with them.

Psalm 127

Unless the Lord builds a house, those who erect it are wasting time and effort. Unless the Lord protects a city, the watchmen are worthless.

Psalm 139

O Lord, You know my innermost thoughts. You know everything I do and my considerations for the future. You are with me when I work or sleep, and nothing takes You by surprise. You know every word I speak and every thought I think.

This thought is more than I can comprehend: Where could I go to evade You, or where could I hide to escape You? If I were to glide on the wind to the uttermost part of the sea, You are there. If I were to take my life, in my death You are there. If I were to fly into space, You are there. Darkness cannot conceal me; You see in the dark as if it were light. Wherever I might go, Your hand is upon me, You are there to lead me. I praise You, for I am amazingly and wonderfully made. Your creation is awesome. You knew me when I was still a fetus. As I developed day by day, You controlled my body before I was born. I worship You.

Your thoughts are precious to me, Lord. I contemplate them. Search me, O Lord. I open my heart and mind to You. Evaluate me and my thoughts, and give me insight into any wicked ways within me. Lead me in the way of everlasting life.

Praise 150

Praise the Lord. Praise God in His sanctuary and in the universe which is under His power. Praise Him for His tremendous acts and for His excellent greatness. Praise Him with music and dancing, cheers and celebrations. Let everything alive praise the Lord, Yes, you, praise the Lord.

SELECTED PROVERBS

WISDOM

A wise individual will listen and increase knowledge, and persons with understanding will consult wise counselors.

The fear of the Lord is the beginning of knowledge, but fools despise wisdom and instruction.

Do not have an inflated opinion of your own cunning, but fear the Lord and flee from evil.

Happy is the one who obtains wisdom and understanding, for it is more valuable than wealth or all the other things you could want. Wisdom gives long life and honor with contentment and peace.

Give instruction to wise persons and they will grow wiser. Teach a just person and that individual will benefit from it. The fear of the Lord is the starting point of wisdom, and acknowledging the Holy One is a requisite for correct understanding. Fear the Lord and you will enjoy a long life.

The way of a fool is right in his own eyes.

A fool's anger is quickly shown, but a prudent man controls it.

Where no counsel is sought, the people stumble, but in many counselors there is stability.

A wise person respects the law and avoids breaking the rules, but a fool curses the law and brags about his illegal exploits.

A white head is a crown of glory if it follows the Lord.

A word of correction does more good for the wise than a beating does for the stubborn.

Even a fool, when he keeps his mouth shut, is thought wise.

He who makes up his mind in a matter before he hears both sides of the issue is foolish and shameful.

One who continues to rebel in the face of counseling shall suddenly be destroyed without hope.

There is a way which seems right, but its destination is hell. There are religions and philosophies which sound good to human reasoning, but they lead to eternal death.

The righteous bear fruit like a tree of life, and a soul winner is wise.

Guard your heart and mind for they control the issues of life. What you love and what you think about determine what you become.

Trust in the Lord with all your heart. Don't rely on your own ability to figure things out. In everything you do, consult the Lord and He will direct your life.

GOOD PARENTING AND WISE YOUTH

My son, follow the instruction of your father and do not forsake the precepts of your mother. When sinners entice you, do not consent. Don't consort with them; avoid their hangouts. My son, do not forget my law, but keep my commandments sincerely from your heart. Then you will have a long and peaceful life. Do not forsake mercy and truth; write them upon the tables of your heart and you will find favor with God and man.

Do not despise the discipline of the Lord or get discouraged with His correction. The Lord corrects those He loves, as a good father disciplines a son.

A wise son makes a glad father, but a foolish son makes a heavy-hearted mother.

Discipline your child while there is hope, and do not let crying cause you to forgo discipline.

One who will not discipline a child hates him, but one who loves his child will punish him at the proper times.

Even a child develops a reputation by his actions. Choose a good reputation over great riches.

Train up children in the way they should go and when they are old they will not depart from it.

Foolishness is natural in the heart of a child but a judicial spanking will drive it from him.

The rod and reproof give wisdom, but a child allowed to do whatever he wants will bring shame and sorrow to himself and to his parents.

TEMPORARY RICHES AND TRUE WEALTH

Better is a little with fear of the Lord, than great wealth with anxiety.

It is better to live peacefully in a crackerbox than in a mansion with a bawling woman. It is better to live happily in the woods than in a castle with a contentious and angry woman.

Riches are uncertain. They grow wings and fly away. Therefore, don't worry about being wealthy or fret to be rich.

Do not refuse good to one to whom it is due when you have the capability to give it.

Do not fight with another without cause. Do not envy oppressive individuals, and do not follow their ways.

Better to be poor and honest, than dishonest and rich.

Many seek the favor of the government or the rich, yet it is the Lord who will judge us all.

PROMISCUOUS LIVING

My son, the lips of a strange woman ooze sweetness like a honeycomb and her mouth is smoother than fine oil. But her touches bring bitterness, she leads to death, and then on to hell. Stay away from her, do not even get near her house, or you may lose your possessions to those you never before met, and end up working for strangers. At the last you may be wasted with sickness and disease. Then you will say, "Why did I not listen to advice and follow wise counsel?"

Drink water out of your own well, enjoy only your own wife. Let her breasts satisfy you always and be ravished only with her love. The Lord sees all your actions no matter where.

My law is light, my reproofs are the way of life to keep you from the flattery of the strange woman. Don't lust after her beauty or her fluttering eyes. A promiscuous woman will bring you to poverty and even cost you your life. You can not embrace fire and not be burned, nor can you lay with another man's wife and get away with it. Even one who steals food to survive is made to repay, but jealousy because of adultery is a rage in a man, and he will stop at nothing to get vengeance. Commit adultery and you destroy your own soul and invite poverty. Stolen water is sweet and bread eaten secretly is pleasant, but realize that the dead are there and the prostitute's guests are in hell.

Let not your heart decline to the thrills of a prostitute. She has ruined many weak men and destroyed many strong men. Her house is the gate to hell and her rooms are chambers of death.

WORK AND ATTITUDE

Go observe the ant, consider her habits and be wise. She works through summer and harvest, providing her food. How long will you sleep? Until poverty overtakes you?

In work there is profit but in talk there is nothing.

Where there is no vision the people perish.

Pessimism in one's heart makes it heavy, but a positive attitude makes one's heart glad.

Don't brag about what you'll do tomorrow; you can't tell what may happen.

Commit your work to the Lord and your mind shall be at peace.

GUARANTEEING A LOAN OR LENDING VS GIVING

If you've become a guarantor for either a friend or a stranger, you have trapped yourself. A loan cannot buy friendship, but can lose friend and money.

A friend loves at all times and a brother is born to help in adversity.

One who has pity on the poor gives to the Lord, and that which is given will be repaid.

If your enemy is hungry, feed him; if he is thirsty, give him drink; for in doing so you smoke out his conscience, and the Lord will reward you.

PRIDE VS HUMILITY

The Lord hates these seven things: pride, lying, murder, vandalism, evil conniving, a false witness, and one who turns a brother against brother.

Respect for the Lord equates to hating evil such as pride, arrogance, unlawful living, and willful talk.

Before honor is humility.

Pride comes before destruction and a haughty spirit before a fall.

ANGER VS KINDNESS

Hatred stirs up strife but love reconciles all errors.

One who conceals hatred with lies and one who slanders is a fool. In a profusion of talk is often found sin, but one who restrains his tongue is wise.

After a person dies, our memory of a good, law-abiding person is happy, but the name of a wicked person decays.

A soft answer turns away wrath, but grievous words stir up anger.

A merry heart is a good medicine, but a broken spirit dries one up.

FRIENDSHIP

One who chooses wise friends shall be wise, but a companion of fools shall be destroyed.

Don't be friends with a man controlled by anger -- you'll become like him.

One who wants friends must be friendly -- and their is a friend who is closer than a brother.

A gossip tells secrets, but a loyal friend keeps a confidence.

Wait for others to praise you, not praising yourself. Faithful are the wounds of a friend but the flattery of enemies is hurtful. As iron sharpens iron, so a friend will sharpen his friend. As a mirror, so a friend will be truthful with his friend.

HONESTY

To falsify a balance is hated by the Lord, but honest accounting is His delight. Integrity guides the honest, but the perverseness of the dishonest shall destroy them. The goodness of good people stands them in good stead, but the wickedness of wicked people catches them in their own traps.

The wicked run scared even when no one is really after them.

The eyes of the Lord see everything, everyone, every where.

NATIONAL CONDUCT

Righteousness exalts a nation, but sinfulness shames any country.

ALCOHOLIC DRINK

Wine will mock and strong drink will enrage you. Do not be deceived by alcohol.

A VIRTUOUS WOMAN AND A WIFE

A virtuous woman is a crown to her husband but she who shames her husband is like a disease. A beautiful woman who is promiscuous is like a jewel in a pig's snout.

He who finds a wife finds a good thing.

The value of a virtuous woman is above jewels. Her husband trusts her, and he and her children call her blessed. Favor can be deceitful, fair skin can be disappointing, and beauty is empty, but a woman who fears the Lord shall be praised.

"The **Y** - Knot" ™

Why Not Believe?

◆ · ◆

AN ENDLESS MESSAGE

Now that you've completed THE GOSPEL MESSAGE, it's not over.

Read THE GOSPEL MESSAGE again and again. Let its content grasp you, its theme saturate you. Think on these things. Store these thoughts in your heart. Carry it with you. Give it to others.

These are heavenly ideas. **Earth's daily necessities are natural concerns, yet living expecting eternity, focusing out yonder, can alter the necessities.** God's message is a basic, practical necessity. Review it until you comprehend the overview and understand the detail. Study the Bible.

Now, let faith instruct, mold, train, lead, govern, comfort -- moment on moment controlling you. Just willingly do it. Take God at His word. "Trust and obey." Then, one day, we'll all be together, family, in that home in His glory, as planned, faultless in His presence. "Faith comes by reading the Word of God." Got the message?

<u>MY PERSONAL</u>
<u>COMMITMENT</u>

• In accordance with Romans 10: 9,10 *(pg 46)* --

       I right now admit that *In my true inner self I believe that Jesus is the Christ (God The Son, The Messiah of the Old Testament, the promised Savior).*

       I state out loud right now that *I know I'm imperfect, a sinner, and I believe that Jesus is alive from the dead after dying as the infinite sacrifice for my sin.*

       Therefore, right now, **BY FAITH**, *I am trusting Jesus, and Him only, for my everlasting salvation from sin and for eternal life. I want Him to come into my life and take control.* (See Rev. 3: 20 *pg. 219*)

• Based on God's promises such as 1 John 5: 9-13 *(pg 6)* --

       Right now, **BY FAITH**, *I know that I have eternal life and am a member of the family of God.*

As testimony to myself & to the world, I execute this Commitment because **I know I am believing RIGHT NOW**.

DATED _____

              SIGNED _____

VICTORY AT THE CROSS – JOY AT SUNRISE

It was a dark, stormy, seemingly hopeless night. It looked like defeat, but God turned it into triumph. Jesus got the victory at the cross, as God planned. There would be celebration Sunday morning.

All the forces of darkness, sin, death, satan and hell were against Him on the cross, but Jesus was victor. There would be joy at *Sonrise* -- at the open, empty tomb.

You and I face our storms, sorrows, sins, sickness, deaths, even our hells, and those we've caused for others. Praise God, through Jesus there is victory and joy, hope and healing, forgiveness and cleansing, peace and a new day.

Our treasure, hope and comfort is not of this world. The living Jesus is coming again. Because of His victory at the cross, we'll share joy at sunrise and fellowship in the light of His eternal dawn. Aren't you glad that's the way it is! See you there, believer.